PRAISE FOR

M000309266

'In *Exhumation*, the illumination of a family secret sheds a coruscating light on Britain's colonial past. Part memoir, part history, Dhingra's lively examination brings the events leading up to Partition to vivid and immediate life. Madan Lal's story has, until now, been little known in Britain; this important book ensures that will no longer be the case'
Erica Wagner, author of *Chief Engineer: Washington Roebling, The Man Who Built the Brooklyn Bridge* and *First Light: A Celebration of Alan Garner*

'This inter-generational dramatised version of Madan Lal Dhingra's life gives rare glimpses and deeper understanding of a man who paradoxically was regarded as both a beloved revolutionary in India and a cruel murderer in Britain for which he was executed in 1909. In exhuming his memory, the author, who is also his grand-niece, deals movingly with turbulent moments in her family history as well as the agony, violence and transformation so many young Indian students like Madan Lal in Britain underwent, with Veer Savarkar guiding them, towards India's Independence. A fascinating read'
Kishwar Desai, author *Jallianwala Bagh, 1919: The Real Story*, and Chair of the Trust that set up, in Amritsar, the world's first and only Partition Museum.

'As soon as I finished this spectacular book, I started it again, unwilling to leave the vivid world of these people – heroic and touching - whose lives, devastated by British colonial decisions long ago, are so very relevant to today's culture wars. Ghosts of colonialism are alive here'
Victoria Brittain, author of *Love and Resistance in the Films of Mai Masri* and *Shadow Lives, The Forgotten Women of the War of Terror*

'Leena Dhingra vividly recreates how her family, well ensconced in the British Raj, was drawn by 1900 into a multicommunal nationalist campaign. Independence was achieved in 1947 at great cost by way of death and displacement. Will Indian PM Modi, empowering *Hindu* nationalism, repeat the horror?'
H. O. Nazareth, writer and film-maker

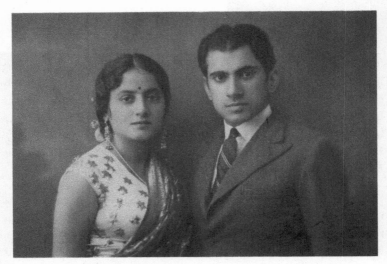

Wedding of author's parents

Family gathering

LEENA DHINGRA was born in India and came to Europe after the 1947 Partition. She is a writer and actor. Her first novel *Amritvela* was published in 1988. As an actor, her credits include *East is East, The Bill, Prime Suspect, EastEnders, Coronation Street, Casualty, Doctor Who* and *Ackley Bridge*. A Londoner for almost sixty years, Leena Dhingra now lives near Manchester.

Author (left), flying to India with her sister 1956

1948 Independence celebration

Exhumation

The Life and Death of Madan Lal Dhingra

Leena Dhingra

SMALL AXES

HopeRoad Publishing
PO Box 55544
Exhibition Road
London SW7 2DB

www.hoperoadpublishing.com
@hoperoadpublish

A CIP catalogue record for this book is available from the British Library.

Supported using public funding by
ARTS COUNCIL
ENGLAND

ISBN: 978-1-913109-82-0
eISBN: 978-1-913109-16-5

Printed and bound by Clays Ltd, Elcograf S.p.A

For Remmy, my beloved grandchild.
'What will I do alone in the English countryside?' said I.
'You're an author, Nanima, and authors need quiet.'

PROLOGUE

2019: Doctor Who *and the Photograph*

'You know, when a trauma is undigested, it gets repeated. It's a known fact. Partition was a terrible trauma and nobody ever talked about it. And it got repeated again and again. In Mummy's life, in Daddy's life, in my life, in your life. We never had a country, a family, a home, a room of our own.'

In the summer of 2018, as a jobbing actress, I took the train to Cardiff to play a role in *Doctor Who*. Since it's a cult show, its producers are very secretive about content and so I had not been sent a script and when I arrived at the hotel I was given only my two scenes.

My part was Nani Umbreen, an elderly Pakistani woman aged around ninety, living in Sheffield, having a birthday party with her daughter's family and handing over gifts and mementoes to her two granddaughters through which we learn that the old lady has a story and a secret – something she can't or doesn't want to talk about.

Arriving on set in my big grey wig I asked what the episode was about.

'It's about the Partition of India.'

'Oh my God.' I replied, 'Really! I can't believe it. That's my story, my history, my trauma, my mystery. It's why I'm here.'

It was also why my character, Nani Umbreen, was in Sheffield.

The young director walked across to greet me.

'Hello, I'm Jamie,' he said. 'Welcome to *Doctor Who*.' He then squatted down beside my chair to be on a level with me and said, 'I never knew about this, about Partition, never learned about it in history and I certainly never knew that we were implicated in any way in this terrible, terrible tragedy.'

I vaguely raised my shoulders and said: 'I know. I always found it hard when I was a growing up here and I would mention Partition and no one knew what that was.'

'I'm so, so sorry.'

I could feel a wave of emotion beginning to well up and immediately sought to diffuse it – so I said, in full theatrical mode: 'It's not your fault, darling, you weren't even born and had it been left up to you, you wouldn't have done it like that.'

Jamie, by then, was busy scrolling his phone to show me the various books he had been reading to inform himself whilst shaking his head and repeating under his breath that it was all too shocking. As he did this, I told him about a character in *The Satanic Verses* called Whisky Sisodia who stutters: 'The trouble with the Engenglish is that their hiss hiss history happened overseas so they dodo don't know what it means.'

The episode, entitled 'The Demons of the Punjab', by Vinay Patel was aired on 11 November 2018 – Remembrance Sunday. The plot involved time travel to Sunday, 17 August 1947, the day the Radcliffe Line demarking the Partition border was announced.

It had been arranged that I would watch the episode with my daughter and her family, all great *Doctor Who* fans who thought it was really, really cool that I was playing a grandmother in one of their favourite TV programmes. After it was over, for some reason I felt impelled to return home at once. The family was surprised that I didn't stay for a cup of tea – and so was I, and I felt a bit bad leaving.

Walking home, an incident with my late sister some twenty-five years earlier came to mind. We were having a coffee in Polly's Tea Rooms overlooking one of the approaches to Hampstead Heath when she suddenly said with great intensity: 'You know, when a trauma is undigested, it gets repeated. It's a known fact. Partition was a terrible trauma and nobody *ever* talked about it. And it got repeated again and again. In Mummy's life, in Daddy's life, in my life, in your life. We never had a country, a family, a home, a room of our own. Have you ever thought about it?'

I didn't reply, just vaguely nodded.

'That's the trouble with you Leena, you *never* know what's going on. You just switch off. You block out your feelings and go into denial.'

My phone in my bag was pinging messages as these memories were coursing through me.

'You see,' she'd continued in a slightly softer tone, 'when one has had an unsettled life like we have had, one of the things that happens is that you lose touch with your instincts. Think about that.'

Back home, my phone still pinging, I was thinking. Did I go into denial? Was that why I'd suddenly felt impelled to come home, to be on my own?

The following day I settled down alone to watch the episode again. As it unfolded, I realised just how much I had drawn on my own mother in the portrayal of my character: her warmth, her humanity, her quirky humour, her knowing looks. When Nani Umbreen says of her life in Sheffield that it gave her a 'home, a life, stability', I felt happy for her – but so, so sad for my mother, as those were the very things Partition took away and that she never managed to restore – a loss and longing that never lifted.

Two weeks before she died, aged ninety-nine, as I was putting her to bed, she asked, 'Are you taking me back to Lahore?'

'Come on Mama,' I sighed, 'Don't you remember Partition and Pakistan?'

'No.' She smiled. 'But I remember Lahore. Do you remember Lahore?'

Watching, and remembering, I found myself weeping and weeping – weeping from sadness and in joy and pity and peace. And release.

In the silence of observing, came a distancing. That story on the screen was a part of me, but I was also apart from it. As that realisation unfolded, identification dissolved and its concomitants – timidity, fear, failure, invisibility – floated away, like steam.

'For the eye altering alters all.' As the great poet William Blake wrote.

I called my friend Ginny, an experienced drama therapist whom I'd known since we were teenagers at drama school. 'You know what darling,' she said, 'I think you are in the process of releasing that inherited trauma.'

Walking in the park one sunny and surprisingly mild December afternoon, I reflected on all the coincidental elements of my experience of *Doctor Who* – that of all the stories that could be told, it was Partition; of all the moments of time travel, it was to the actual day the infamous Radcliffe Line was revealed; of all the actresses who could have told the story, it fell to me; of all the days in the year it could have been aired, it was on Remembrance Day. And this year, it actually fell on a Sunday. Remembrance Sunday.

All significant and potent – partition, remembrance, release and time travel.

Exactly two Decembers earlier, I had written a piece entitled 'Being Here and Now', to send out to friends informing them of my move from London to the countryside, my commitment to writing and my search for a project.

But the project I resisted, which was clearly the most significant, was the story of my great uncle, Madan Lal Dhingra – freedom fighter, patriot, revolutionary, terrorist, misguided youth, murderer, martyr – and of his execution at Pentonville Prison in 1909.

The story had haunted me since I first heard it as a child. It would lap at the edges of my mind and every so often flood it. I had tried to find, grasp and tell it in so many ways: as a play, a film and finally a novel. This needed revisiting. But it felt daunting and painful. The trauma of my forebears had tangled with the trauma of my own immediate family and created a knot.

Maybe now that, too, could be resolved with the touch of *Doctor Who*?

I returned home with a resolute step and a clear purpose. In my garden the shy snowdrops were in bloom. I wondered what colours and flowers there might be by the time I had finished.

I started to prepare my working space, retrieving the material, the existing manuscript, folders and notebooks – and laying them out on my desk. In my hand I held a yellow duster and in my mind was the intention of wiping away the layers of fear, failure and pain, along with the dust.

And just as I had done on previous occasions, I pinned the photograph on the wall above my desk – the photograph around which I had written a prologue in my original manuscript. I started to read it:

THE PHOTOGRAPH
Dhingra the Immortal

'Dhingra has behaved at each stage of his trial like a hero of ancient times. He has reminded us of the history of mediaeval Rajputs and Sikhs who loved death like a bride. England thinks she killed Dhingra; in reality he lives forever and has given the deathblow to English sovereignty in India. In time to come, when the British Empire shall have been reduced to dust and ashes, Dhingra's monument will adorn the squares of our chief towns, recalling the memory of our children to the noble life and the noble death of him who laid down his life in a far-off land for the cause he loved so well.' (Har Dayal, 1909)

On the board above my desk I have pinned up a photograph of you. You are wearing a striped lounge suit with a contrasting waistcoat in lighter material. You are sitting in a chair, in a garden. It is a bentwood chair, rather like the ones I have. Your legs are crossed, your hands are in your lap, you look relaxed and your face bears a forthright and determined expression. You are looking straight through the camera, and across the years, at me. Sometimes that feels very strange. I remember the first time I saw this picture of you, when my Canadian cousin sent me a copy. It was a few years after my father died, and I was struck by your resemblance to, a particular photograph, taken on the porch of Villa Nova, my grandfather's house in Simla. My grandfather, your elder brother. My father is there in the last row of a formal family photograph that is hierarchically arranged – expressing a patriarchal, colonial culture. They all look like proud examples of Macaulay's 'Minute': 'to form a class of persons Indian in blood and colour, but English in tastes, in opinions, in morals and in intellect'.

There's a look in my father's face, a rebellious almost wild look that I imagine you might have recognised. It's as though he wants to burst out of the confines of his straight, double-breasted jacket.

Your photograph is in the form of a postcard. On the back and across the two halves marked 'Communication and Address', is written:

The last photograph of Deshbhakta Madan Lal Dhingra (d.17.08.09).
To the members of his family, from D. S. Madhava Rao. Paris, 19 août 1947.

This photograph was taken in the summer, quite possibly in June, maybe even sometime around when my father was born, on 16 June 1909. Just a month between his birth and your death

It is a photograph of you becoming an icon, and I imagine that is what you were thinking about when it was taken. Thinking determination. Thinking sacrifice.

Sacrifice means to make sacred.

I have often wondered about my wanting to know you, and at the same time about my resistance to finding out. And you have now been around a long time.

There is violence at the heart of each of our stories. Violence and silence.

Will telling set us free?

January 2019

Alongside the photograph I have now pinned a poster. One hundred years separates the two. The photograph was taken in 1909, and the poster was made in 2009 by the Indian Workers' Association to commemorate the centenary. It is a headshot in colour.

Across the top is written:

'The only lesson required in India today is to learn how to die and the only way of teaching it is to die ourselves. Therefore, I die and glory in my Martyrdom.'

And below:

'First Freedom Fighter to be hanged on foreign soil. England. GREAT MARTYR MADAN LAL DHINGRA. Indian Workers' Association (G.B.)

Resonant images. I look at them both and remember that it was a request by the Indian Workers' Association in 1976 that I should find a photograph, that finally made me take an interest in Madan Lal and made me embark on my quest for his story in the archives of the city. And although I didn't find the photograph then, my connection and commitment was cemented.

My mother's voice drifts into my head:

'Madan Lal Dhingra was your father's chacha, *that is to say he was your grandfather's younger brother. But I am told your grandfather,*

Sir Behari Lal, never allowed his name to be mentioned in the house.

'*Then, when we were in Paris, we met this man. He'd known Madan Lal in London. I remember your father was so happy to meet him.*'

'This man' must have been Madhava Rao. I unpin the photograph to look at his handwritten message on the back:

The last photograph of Deshbhakta Madan Lal Dhingra (d.17.08.09).
To the members of his family, from D.S. Madhava Rao. Paris, 19 août 1947

As I look at it a parallel emerges. Violence and silence are there in the dates, for the 17 August 1909 is the date of the execution.

And 38 years later on 17 August in 1947, the Radcliffe Line demarcating the boundaries of the Partition was announced. Overnight some 15 million people were on the move and more than a million people lost their lives.

Both events were silenced.

The short, handwritten message is redolent of the past and rich in intimation of what would come. I read: *To the members of his family ... Paris, 19 août 1947.* And I think of my young father holding the photograph, being so happy to learn of his mysterious uncle, Independent India being four days old. Maybe he thinks of his return the following month to resume his teaching at Government College in Lahore. Not realizing that the Radcliffe Line had placed Lahore in Pakistan. That he would never return. That he would stay and die in Paris – far from me. It was all a long time ago – and yet, how does time work?

As I am settling to write, I receive an article forwarded by a friend from the *New York Times* entitled, 'The Malign Incompetence of the British Ruling Class', in which the writer Pankaj Mishra draws analogies between the historic incompetence of the Partition of India and the present incompetence of Brexit.

'It is actually more accurate, for those invoking British history, to say that partition – the British Empire's ruinous exit strategy – has come home. In a grotesque irony, borders imposed in 1921 on Ireland, England's first colony, have proved to be the biggest stumbling block for the English Brexiteers chasing imperial virility. Moreover, Britain itself faces the prospect of partition if Brexit, a primarily English demand, is achieved and Scottish nationalists renew their call for independence.'

More parallels: Partition and Brexit. My past, present and future.
Now for some time travel ...

1.

23 JULY 1909:
PENTONVILLE PRISON,
LONDON

The door shuts with a heavy metallic clang. The sound seems to go on and on, echoing in the prison corridors outside, reverberating from the walls of the cell and through the young man who has just been led in and left. He stands there, rooted to the spot, waiting for the deafening noise to subside, the interminable clanking of keys in locks and the echo of footsteps. He listens carefully, trying to count the footfalls. Are all three leaving? Or is it only two? Soon they are lost among other sounds, more doors opening, slamming, voices shouting. Is he alone? He senses he is still being watched as he quickly surveys the cell: bare brick walls, bed, bucket, window. Three paces long, two-and-a-half wide, he guesses, as he strides across to verify his assessment. A slight breeze catches him. In the window above, a tiny pane, not much bigger than the palm of a hand, is open. He reaches up, and as he does so the coarse cloth of his prison clothing rubs up against his neck. He grips the wall to balance himself as he feels the tears welling up behind his eyes. The urge to cry out loud is almost irresistible.

'Hey Ram'! He implores. 'Help me God! Help me! I must not, I will not, break down now! Please help!'

He conjures the memory of just a few hours earlier, standing up, erect in the court watching the judge as he put on his black cap for the sentencing.

He'd bowed and said, 'Thank you, my Lord. I am proud to have the honour of laying down my life for my countrymen.'

He had felt weightless then. Possessed of an energy and lightness from the ether. Now, alone in his cell he willed the memory to sustain him, to help him stay erect when all his body wanted to do was to crumple.

Down the corridors there is a scream, followed by the sound of running feet. From the door outside his cell footfalls move away. He is alone. At last. Then he starts to breathe rhythmically and becomes composed. Straightening himself out, he wipes away the dampness that has squeezed through his clenched eyelids, tidies his prison clothes – a habitual gesture from smarter days – and looks again at the room. His gaze stops at the small parcel of his belongings on the bed: a book, a notebook, some letters and a pencil that he has been permitted to retain – all wrapped, tagged and labelled.

'Madan Baba, this time you are going properly ...' Ratan's words flash through his mind, together with the image of himself three years earlier standing in the outer courtyard of the family house. Alongside Ratan, the old family retainer, inspecting the tags and labels of the trunks that will make the voyage with him from

Amritsar to London. 'Cabin', 'Not wanted on Voyage', 'Wanted on Voyage'. Trunks freshly painted with his name: Madan Lal Dhingra. 'Madan Baba, this time you are going properly, like the son of a noble house.' Images flash into the mind's eye: Ratan, with his misty eyes, oil lamps and incense, *kumkum* and rice, flowers and coconuts, blessings and goodwill, embraces, touching feet, taking leave, waving at the station, Bhajan running alongside as the train steams away, darkening the day with its grits and smoke.

'Madan Lal Dhingra, now prisoner number 9493, is that me?'

The sound of his voice in the cell feels strange, solitary, trapped. What do you do when nothing remains for you of the outside world, other than a slight breeze and a small patch of blue? When images flood your mind of all that you will never do again: laugh with your friends; shadow-box with your brother; embrace your mother; touch your young wife; chase the *jugnu* fireflies on the roof terraces at night to trap them in a bottle to read by their light; walk along the Thames in the moonlight, like that long, last walk.

'What do you think when they have put you in a condemned cell, taken away your clothes and shoelaces, given you a number instead of your name?'

'My statement! My statement! Pompous, arrogant hypocrites in your wigs and gowns who wouldn't read my statement. But how did I forget it then, when I remember it all now?'

The walls slap your words back at you, beating you down from your feet on to your knees and racking your body with breaking sobs, which slowly let way into a great, yawning weariness. You lie crouched on the floor, feeling broken and beaten. How long? Until a faint breeze stirs the stillness and touches your forehead. You move. Slowly. Drag yourself across to and onto the bed. But just before the weariness engulfs you, you invoke the goddess riding resolutely on her tiger: 'Mother, I vowed my unflinching devotion to you. Help me to fulfil myself.'

You sleep, your damp locks streaking your face. In your dream it is the face of your own mother that smiles at you.

'I fed the sweet rice to the fish, my son. You will have a safe journey.'

Gently she lifts the tangled curls from your forehead to mark it, first with the red vermilion *kumkum* and then with the grains of rice. In your sleep you smile.

2.
1956: TRAIN JOURNEY
FROM BOMBAY

*'When you are in India, you call people who are older
than you "uncle" or "aunty" and if they are children
you call them "bhai" or "bhen".'*
'Yes, Daddy.'

I was thirteen, an English schoolgirl in Parisian clothes. I landed
in Bombay to go to a new school in South India. It was a two-day
journey by train and, having been equipped with the necessary
bedroll and clothing from the school lists by family friends in
Bombay, I met up with the school party to make the long journey
south.

It was my ninth school in as many years and my third in India.
There had been three in Switzerland, two in France and one in
England. Partition had had left us displaced in Paris waiting to go
home. I now felt like a proud trailblazer who had come home and
was paving the way for the others.

My parents had informed two family friends of my arrival and both had come to the airport to meet me. 'Uncle' had sent his secretary and 'Aunty' had come herself. It was agreed that I should go with aunty and visit uncle the next day.

Standing there in the muggy heat and bustle of Victoria Terminus – the steam, the whistles, the chatter, the clatter – I wished I'd worn one of the new Indian cotton dresses that Aunty had had stitched for me, as she'd suggested I do. But on the morning of my departure I wanted to put on the special going-away dress that had been bought for me the previous month at Galleries Lafayette. I had gone there with Marie Thérèse, one of my father's friends, 'We'll get something *très jolie, à la Parisienne*,' Marie Thérèse had said. 'Something in which you will feel confident.'

Now my tailored attire made me feel conspicuous. I noticed a group of girls who eyed me with curiosity. Then one of them smiled. A tomboy in plaits, she detached herself from the group and strode over as the others turned to throw side glances.

'Hello! You're new, aren't you? What's your name?'

'Leena.'

'Good. I'm Amrita. Welcome!' She thumped my arm. 'Come!' she commanded, both to the group and me. 'Come on, you guys!' The group of girls moved forwards, and we met halfway for the introductions: 'Charu, Anita, Sheila, Vijaya.' All around my age.

They took in my clothes as discreetly as their curiosity would allow. 'Are your parents posted overseas?' ventured Charu.

'Well, no ... not quite ... but well ...I don't know, but sort of, I suppose. My father works in Paris, actually.'

My flustered reply was because we were not 'posted'. Posted meant that you were sent from somewhere with somewhere to return to, whereas we were displaced by accident. My father, a lecturer in English at Government College, Lahore, had taken a six-month job with the new UNESCO in Paris. My mother had come to join him for a short holiday and six weeks after her arrival, and two months before they were due to return and reclaim my sister and me from the boarding school in which my mother had left us, Partition took place and there was nowhere to return to.

'Your parents are quite right to send you to India for your schooling. This is where you belong.'

It was warming to think that one belonged.

On the train Amrita asked me what caste I was.

'I'm afraid I don't know,' I replied.

'How can you not know what caste you are?!' She sounded incredulous. 'You must write to your parents and find out.'

My father replied by return of post and stated emphatically: caste was not an issue. I was a citizen of Free India and, as such, of the world, and he was surprised that a girl in a Krishnamurti school should ask me about caste. He suggested I should both remember and remind my friend of what Gandhiji had said.

I wasn't quite sure what that was.

Sitting under the tree in the recess, Amrita was diligently working with a penknife, transforming a branch into a staff for herself.

'Your father is modern,' she said, 'and that's good. But your name, Dhingra. Are you any relation to Madan Lal Dhingra?'

I knew that I was, but didn't know what that meant. A few years earlier, in boarding school in England, my older sister had asked me, 'Have you ever heard about Madan Lal Dhingra?'

'I don't think so ... I can't remember,' I'd replied.

'Well,' she'd continued, 'he was Daddy's uncle, and I've just read about him in a magazine series about famous murderers.'

'Gosh! Was he a murderer?' I shuddered.

'Well, that's what they called him. He shot some important Englishman and was hanged! Funny, isn't it, that Daddy's never spoken about him.'

I hadn't known what to make about this at the time.

Amrita was carving her initials on her staff. 'Are you?' she asked again.

'I think he was my father's uncle. But I don't know anything about him,' I added defensively.

'Your father's uncle! Really?' Amrita stopped and closed her penknife. 'Well, if Madan Lal Dhingra was your father's uncle, then you come from the family of a great patriot – and patriots are above caste!' She smiled at me. 'Here, have this.' She held out her newly made staff. 'They are very useful, you know.' She sliced the air with it to prove her point as we walked along. 'You can use it to knock tamarinds off trees and protect yourself from snakes and scorpions.'

I flinched. 'Snakes and scorpions? Are there many around?'

'Oh yes!' she replied cheerfully. 'But most of the time they hide away – and only a few are dangerous.' We walked along towards the 'summoning bell'.

'Did your parents go to jail?'

'No. They didn't. My mother always says it's her biggest regret.'

'What is?'

'That she didn't manage to get to jail.'

Amrita laughed. 'Well, my parents only went to jail during the "Quit India" movement, but my grandfather was in and out for much longer and it ruined his health.'

'Gosh!' I exclaimed, quite impressed.

'It was my grandfather who told us about Madan Lal Dhingra and the inspiration he had been.'

'What did he say?'

'That he was a great patriot who sacrificed his life so that India could be free, and that we must never forget him and the many others who died so that we could regain our self-respect. It's our duty to remember.'

Throughout my year at the school in India, Amrita remained my staunch friend, investing me with a respect I felt I hadn't earned. In the beautiful valley where our school was set we went for long walks. She taught me many skills: how to scale tall trees; how to dig groundnuts and boil them in salt water over a campfire; how to drink water without touching the ladle to my lips; how to avoid snakes and scorpions, and what to do in case I couldn't; how to wash my feet under a tap without using my hands but skilfully rubbing one foot against the other in an intricate dance that scrubbed them perfectly clean. She also taught me some nationalist songs: *Bande Ma-tar-a-am Bande Mata-Rum*. The hills would echo them back.

'When you grow up,' Amrita announced on one of our jaunts, 'you must find out about Madan Lal. We must never forget.'

I wasn't surprised that I knew so little. I had left India as a small child and been moving around since, so there was lots I didn't know. My tangle of bewilderment would disappear into a dark well in my mind labeled 'Partition', full of fears, confusions and unformulated questions.

'You might need to go to London for that. Because that's where Madan Lal was.'

At the time London was nowhere on my radar. My parents were in Paris, I had come home to India and the rest of the family would soon follow. That was the plan.

19

But life had other plans. My level of maths was way below that of my peers. So I'd have to lose at least a year.

'How could I keep you there,' my mother would explain later. 'They said you would lose a year at least. Rishi Valley was a small experimental school.'

So my mother moved me, probably on the advice of her family – who I can imagine might have said: 'You should send her to a proper school. None of this Krishnamurti experimental nonsense. Send her to MGD, Maharani Gayatri Devi Public School for Girls in Jaipur. That's a good school.'

I was placed in MGD, a school for princesses, which after the magic of Rishi Valley felt like a strange and stifling anachronism.

5.

1906: TRAIN JOURNEY TO BOMBAY

It was in the blistering May heat that Madan Lal left Amritsar, bound for Bombay on his way to London. Although the train left in the late afternoon, the ground was still giving off waves of heat so that his last image of the family group gathered on the platform was of them melting away into a blurry haze before being swallowed up and lost in a cloud of steam.

Madan watched the city disappear before joining his elder brother. He was travelling with him as far as Delhi in a specially appointed first-class carriage. His brother, Dr Behari Lal, was deeply engrossed in a medical book on eugenics. Madan sank down comfortably by the window, opposite a fan circulating ice-cooled air and peered out of the half-closed Venetian blinds.

The train rocked and hooted on its way across the Punjab, casting long shadows and clouds of steam over the parched, sun-baked plains. It was difficult to imagine that this dry landscape would suddenly burst into a lush green when the rains would come in six to eight weeks' time. In eight weeks' time, Madan calculated, he would be on his own and settled in his London lodgings. His eldest brother, Kundan, who was briefly working in England, had arranged to stay on to meet him. In eight weeks Kundan would have finished his duties and be sailing back to India. He smiled and caught his reflection in the window: his smart summer suit, soft powder-blue turban, round gold-rimmed spectacles, and the last traces of sandalwood paste and vermilion powder on his forehead from his mother's parting prayers. She had also given him this same blue turban, and he resolved that when he returned to Amritsar he would wear it. But that was at least three years' away. Now he was leaving – 'going properly', as Ratan had said. *Well, Ratan Kaka, this time I am going more than just properly; I'm going in pukka style, in luxury, like a Raja.*

The compartment was freshly painted, lined with fine wood panelling and fittings of polished brass. On the opposite, sunny, side the wooden shutters had been pulled down and four electric fans circulated ice-cooled air. Madan stroked the smooth finish of the furnishing fabric and watched the uniformed bearers prepare the tables for tea. Dinner, by invitation, would be in the dining room of the adjoining private saloon of the Maharaja of Jind, ruler of one of the independent states of the Punjab, where Dr Behari Lal served as Chief Medical Officer.

These special travel arrangements had been made because Madan Lal left Amritsar when he did. For the middle of May was also the season during which the various departments of the British administration made their annual migration from the heat of the plains to the cooler hills of Simla, which until the middle of September became the summer capital of the British Raj. As was the fashion, the local maharajas, nawabs and other princelings also made their way up to the hills for the summer, and it was because of this that Madan Lal made the first part of his journey to Delhi with his elder brother.

Dr Behari Lal was returning from Lahore where he had accompanied the Maharaja for some delicate negotiations with the British resident for the independent states. For the Maharaja, Dr Behari Lal was more than Chief Medical Officer; he was an invaluable asset in dealing with the British administration. He was familiar with the peculiar English ways and knew just how to handle things in such a way so as to elicit both the respect of the government and the unmitigated admiration of his employer. Even though Jind was an 'independent native state', this independence could only be maintained by a cautious and delicate diplomacy.

At Ambala the Maharaja's saloon would be detached to go on to Kalka and the hills whilst the others continued to Delhi. Madan would then complete the rest of his journey on his own and, after a few days in Bombay, board the 'homeward bound' P&O *Macedonia* steamer to London.

Madan thought about his journey and again smiled to himself. Behari Lal, glancing up briefly from his book to turn a page, caught a glimpse of his younger brother's smile and the corners of his own mouth flickered slightly as he felt a warm sense of satisfaction. He closed his book and smiled at his brother. It pleased him that Madan was going to England to study, that he was going properly this time. Behari Lal's satisfaction stemmed in part from the role he had played in enabling this present turn of events. It was as it should be and was his due as the son of Dr Ditto Mal, the first Indian civil surgeon of the Punjab.

Of the seven brothers, all the five older brothers had been to Europe for their further education. In his own case it had been for medicine in England and Belgium, and it was only right that the youngest two, Madan Lal and Bhajan Lal, should have the same opportunity. In Madan's case, however, this did not happen smoothly.

Over the years, Dr Ditta Mal had amassed a considerable amount of property in and around Amritsar, in addition to the family lands in their native district of Sahiwal. With his five eldest sons well-established in a profession, two as doctors, two as barristers and one as a successful businessman, he began to entertain the idea of keeping at least one of his two younger sons to help him administer the family estates. The youngest, Bhajan Lal, had quite early on expressed an interest in law. He often spent time in the chambers of his elder brother, Chaman Lal, a pleader at the Amritsar Bar, who took it upon himself to persuade their father to send Bhajan to England, to join Gray's Inn, be called to the Bar, and then, maybe, to join his practice in Amritsar. So it had been decided that Bhajan Lal would be sent off to England in three or four years' time when he finished his studies in India and that Madan Lal would be the one to help his father. As Madan had never shown any particular enthusiasm or definite direction in his choice of career, it appeared to Dr Ditta Mal to be a natural choice, and he decided to train him himself or at least to keep him near him and oversee his training.

None of the brothers thought this was the right course of action, neither did they feel that Madan was suited for what had been planned for him, but their father was adamant. Dr Ditta Mal was a highly intelligent, self-made, strong-willed man with an independent mind and he was used to having his own way. It was not easy to argue with him and neither was it in the scheme of things to question or contradict a father's wishes.

Behari conferred with his older brother, Mohan Lal, and they both agreed that Madan was maybe too much like their own father in character to fall neatly into a preordained course that was not of his own choosing. At the same time, they also conceded that there was nothing very much they could do about this.

Dr Ditta Mal in no way felt that he was doing his son a disservice. Quite the contrary. He was a pragmatist and knew that however well his sons did in their respective professions, they could never earn as much as they would from the rents of the properties he had amassed. In training Madan for the business, he would leave him both skilled and well settled. He decided that Madan should be called back to Amritsar from Lahore, where he was pursuing his studies at Government College.

Madan returned to Amritsar. He withdrew into himself, confiding in no one, not even Bhajan or Ratan Kaka. He fulfilled his obligations, did what was expected, but never smiled any more. Behari came to know about this from different sources: messages from his younger brothers, other members of the family and finally a letter from his mother in Bhajan's hand requesting him to come and speak to his father as the two eldest, Kundan and Mohan, were both away. It was agreed that he would arrange a visit to Amritsar, purportedly on Jind state affairs, and in the ensuing interview with his father would broach the issue of Madan's education. What puzzled the brothers most was that their father, who had long upheld the view that a spell away from home was important for developing his sons' independence and character, should not treat Madan in the same way as he had treated his other sons.

Behari sipped his tea and remembered the first time he had intervened on Madan's behalf. It had been in January, a day before

Lohri, the festival that marks the coldest day of the year. That particular year it had been exceptionally cold, so much so that he had unpacked his Swiss winter coat for the journey to Amritsar. A sharp chill had greeted him as he stepped out of the carriage. In the stables, piles of wood had been gathered for the Lohri bonfires of the next evening, and outside the kitchen the long sugar canes lay waiting to be chopped for the celebrations.

Later that evening he remembered feeling another shiver, this time owing to something other than the cold, as he stood in the 'English' drawing room collecting his thoughts before confronting his father. He thought how much easier it was to deal with the most officious British official than to deal with his own father. The English drawing room with its stiffly upright Victorian furniture served as a formal reception area. Across it, behind the heavy velvet drapes, a door led into the *baithak*, the informal sitting room/study, furnished in Indian style and known by its Indian name. Behari stepped out of his shoes and into the room that greeted him, warm and bright. Each of the five low divans was covered with a white sheet, the floor was carpeted with rugs and on the walls hung the framed certificates, honours and portraits of the family. Two lighted *sigeris* gave out smokeless heat from their charcoal embers and Dr Ditta, comfortably resting on the *gao-takia* bolster, a shawl draped over his legs, gently pulled at his hookah that responded with a resonant purr.

'Come in, my son, come!' His voice had been warm and welcoming. As Behari rose from touching his father's feet, Dr Ditta added, 'Your mother told me she was writing to you.'

'Yes father, we are all concerned about Madan.'

'I am concerned, too. He is also my son and I have resolved to send him away for further training.'

'I am glad, father. A young man needs an independent profession, especially these days when there is so much opportunity for advancement. But then I am only expressing your own views.'

'Quite so. I have myself observed that Madan is not quite himself, and I am making arrangements for his future. Do not worry. I have told your mother as much. But I am glad you are here. You will be with us for Lohri and there are some matters upon which I would welcome your opinion.' And Dr Ditta proceeded to discuss some medical matters with his son.

The next evening the Lohri bonfires were lit and everyone gathered around, pushing in their sticks of sugar cane, then retrieving them to suck the warm, sweet juice whilst loudly singing the Lohri song: 'Sloth and torpor now burn away. Light and energy fill the day!'

Behari saw Bhajan laugh and Madan smile and, though not normally demonstrative, he walked over to embrace his two younger brothers. It even crossed his mind that his fine Austrian coat would, with a few alterations, serve Madan well for the English winters. It would even suit his brother's fastidious tastes.

In retrospect he should have realised that his father and he were talking at cross-purposes, but he hadn't, so he was genuinely surprised when he learned that Madan had not been sent abroad but instead to Kashmir, to work for six months in the Settlement Department.

Six months later came the shocking news that in Jammu, Madan had signed on as a lascar in the merchant navy – to work as a stoker! Behari winced at the memory. Clearly it was an act of desperation. Why else should Madan Lal, the son of a Rai Sahib, of

Dr Ditta Mal Dhingra of Amritsar, a young man who could enter any of the new professions, sign on to work as a simple seaman, an ordinary lascar? When he returned, some nine months later, Madan had said that 'he had wanted to travel'. Then it had taken all the brothers, Ammaji their mother and many hours in the *baithak* to convince their father to send Madan abroad.

Now he glanced at his younger brother with a warm sense of satisfaction. Indeed, he thought, everything was at last turning out as it should and engineering, he was sure, would be eminently suitable for Madan's temperament, and for the many opportunities opening up in the Punjab.

Madan briefly caught his brother's glance, but also noted the fine tailoring of his suit and thought that now he, too, would be getting a new outfit made by W. J. Pickett, the family tailor in New Bond Street.

He got up and was opening up the Venetian blinds as the train slowed to enter a station. 'Jullunder', it read. The carriage lined up alongside a goods train; the station platform was on the opposite, shuttered side of the compartment. The two brothers watched the loading, the bales of cotton, the sacks of wheat, grains and pulses – the rich exports of the province – bound for the ports of Karachi, Bombay or Calcutta.

'These English *Ferengee*,' Babu Ram would say, shaking his head and rolling his eyes, 'they are very clever. They give us land, make us grow what *they* want, and then buy it from us at *their* price. And we, we say: "thank you, thank you".'

Madan caught his elder brother's eye looking out with pride. He said: 'With the new irrigation canals, output has doubled, trebled, with at least two harvests a year. This is all produce from the newly reclaimed canal colonies.'

Madan nodded.

'It really is a remarkable achievement, and when you return qualified you will contribute your part to it. Wastelands have been reclaimed. People have been given land free, as well as seeds. The benefits of this administration are great indeed. And also,' he added more pointedly, 'it is a feat of engineering.'

Madan nodded again. 'Yes Behari Bhai, it is a remarkable feat, of engineering.'

4.
1957: PARIS, PARTITION, PAPA

'Remember we are refugees. Everything we had was lost in the Partition, so everything we now have is by God's Grace. Therefore, you must always remember to share your good fortune with those less fortunate than you.'

When the summer holidays came along, I returned home. To Paris. And the little apartment on the fourth floor of Avenue Niel in Paris 17. Central, noisy, sooty, its only view was stone apartment buildings and the narrow street below.

The apartment itself comprised two rooms, which had been opened out to form a single larger one, a bathroom, an eat-in kitchen and a hall with an enormous built-in cupboard. It was ideal for a single person or a newly married couple. But for a family of four it was unsuitably small and therefore we could rarely be there together for any length of time.

It was intended to be temporary, until a larger flat could be found, a permanent job came along or until we moved on and returned home to India. But it was also cheap and convenient: ten minutes to the Arc de Triomphe, fifteen minutes to the Champs Élysées and two minutes from a most wonderful fruit and vegetable market.

And so it became home and a haven, a magical space, a little floating oasis, chock-full of books, curios, pictures – and light. My parents, each in their own way, had tried to fill the emptiness and longing that their loss of home had left.

Post-war Paris was the cultural and intellectual hub of the time, so for my father, with his fluent French and philosophical bent, this emptiness was filled by books and the rich cosmopolitan cultural life of the city, the intellectual ferment and torment following the war, the crumbling colonial reigns and the search for new meanings, meetings and cross-cultural dialogues. He would share this through articles in various Indian newspapers and his regular monthly column: 'Leaves from a Paris Diary' for *The Aryan Path*, the journal of the Theosophical Society.

My mother's way was more tangible and located primarily at the Marché aux Puces, the flea market, to where she would make systematic forays to reclaim the imperial loot, long-languishing and unvalued. She sought and found Thai buddhas, Tibetan thankas, Chinese carvings, Indian bronzes, but in particular she would seek the splendid Jamevar shawls from Kashmir. Steadily these finely woven paisleys, red, maroon, ochre, black, blue-green, would find their way into our small apartment, in transit, waiting to be shipped back to their home in India where they rightfully belonged and could be fully appreciated. In the meantime, we slept over them and under them. Four trunks of shawls with a mattress on top made a bed, and my sister and I each slept on one of these. Shawls also served as blankets, as bedcovers, and my mother would put them to their proper use by wearing them instead of coats. In fact, she resolutely refused ever to wear coats or closed shoes; she was, she insisted, an Indian woman – so why should she dress like a European?

I was thrilled to be back with my parents and their different ways, the sunny flat, the familiar *quartier* with its daily market, Madame Nicole our concierge who filled me in on all the latest gossip ... and I was pleased to find that the little under-used, inaccessible kitchen cupboard I had appropriated as my trove when I was nine-and-a-half when, as now, I'd returned from a school in India, was waiting for me. All my books and personal things were there: *Les Contes de Perrault*, *Les mémoires d'un âne*, *La Comtesse de Ségur*, *Ride with the Sun* ... All had been left as they were, untouched.

In Paris everyone was busy and following their own preoccupations. My elder sister was studying at the Sorbonne and living in the University residences. My father was at his office during the day and was also in the last stages of finishing a book entitled *Through Asian Eyes* and another book of Indian stories which had just been published in French, called *Le Collier D'Étoiles* and dedicated: '*Pour ma fille Leena*'. I liked that.

My mother, who didn't speak French, although she tried to learn, didn't wear glasses although she was very short-sighted, didn't enjoy housekeeping but produced delicious 'lazy cooking' food, was often floating in what she called her 'dreamland', a perfect universe of loving family, long friendships and projects to help refugees, which was also an endless font of stories, including some about bad housekeepers. In this dreamland she was designing a house to be built in Delhi to replace the one lost in Lahore. She had recently sent some money for a plot in a large tract of land she had sourced and encouraged her sister to buy into as well – so that dream appeared to be solidifying. She was happy and so was I. We would have a place to live and be able to go home! The French notebooks, bought from our local *Prisunic*, had squares rather than lines and were perfect to measure out the feet and inches of rooms, furniture, dreams ...

Stretched out on the big bed covered in a paisley shawl in her purple sari with a yellow border, she would enunciate: 'In life you have to have a dream and then you have to dream it. From the time I was quite small I always had this dream of building a house to my design.' She would close her eyes as she reminisced. 'Everyone laughed at me. I let them laugh. They laughed, I dreamed and I built my house. I was the first person in my family to build a house. And it was a beautiful house. And in the house we would have parties – dancing parties, fancy-dress parties, literary parties. Once I went as Helen of Troy and your father as Marlowe ... "Was this the face that launched a thousand ships?" ... It was such a wonderful life.'

Or sometimes she might look wistfully out of the window and ask the grey Parisian sky, 'Why did these Britishers always make these partitions? Creating endless suffering. Tell me. Why?'

The sky had no reply.

As a small child I never quite knew what Partition was; was it a mighty machine or a mean monster? I only knew that it was something bad, that it had hurt my darling Mummy and Daddy and that it upset them to talk about it. And I didn't want to upset them. I loved them too much for that. I wanted to help them and for that I needed to be a good girl, do as I was told and not ask too many questions.

'Mama why won't Partition give us back our house?'

'Shh, darling. Go back to sleep.'

'When I grow up I'll find that Partition monster, I will ...'

Both my parents were storytellers. But Partition was never a story that could be told, and my attempt to clarify what it was only led to more confusion. Lahore was our home. We couldn't go back to Lahore, because it was no longer in India but in Pakistan, which was a Muslim state and we were Hindus. And, no, of course it didn't mean that Muslims were our enemies! Where did I get such a silly, idiotic idea? After all, Uncle Bashir and Aunty Sara, Uncle Aziz, Azim, Aunty this and Aunty that were all Muslims. Indian Muslims were our friends and, yes, so were some Pakistani Muslims, though sometimes they weren't always allowed to be because the governments didn't want them to be. And so that was why my father and Uncle Akhtar never met in Paris but would instead drive out in separate cars to Jean's place in the countryside. This was because even though Uncle Akhtar was a good friend, had been my father's student in Lahore, and the families had known each other for generations, Uncle Akhtar now worked in the Pakistani embassy and we were Indians. Yes, that's right, Uncle Akhtar had been an Indian before Partition, but now he was a Pakistani, although he had a brother who was still an Indian because he'd stayed on in India. But, no, we couldn't go to Lahore because it was in Pakistan.

The conversations would usually end with my being told it was rude to ask so many questions, and to remember that although we had lost everything and were refugees we must be very grateful and always remember to share our good fortune.

One long and wet weekend after my return, when my father was away annotating the proofs of his book and my mother had not gone to the flea market and was engrossed in her notebook drawing plans for the house in India, I asked: 'Mummy, have you ever heard about Madan Lal Dhingra?'

'Hmm,' replied my mother, from some distant somewhere in her own world.

'You're not listening to me are you? Madan Lal Dhingra. Have you heard of him?'

'Madan Lal Dhingra? Ah yes. Madan Lal.' She enclosed the pencil into her notebook and put it to one side. 'Madan Lal.' She was nodding her head and looking up at the ceiling as she gathered the story from its place in the air as though it was suspended there. Then she unfolded her narrative in the special tone reserved for the stories I was encouraged to remember.

'Madan Lal Dhingra was your father's *chacha*, that is to say he was your grandfather's younger brother, but your grandfather, Sir Behari Lal never allowed his name to be mentioned in his house.

'In those days the Britishers used to rule and we had to do what they wanted. They didn't understand us at all but kept telling us that they were there for our own good. We had no say, no say at all. If Indians did say anything the Britishers didn't like, they could be beaten, killed or sent off to Kala Pani – that's the Andaman Islands. Madan Lal had come to London as a student, and had become a member of a revolutionary group. These were young men who were prepared to sacrifice their lives to make India free once again. And that's what Madan Lal did, sacrificed his life. He was fearless. He said in court that his only wish was to be reborn so that he could die for the same cause until India was free. Churchill wrote a book called *Great Speeches in Court* or something and your Uncle Madan's speech was in it.

'When we first came to Paris, we met a man who had known Madan in London. Then your father went to see him and met another person I think who had also known Madan. Your father was very happy.

'You see, it is only through great sacrifice that India is free today. Remember that. We all have a duty and a debt – to make her strong again. You must make yourself strong and clear so as to know your duty to your Motherland.'

But before I could fulfil this destiny/duty to a distant homeland – which was in the future – in the present, I needed to finish my schooling.

On returning from India I had said to my father, 'You know, Daddy, you send me to a Quaker school and then a Krishnamurti school and then expect me to fit into an authoritarian Indian/English public school where your letters are opened and "treats" are compulsory. And they can quite be cruel, too.'

My father laughed, and said simply, 'Well you don't have to go back there if you don't want to.' And then to himself he added: 'In any case, I've never liked uniforms.'

So to finish my exams, my mother and I embarked for London. My father had written to his friend Mr Knaster who had organised a tutor for my GCEs and a drama teacher to prepare me for drama school. The story went that when I was ten I'd asked my father:

'Daddy what do you want me to become when I grow up?'

'An actress, of course.'

'Oh Daddy, how can I become what I already am!'

'Don't forget to say goodbye properly to Madame Nicole before you leave. Get some flowers and chocolates and spend a bit of time with her. It's important.'

'Yes, Daddy.'

At the Gare du Nord after we had checked in our cases to be collected in London, my father handed me an envelope

'When you are in England and anyone invites you over, the first thing you do when you get home is you write a thank-you card and post it the very same day. It's important. It's how things are done. There are some in this envelope and always keep a supply handy.'

'Yes, Daddy.'

I slipped the envelope in the yet-uncut pages of my father's book beside a story called: *Un Tigre est un Tigre (A tiger is a tiger)*

'And take care of your Mummy.'

'Yes, Daddy.'

As the train pulled out of the Gare du Nord, my father stayed on the platform watching it go, concerned and willing us well. I watched from the window until he disappeared into a cloud of steam and I could see him no more. The image stayed with me. I was sad to leave him behind.

But Madan Lal came with us. And from the beginning his story started to merge and weave in and out of my mother's story, and the story of India.

Although I had travelled to England before, it had always been by air as an unaccompanied child, so the train and then the sea was a new adventure.

'I suppose Uncle Madan Lal must have come by sea.'

'Of course. Even the post came by sea, then.'

On the ferry my mother reminisced about her European tour in the mid-thirties, her good fortune to have been able to go, of tasting olive oil, kissing the pope's ring, meeting Mussolini, getting his autograph and absent-mindedly walking off with his pen:

'Then they came running after me waving their arms and shouting, 'Il Duce's pen, Il Duce's pen.'

She laughed at the memory.

'Now I didn't hear about Madan Lal in the family because they didn't talk about it. I heard about it from Aunty Sarlata. She was family in that she'd married your father's uncle who used to be the Chief Medical Officer in Kashmir. He had died some time back, outside India. I think he may even have died in Paris, but Aunty Sarlata continued living in Kashmir.

'In the summers when it was very hot in the plains and there were vacations from Government College, we would go to the hills. Either to Simla, or to Kashmir or Dalhousie. That summer we went to Gulmarg in Kashmir, and I went to visit Aunty Sarlata. She was very ill and living all alone. I stayed to look after her. She was a Bengali lady, the great, great granddaughter of Raja Ram Mohan Roy. You know about him, of course?'

'No. Who was he?'

'Haven't I told you about Raja Ram Mohan Roy?' She shook her head. 'You should know about him, he was great reformer. A very great man. He believed in women's equality, set up the Brahmo Samaj and travelled a great deal. He came to Paris at the time of the French Revolution. He died in England somewhere.

'Then one evening Aunty Sarlata and I were sitting on her porch looking out at the great mountains when she suddenly told me that she had only married into the Dhingra family because of Madan Lal. Naturally I was very intrigued. She said that at the time when it all happened, the trial and all, she was just a young girl, but that she'd remembered everything. It had created a sensation in Calcutta and everyone in Bengal talked about it. She used to have a photograph of Madan Lal and people knew his speech by heart. She said the impact was enormous and that someone got up in the English Parliament and said that from that day onwards the history of India would no longer be the same, or something like that.

'You see, I understood her completely. When I was a young girl, they hanged Bhagat Singh and he was a great hero. He, too, was only in his early twenties, and all he wanted was that India should be free. And they hanged him. They feared trouble and they kept the date a secret, so we never knew when it was going to happen. We would guess and there would be rumours. There was this big Congress session in Lahore and before the session we all sang *"Bhena tusi gao kodiya, Datta Bhagat Singh chad gaye ghodian,"* which means "Sisters sing auspicious songs, Datta and Bhagat Singh have mounted their bridal horses." I wept and wept and wept. We all did. The whole hall was weeping.' My mother tugged at the end of her sari and wiped away a glistening of moisture from her eyes.

5.
1906: SEA VOYAGE

Arriving in Bombay, Madan Lal was overcome with a feeling of exhilaration. The proximity of the sea and everything associated with it invariably had this effect on him. He'd felt it that very first time, some ten or eleven years earlier, when their eldest brother Kundan had taken Bhajan and himself to Bombay. He remembered how immediately his spirits were uplifted, how his lungs had felt clear and how everything had taken on an almost magical quality: the sea, the sounds, the smells, the air, and even the muggy humidity. It did more than just uplift his spirits; it was as though it enabled him to think more clearly, as though he could almost see his thoughts and observe them instead of their simply remaining a noise in his head. If he closed his eyes and conjured up an image, he could open his eyes and project the image on to the sea and watch it.

'Would you be requiring a fan, sir?' asked the purser as Madan completed the formalities on arrival on the ship. 'There is an extra charge of one pound for the duration of the journey.' Madan nodded his head. 'Very good sir. We will add it to your bill.' In the four-berth cabin, two of his fellow travellers had already boarded, although they were not in the cabin when Madan came in. He put away his things in the cabin trunk, tidied himself and stepped out on to the spar deck to look out once again at the sea.

He wondered at himself, a land-bound Punjabi whose natural affinity should have been with the plains and the mountains that had always surrounded him, but who instead was drawn into such a rapport with an alien sea. Then again, he'd always been different, an outsider, who couldn't quite see things like others or fit in with their ways. Especially the ways of his father and older brothers. His father, Baoji, loved the mountains and probably thought that Madan loved them just as much. Madan remembered that each time his father had sent him away from Amritsar it was to the hills. First, he had apprenticed him to Nanda Sahib who ran the Kalka to Simla *tonga* service, and then he had sent him to Kashmir to work with the settlement department. Both had been upsetting experiences, nothing to do with the natural heights of the landscape but all to do with the lofty arrogance of the English rulers. Madan had found Nanda Sahib's smarmy subservience intolerable, and in Kashmir had resented the nature of the work, which was to record the local revenue settlements for the purposes of taxation. 'The produce is taken away and the land that produces it is taxed as well.'

It wasn't the mountains; the mountains were wonderful, majestic and awesome. They were like the Titans of old who had dared to rebel and were left imprisoned in the earth reaching up to the unattainable: the sky. Madan, in the idyllic landscape of Kashmir, the garden on the roof of the world, had also felt imprisoned.

The sea offered an escape. It offered unchartered territories, different and changing horizons. It offered untameable turbulence. And it was from its depths that the Amrit had been churned up. Madan closed his eyes and saw his brother Bhajan and himself,

41

aged about four and five years old, sitting cross-legged on the floor and listening attentively to their mother telling them the story of the churning of the ocean. Now, opening his eyes to look at the water, he could almost see the great snake Vasuki being tugged and pulled as the ocean was churned to produce the pot of the sacred Amrit, the nectar of immortality. He would often think of that story. He and Bhajan had shared in the making of the special sweet rice, which would be taken down to the river to be fed to the fish.

'Speak to the fish,' his mother had told them. 'Tell them to tell their brothers and sisters in the sea to protect your brother and give him a safe journey.' Their mother would place a handful of rice in their hands for them to throw in. When he'd grown older, he'd stopped accompanying his mother to the river. But on the day of his departure his mother had placed a tiny ball of sweet rice in his mouth. 'I fed the sweet rice to the fish, my son, you will have a safe journey.' Even now he could almost taste the sweetness.

He looked down at the waves below him, rushing up and lapping against the ship, frothing at the edges and retreating back before surging forward again and again.

'Ruling the waves!' he said to himself. 'What an arrogant presumption and how typical of the English, to imagine that they can rule the waves! No one rules the waves; very soon the English will be cut down to their true size. The sea that brought them here will take them away, and on that day, I shall stand on the quayside and watch them go and laugh as I have never laughed before.' Madan smiled at the idea as he walked along the deck, past the smoking room, to where he could overlook the port and the city.

Nothing in his demeanour betrayed his thoughts. Standing there, he looked what he was, a young man in his early twenties from a privileged background, undoubtedly going to England for further studies that would enable him to enter one of the new professions that had been concomitant with British rule. Leaning over the balustrade, watching the passengers board and the ship being loaded, he cut a most agreeable figure, dashing even. He was tall, with fine features and dark, steady eyes marked with an intent gaze. His head was crowned with thick, black curls, neatly tamed into place but occasionally requiring a bit of coaxing to stay put, which he achieved with a characteristic gesture. His clothes, tailored and tasteful, revealed a streak of the dapper, betraying a buoyant youthfulness beneath his otherwise controlled reserve. The reserve was part of his disposition and the control something he had early learned to express. The intent gaze, although shielded by spectacles, revealed to the discerning observer the look of a man who had witnessed a lot – much more than a typical man of his years.

Indeed, Madan had witnessed a lot in his twenty-two years. He was already aware of the wider world beyond the protected precincts of family and privilege.

Taking leave from his brother he had on impulse asked, 'Behari Bhai, may I keep the newspapers?'

'What? These old newspapers?'

'Yes. Newspapers of the day I left Amritsar. I would like to take them with me to London.'

Behari had smiled as he handed over the papers, all perfectly folded back into their original state. He had always suspected his younger brother of having a touch of eccentricity, but this sudden expression of sentimentality, as he saw it, was quite new. He smiled at Madan and gave him a gentle pat on the shoulder before the farewell embrace. On Madan's part, asking for the papers had been quite spontaneous; he hadn't been aware of a particular reason. But he knew that the India to which he would return would be different from the one he was leaving behind. He knew this from what he had seen and heard beyond the peaceful Punjab, but he knew it also from some deep, indefinable instinct, a connectedness to the spirit of the age – the *zeitgeist*. It gave him flashes of foresight and foreboding, and feelings that it was not always possible to understand or contain. He knew for certain that India was on the threshold of an enormous change. Most people didn't know this. Those two students boarding, did they know? Or that band of Tommies and the English family with their two children, a boy and a girl and ayah all climbing the ramp to board the homeward-bound *Macedonia*; they didn't know and probably didn't want to know.

'*Ek din inke sab jahazey*. One day, all their ships will take them home,' Babu Ram used to say, and Mohammed Ali would laugh. 'And all their fires they will also have to stoke themselves.'

'Babu Ram.' Madan silently mouthed the name, and conjured him up in his mind's eye so clearly that he was astonished when he actually saw him, or what looked like him among a group of lascars on the quay. 'Extraordinary,' he said out loud, and sliding quickly along the balustrade to go towards the ramp, he collided with a fellow passenger, another young Indian who, in turn, collided with another, a white man, incurring his wrath: 'Watch out, you silly nigger.'

When Madan looked again, the group of lascars had moved closer. He was now no longer certain that the man was Babu Ram. Madan tried to squint through his glasses whilst leaning over the railings. A voice behind him said, 'Would you like to borrow these?'

Madan turned. An Englishman in his sixties, with a kindly face and ruddy complexion from exposure to the elements, was offering him a pair of binoculars.

'Thank you.' Madan flushed slightly and accepted the binoculars. 'Thank you,' he said again when he returned them. 'I thought I saw someone I knew.'

'It wasn't him?'

'No, I'm afraid not.'

'I am sorry.' The man smiled genially. 'You're from Bombay?'

'No. I'm from the Punjab.'

'The Punjab, eh? Fine province, the Punjab, and fine people, too.'

Madan bowed. 'You are very kind, Sir.'

'I was posted in the Punjab for a while. Colonel Dane of the Rajputana Rifles.'

'Madan Lal Dhingra, from Amritsar.'

'What will you be studying in England? I presume you are going to study?'

'Yes sir, engineering.'

'Oh, excellent. Plenty of scope for that in the Punjab: canals, bridges, railways, still lots to be done.'

'Indeed, Sir.'

'Yes, and I'm sure the public works department will do well with a fine young man like you.'

Madan bowed again. 'You are very kind, Sir.'

'Yes, well, good day to you, young man. We are sure to meet again.'

Madan returned the smile, and then glanced to where the group of lascars had been standing. They were no longer there.

Madan was still thinking of Babu Ram and his last time at sea when he entered the cabin to change for dinner, to discover that the young man he had collided with earlier in the day was in the berth next to him.

'Harish Chandra Koregaonkar.'

'Madan Lal Dhingra.' They soon discovered that they were the same age and both on their way to London, where both planned to study civil engineering. They went in to eat together like old friends.

That night, long after the others had gone to bed, Madan stayed out on the deck, intoxicating himself with the sea air and a sense of – what was it? – freedom, adventure … and something else. So many things. A whole host of feelings raged within him, demanding attention and pushing away the need for sleep. There was excitement about going to England for the first time. He wanted to see this place, this magnet that both attracted and repulsed him. He wanted to be independent, to follow his own way. Civil engineering was a good idea, it would enable him to travel and he'd always loved that. Moving around, seeing new places. He stopped walking and looked down into the dark water, shot through with shafts of light from the ship, and watched as it transformed into the inner courtyard of the house in Amritsar. He thought of his father and felt grateful to him. He could see Ratan placing hot charcoals in the hookah and carrying it up the stairs into the *baithak*; he could see his sisters-in-law laughing as they churned the buttermilk; and the children playing *chowpat* by the swing. The inner courtyard was the heart of the house, Ammaji's domain. It connected all other parts of the house, the various roof terraces, the balconies, verandas, all the rooms, the other courtyards, the stables. But it had no direct access to the street. It was the protected space of the home. Like Ammaji herself. It was thanks to Ammaji that he was now on this ship sailing to England. Because it was Ammaji who had intervened to make it possible when Baoji was adamant that he should stay. Of course, everyone had tried to persuade him, all his older brothers and particularly Behari Bhai. But only Ammaji could ever change Baoji's mind. As he thought of Baoji, Madan lifted up his head, looked out into the sky and thought that he would not like to disappoint this father again.

6.

1906: AMRITSAR – SAHIB DITTA MAL

Rai Sahib Doctor Ditta Mal, returning from his early morning ride, directed Rani his grey mare into a gentle trot as they re-entered Amritsar. The city was now waking to a cacophony of birds, dogs, goats, cows and the various calls from the mosques, temples and gurdwaras. Later in the morning he would accompany his wife to the Darbār Sahib, whose famous golden dome he could see in the distance.

He loved these early morning rides that had formed part of his routine since his youth, apart from the time when he was a medical student in Lahore and there were no facilities to keep a horse. But even then, Amritsar was only thirty miles away, a short journey on the railway. He'd been aged sixteen when the railway had opened and his father had taken him to Lahore, the legendary city that all the poets had written about, and he'd not been disappointed by its many delights. At one time he had briefly toyed with the idea of settling in Lahore upon his retirement and had shared these embryonic thoughts with his wife Vidyavati. She had nodded her head and listened, but when she'd been asked about what she thought the idea she'd been very definite.

'Lahore,' she'd said, 'is a grand city, a legendary city, a city of art, culture and sophistication, about that there is no doubt. It is also a cosmopolitan city, full of opportunities and appeal, and it is the capital of the Punjab.'

He'd known straight away where she'd stood but he heard her through.

'But why,' she'd asked, 'would you wish to leave Amritsar, the city in which you grew up, the place your family chose when they moved from Sahiwal? Amritsar is a city with many advantages. It has the advantages of both city and country. As it is closer to the hills its climate is more temperate than Lahore, which in any case is so near that it is considered almost a twin city. The people are less sophisticated than Lahoris, rustic cousins, maybe, but they are also down-to-earth and straightforward. Amritsar is a centre of manufacture, commerce, a trade route, a place of pilgrimage. Whereas Lahore might be the seat of power, Amritsar is the heart of the Punjab. It is a holy city, the centre of Sikhism, the faith that the Punjab itself had engendered, founded on the beliefs and ideals of the great saint Guru Nanak, who was venerated by both Hindus and Muslims. And hadn't Guru Arjan Singh asked the Muslim *pir* Mian Mir of Lahore to lay the foundation stone of the great temple? Amritsar is where you belong and where you will make the best contribution.' She reminded him that in Lahore there were many physicians. In Amritsar he would be able to provide better facilities for the patients who attended his practice.

Ditta Mal liked Amritsar and his wife's opinions echoed much of what he felt. He already had property in the city along the Grand Trunk Road. Shortly afterwards he purchased land in the Khatra Sher Singh, just outside the Hall Gate, on which he gradually built up a row of twenty-one houses that formed his home, his eye clinic and provided the necessary accommodation for the princes and chiefs and their large retinues that featured amongst his patients. Alongside, he ran a free clinic for the poorer citizens of the city. The doctor was also an active member of the municipal committee where his particular area of interest, other than health, was the education of women – on which he held very progressive views, which he made a point of expounding with passion.

'Madan's letter should arrive any day now,' Dr Ditta announced that evening to his wife, having calculated in his head the earliest date when it could arrive. 'Maybe even tomorrow.' Sure enough, the next morning the letter was brought to him as he sat in the *baithak* taking his breakfast of fruit and buttermilk. He scrutinised the postmark, and was pleased to note that his son had dispatched it first thing upon his arrival in Bombay. It was the punctiliousness that he appreciated, which a lifetime of service in the British Indian administration had led him to expect. He had made every effort to inculcate these sound habits in his sons, never tolerating lateness or slipshod ways. He felt gratified that he rarely had cause for complaint.

Dr Ditta folded Madan's letter and slid it back into the envelope. He thought of Madan, his seventh child and sixth son whom he had been reluctant to send abroad. Madan, who had always been 'at odds', different, searching, but for what? He had always showed character, determination, fortitude. They had a similar temperament and neither was at ease with talk. Bhajan was much more affable, like his mother. He hoped when the brothers were together in London they might help one other. All his sons would have finished their studies away from home. He himself had never been out of India. If he tried to imagine his sons in England he always saw them in black and white like the photographs they sent home.

7.
1957–60: London and the Big Betrayal

At Dover we got off the boat to go through immigration and take the train. There were two queues, 'British' and 'Aliens'; it looked as though we were the only Indians.

My father had told us to wait on the platform when we got to Victoria station as he had arranged for us to be met. I spotted an Indian gentleman in a maroon turban, and, as I was telling my mother, who was short-sighted but never wore glasses, he waved and started to walk towards us. From behind him came another wave in our direction; it was an English gentleman, complete with bowler hat and rolled-up umbrella, also striding in our direction. A Mr G. B. Singh, who had been a student of my father's in Lahore, and a Mr Knaster, who'd been my father's 'guardian' when he was a student and had become a friend, introduced themselves to us – and to each other. As it turned out that they both lived nearby in South Kensington. Our host, Mr Singh, suggested we go to his flat in Manson Place for tea.

Over tea, Mr Knaster informed us that he had found me a tutor, a Mr Bussel, who had successfully tutored my father for his

Cambridge entrance and would be happy to help me with my O levels. He had also been in touch with a local drama school that had recommended a Mrs Brent as voice and drama coach. They were both within walking distance from Manson Place, where we were staying temporarily, and he suggested we might look for more permanent accommodation nearby.

My mother lost no time in enquiring if there was a flea market, or places where she might pick up 'old Indian things' and Mr Knaster obligingly offered to take her to the Portobello Road.

Previously, London was not a place I knew but simply a place I passed through on my way to school, which had usually meant the air terminal, where we arrived, Uncle Bashir and Aunty Sara's in West Hampstead, where we stayed, Oxford Street, for last-minute shopping, and King's Cross to catch the train to Letchworth. At the same time, it had a strange familiarity. I knew it from the Monopoly board and from stories. In India my peers automatically assumed that if I had come from 'overseas', I had come from London.

'Paris? You mean you don't live in London?'

Now I could write and say that I did. London was connected to India and it felt right that I should be here, like a rite of passage, or a promotion. Even though Queen's Gate and Kensington didn't feature on the Monopoly board, Park Lane was not far away – so that was okay.

We decided that for the short term we would look for a room to rent. As my mother was not comfortable with phones, this was left to me.

'Where have you come from?' said the voice on the phone.

'We've come from Paris.'

'Are you French?'

'No. We're from India.'

'Oh. I'm so sorry, dear, but we can't take coloureds here. In any case, the room won't be free for another month.'

I put down the phone feeling intensely awkward.

'Are we coloured, Mummy?'

'No. We're Indians. And don't call me Mummy.'

'Sorry, Mama.'

Uncle G. B. laughed. 'Only some are like that. You just hit on a bad one. But there are lessons to be learned. We might be citizens of Free India anywhere else, but here in England we are still subjects of their Empire.' It was further explained to me that there was a name for the way the woman had behaved: colour prejudice. Some people had it and others didn't. Like hay fever.

We found accommodation without much difficulty: a large, twin-bedded room on the top floor of a building on the Cromwell Road. It was all beige and brown, but had the essentials: washbasin, gas fire, cooking ring, and some sad, heavy, brown furniture. But it had plenty of sun and we could get on with our routines.

Gardiners Tutors in Lexham Gardens was my tenth educational establishment in as many years. Four bus stops down the road or a twenty-minute walk, Mr Bussel's teaching room on the first floor was a busy space. Bookcases lined the walls, the large table in the middle was covered with files and papers, an armchair sat on either side of the gas fire and on the mantelpiece above was a row of pipes and tins of tobacco. The room was infused with the smell of his 'Old Holborn'.

On the wall on either side of the window were some etchings, and Mr Bussel would look at them regularly, close his eyes and be transported elsewhere. Once I followed his gaze and he explained that they were by Eric Gill, an artist Mr Bussell knew and admired and with whom he also shared his Catholic faith.

I, too, closed my eyes as I recalled Mireille, my hopscotch friend from when I was eight and we lived in St Cloud, sitting on the steps of our house and showing me the holy pictures she had received at her first communion.

'Who do you pray to?' she'd asked.

'The Divine Spirit within me,' I'd replied.

'Oh. We have him, too. We call him the *Saint Esprit*.'

Five minutes' walk away from Lexham Gardens was Collingham Place and Mrs Brent my voice and drama coach. A large room on the first floor featured a grand piano on which there was a huge vase with an abundance of flowers. She herself was a large lady with carefully arranged blue-rinsed hair who positioned herself by the window from where she could admire the flowers, survey both the room and the street below – and throw down the front-door keys to her pupils when they arrived.

Apart from elocution … '*Peter Piper picked a peck of pickled peppercorns* ... I would learn poems: '*I am—yet what I am none cares or knows ...*' and audition pieces: '*The quality of mercy is not strained ...*' She would enter me for competitions so I could get used to performance, presentation and projection.

'It's byoot-ful. Byoot-ful, not beauty-full.'

London was new for my mother, too, and so – cocooned together – I was enveloped by the folds of her worldview, her dreamland, her stories, her family, India, the plans for our return, the house she was designing near her sister Painji, and her preferences and prejudices: I was not to call her 'Mummy', but rather *Ammi*, or Mama, and my father *Pitaji*, rather than 'Daddy'. I was also to splash my eyes with cold water every morning and pray every day that 'love and light should fill my heart and overflow from me to all'. And of course we should never forget, as refugees, to share our good fortune with those less fortunate. She was very proud of her middle sister, Danti, who ran a camp for refugees and when we all went back to India I, too, would work for the 'uplift' of my Motherland.

My mother loved walking and talking, so we would go for long, storytelling walks in the various parks of the city, and sometimes go the theatre; and she would read my 'set books' and help me revise the Tudors and Stuarts. The stories of Home, of India, of the Family, the Epics and their sagas would intertwine – how Aunty Sarlata chose her groom and how Draupadi or Sita chose theirs. And, of course, there was always Lahore ... 'the perfect city', the evening walks in the Lawrence Gardens, friends and friendships, family and love.

'At Divali, our Muslim friends would send us gifts and sweets wrapped in red and at Eid we would send them sweets and gifts wrapped in green.' And then there was the house she had built in Model Town, and sold her wedding jewellery to do it: 'An Indian woman was never supposed to sell her wedding jewellery, it was her insurance. But I wanted my house ...' And how, although everything was lost, at least 'one thing got saved: my Roerich painting of the Kulu Girl because I'd left it with my uncle before I left for Paris.'

Then she'd smile and tell me of the new home she would build and where everything would come together. And I would feel reassured that the Partition Monster would be assuaged.

Madan Lal would appear in the strangest places. Once we were sitting on top of the No 9 bus on our way back from the Ideal Home Exhibition, where we had gone to pick up some house ideas, when she suddenly said:

'Imagine Madan Lal, standing up there all alone, so young yet so strong and clear.'

We were passing the Albert Memorial and I remembered Amrita. *'When you grow up you must find out about Madan Lal. You might need to go to London for that. Because that's where Madan Lal was.'*

Well, I thought. I'm in London now, but not grown up, and maybe by the time I am, I'll be back in India.'

My mother would periodically return to Paris, and a chill would enter the cocoon. I would be left to fend for myself: to collect my money from the Post Office, eat at the local ABC cafeteria, sit in the library, listen to the radio and boil potatoes on the cooking ring, which then, mashed up with butter and cheese, would make a meal. Sometimes at the weekend I might visit Uncle Bashir and Aunty Sara would feed me and worry that I was on my own so young and I would make light of my situation to protect my mother.

But in reality, I was bewildered in the big city, far from my father and the familiar surroundings of our *quartier*, and our sunny, treasure-trove flat. Why was I in London, where I didn't know anybody, wasn't in a school and felt at sea? So I created an imaginary world to make sense of it: I was an Indian girl steering myself to return to the land of stories to which I belonged and where we were building a house so that we could go home.

Then came the letter. Forwarded from Paris to Grindlays Bank in Parliament Street. My mother smiled as she slipped it into her bag.

With our one-dish meal of savoury vegetable rice simmering on the gas ring, my mother squatted on her bed and finally read the letter while I sat in the big brown armchair reading *Vanity Fair*. I heard her let out a sigh and then she got up, collected some shilling coins that we kept for the gas meter and told me she was going to have a bath and that I should turn the gas off in fifteen minutes. She had disappeared into her dreamland. But I could sense a disturbance.

I returned to my reading, but kept looking at the open letter on her bed. In the end I went over to read it. It was from my cousin and stated just like that, baldly factual, that the land had been purchased but there was no plot for us as they had decided to keep it in the family. The letter then went on to list the items that she would like bought and brought for her on our next visit.

I felt the frosty chill of the spectre of Partition and understood why my mother wanted a warm bath. I grappled with the implications of the message.

No plot for us … keep it in the family. What did they mean? I thought we *were* family. These were people I was brought up to love and trust. People my mother loved unconditionally, whose demands took precedence over our own. So why were they harming us? I looked out of the window of our garret room at the fluffy white clouds floating across the sky, carrying away all our dreams: our return from exile – Home and Family.

The clouds were shape-shifting into the monster of my childhood: Partition, with the Hydra-headed faces of my aunt and uncle and cousin devouring home, safety, trust, loving kindness … and spitting out the dreaded words: 'you are not family.'

My mother came into the room exuding steam and sandalwood. 'Oh ho! You forgot to turn off the fire.'

'I hate them I hate them I hate them, I hate them …'

My mother turned off the gas and snatched the letter from my hand, saying: 'No, no. No! Never hate! Hate harms you. Pray that love fills your heart …' she continued and, opening the window wider to clear the 'atmospherics', assured me that everything would be all right, and we would soon have a home in London!

I was a girl from India, a girl from Paris, a refugee from Partition, a coloured girl, but beyond those labels, who was I?

Sometimes walking to the bus stop I would pass the houses with their net curtains and wonder if anyone behind them might have the 'hay fever'.

In the London of the late 1950s India was never very far away. There were my mother's stories and many people around had been 'out there'. Soon afterwards, my older cousins and semi-cousins, sons and daughters of family and close family friends, started to arrive to study at various universities around the country. This was their rite of passage in the old colonial tradition, following in the footsteps of their fathers. They brought with them a quaint Indian Edwardiana and ready-made itineraries of places: Speakers' Corner, Fortnum & Mason, India House in the Aldwych, where there were Indian newspapers and a canteen, and the international clock at Piccadilly Circus, which was also the appointed meeting place for 'the gang' on Saturday evenings. My mother often returned to Paris and I lived with my cousin, Anjali, who took me under her wing. I'd tag along with her friends.

They were all older than me, at university while I was still doing my school exams. They called me 'kid' or 'Leena kid' and were here for just a few years, in transit on their way to the good jobs that awaited them with their connections and English qualifications. They talked of India, family, money, the sun, food, and politics, of arranged and non-arranged marriages. I tried to fit in, to understand their ways. But their settled sense of place was not something I shared. I tried to imagine how it might feel – having a home in India to go back home to.

Partition was never discussed, neither did it appear to have been something that had affected them unduly. Their fathers had not lost their jobs, position, possessions or homes and if they had, these had been replaced. They didn't see themselves as refugees, but rather as confident citizens and inheritors of independent India with an attachment to an imaginary England forged out of novels and the Indian public school system.

One Sunday afternoon, tagging along with the gang and strolling around Speaker's Corner we befriended a couple of law students from Calcutta who connected my name and asked if I was related to 'The Dhingra'.

'Who's that?' asked one of the gang.

'Madan Lal, of course,' said one of our new friends, Deben, as though stating the obvious.

The 'gang' hadn't heard of him.

'He was a revolutionary,' Deben said.

'Oh, my God! Surely he wasn't a violent revolutionary like you Bengalis?' asked one of the gang and the conversation drifted into a good-humoured argument about violence and nonviolence. 'Kid' was invisible. Our two new friends, Kajol and Deben, concluded that they had definitely read different history books to those of the gang. I listened and wondered about it all, and the fact that there were those who knew and those who didn't know. Or who forgot. Soon I, too, would forget.

By the end of the decade I entered a new world. I joined drama school. Until then England had been a mostly mysterious place behind the net curtains I passed in the street. Now I was in it and part of it. I was a bit late in joining, but for the first time since I'd left India three years earlier, I met up with people my own age. And I loved that.

'I'm so glad you've come and there's another girl in our term group,' said my new friend Ginny as we sat on the steps waiting to go in to our fencing class. 'Otherwise it was just me and four boys.'

We giggled. 'It's so nice to have a friend,' she said.

'Yes,' I replied, touched by her openness and generosity – and feeling happy.

Although no one around appeared to have the 'hay fever', I was aware that it was out there, somewhere, and I had inadvertently internalised it enough to contrive a nickname for myself – 'Beige'.

8.
1906: SS MACEDONIA

Madan liked to stroll on the decks alone and look out at the vastness of the sea. It was awesome, exhilarating and peaceful. He would often find himself thinking of Babu Ram, the engine room, the nights in the moonlight, and these images warmed his heart. He looked at his hands and smiled.

'I know who you are and you have nothing to fear,' Babu Ram had said. 'Your hands give you away, Sahib.'

Madan had signed on as a seaman, pretended he didn't know English and worked as a stoker. Babu Ram had been a brother, friend, father and teacher.

'Once upon a time on these seas, there were ships from Egypt, Arabia and China, and we exchanged silks and porcelain, spices and stories,' Babu Ram would tell them. 'And then they came with their guns. Now we are robbed and reduced to this: transporting opium tilled with our sweat to poison people who have never hurt us. And what *karma* are we forced to make for ourselves?'

Babu Ram, Mahmood Ali, Gulzari, Lal. Sometimes he'd felt more at home with them than he'd felt in his father's mansion.

Now Madan spent time with Harish and Basu, who were also in his cabin. Sometimes Harish and he would join in one of the activities organised onboard, but Basu never did, although he would stand by and look on. Basu was some ten years older and had lived outside India for some years. He had been based in Paris, knew London, Berlin and Geneva, and frequently travelled to India. He had been in Calcutta during the *Swadeshi* and Boycott agitations and had witnessed the tumultuous events.

'There were bonfires of British goods, and people took their shirts off in the street and threw them on top of them. This partition of Bengal has ripped open the veil and we can now see the true nature of the beast. It is nearly fifty years since their Queen Victoria's so-called "Great Proclamation", which was to bring in such changes and consider the aspirations and self-respect of the Indian. And has anything changed?' Basu made a face and shook his head slowly. 'Nothing will change unless we make it.'

Madan and Harish nodded thoughtfully. Basu lowered his voice. He always talked where the wind would blow his words out to sea.

'In England there are books you can read and people you can meet. You should try to get hold of Dadabhai Naoroji's *Poverty and Un-British Rule in India*, or William Digby. Also, find out about a hostel for Indian students called India House and a man called Shyamji Krishna Varma.'

Sometimes they would have discussions far into the night in an unfrequented part of the ship, near the engine's drone.

'Everything has its time and our lifetimes are little more than a blink in Brahma's dream, and so, too, this grand imperial ship, puffed up with self-conceit, is nothing more than a tiny time-capsule floating on ancient seas, in water that has been in existence since our world began. We are living in a time of great change, great transformation, and we are part of it.'

At Aden they disembarked and wandered through the bazaars and teashops.

'You will find, from now on, that the white man will become more polite. Britannia smiles and Britannia snarls, depending on where she faces and on who and where you are.' Basu smiled. 'There is an Indian lady, Madame Cama, who stands up in Hyde Park on Sundays, denounces the injustice of British rule and argues for Home Rule. She can't be sent to prison or flogged for that in England.' He also reminded them: 'Remember to find out about India House.'

Basu got off at Brindisi to continue the rest of the journey by train while Madan and Harish continued to Tilbury with a growing sense of excitement.

9.

1 JULY 1905.
INAUGURATION
OF INDIA HOUSE,
HIGHGATE

Shyamji Krishna Varma had inaugurated the India House that Basu had told Madan about the previous year. It was 1 July. That morning Shyamji had woken early. The household was still asleep. It was 4 a.m. Shyamji slipped into his dressing gown, closed the bedroom door quietly, was about to go up to his office, then changed his mind and went down the stairs. Across the hall, opposite the front door, was a large red banner – 'Welcome to India House' – and another on the wall above the entrance to the dining room that read: 'The India Home Rule Society'.

Later that day Shyamji's friend Henry Hyndman would officially inaugurate India House. Mr Hyndman was not just a good friend to him but also to India. That's what was important: India, The Cause.

Shyamji stepped into the garden, filled his lungs with the morning air and his spirit with birdsong. Hornsey had been declared the healthiest borough in London, a point he never tired of mentioning, and therefore an ideal place for a student hostel: India House. Its opening was a historic occasion, the culmination of much planning and effort.

Shyamji felt himself to be on the pulse of history. 1905 had already been a tumultuous year. In Russia, the Winter Palace carnage; in Ireland, Sinn Féin; in China, Sun Yat Sen; and events in Turkey, Poland, Morocco, Egypt ... all part of the changing new mood. Everywhere voices long silenced were now demanding to be heard. And India, too, had been set alight with the Boycott and *Swadeshi*. Lord Curzon with his supreme racial arrogance had done them a favour. And Japan's victory over Russia had sent an icy shiver through the ranks of the Europeans.

1905 was also the year that Shyamji had stepped into the fray with the launch of the Indian Home Rule Society and the publication of the first issue of *The Indian Sociologist*, a penny monthly available free to any Indian who wrote and asked for a copy.

Shyamji Krishna Varma was a great admirer of Herbert Spencer and had endowed a £1,000 Herbert Spencer Lectureship at Oxford University, from where he had had the distinction of being the first Indian to be awarded an MA. The masthead of his journal featured two quotations from Spencer:

'Every man is free to do that which he wills provided he infringes not on the equal freedom of any other man,' and, 'Resistance to aggression is not simply justifiable but imperative; non-resistance hurts both altruism and egoism.'

The purpose of the journal was stated in a long opening editorial:

'The political relations between England and India urgently require a genuine Indian interpreter in the United Kingdom to show, on India's behalf, how Indians really fare and feel under British rule ... and to plead the cause of India and its unrepresented millions before the Bar of Public Opinion in Great Britain and Ireland.

'This journal will endeavour to inculcate the great sociological truth that "It is impossible to join injustice and brutality abroad with justice and humanity at home". It will from time to time remind the British people that they can never succeed in being a nation of freemen and lovers of freedom so long as they continue to send out members of the dominating classes to exercise despotisms in Britain's name upon the various conquered races that constitute Britain's military Empire.'

Shyamji was aiming at the conscience of Liberal Britain, which he had come to admire during his earlier sojourn. But on his return to India, he soon found that the fine liberal traditions did not extend very far, and that justice and fairness was invariably superseded by race. He recalled with some irritation a certain gentleman currently at the India Office who, like him, had not long come from India. 'Wyllie! Wily Curzon Wyllie,' he muttered and shook himself as though exorcising him.

Both the journal and establishment of a hostel for Indian students in London were the culmination of much planning and effort. For the last seven years Shyamji had been living quietly in Highgate, preparing, making contacts in the West, maintaining contacts with leaders in India. Some of the leaders would be present at the opening later that day and one of them was staying in the house itself: Lajpat Rai, one of the trio of 'Lal, Pal and Bal'. (There was Lala Lajpat Rai from the Punjab,

Bepin Chandra Pal from Bengal, and Bal Gangadhar Tilak from Maharashtra.)

The plan, of which the India House hostel was a part, was to establish a base in London, where Indians could meet and discuss freely, which they could not do in India, and also to be guided by Shyamji and his team. A number of scholarships and fellowships had been set up to enable Indian graduates to come to England to study, experience life in a 'self-governing country and equip themselves efficiently for spreading amongst the people of India a knowledge of the advantages of Freedom and National Unity'. At present, three scholarship holders had arrived and more were to come. Each recipient was required to undertake a pledge never to work for the government in any capacity, the 'predatory foreign incubus', as his friend Tilak called it.

This morning as Shyamji walked in his garden and thought of all that had been achieved he felt proud. He was forty-eight years old, a self-made man of some considerable wealth with no children, and this was now his life's work. As he went back into the house he remembered that he was also redeeming a pledge, made many years earlier, to his guru and mentor, Swami Dayananda. For a moment as he thought of it, he felt humbled. The house was still quiet when he came back in.

A few hours later, however, the house had become a hub of frenzied activity. Two of Shyamji's team, Sardar Rana and Madame Bhikaiji Cama, who were usually based in Paris but who frequently came to London, were taking charge of the proceedings downstairs, while Shyamji was busy in the library. The student residents, the staff and guests, were all busy. Music filled the air. A record of '*Bande Mataram*' ('Hail Motherland'), banned in India, was freely spinning on the record player in the dining room.

Around the same time in Hampstead, Henry Mayers Hyndman looked up from his desk into the blue sky, put down his pen and walked across to the window. Indeed, it was a very fine day, he thought. Not just because of the weather, which was delightful, but because the inauguration of India House, at which he was to officiate, was a cause close to his heart. For years he had pleaded justice for India; he had spoken out, written, agitated and lobbied for it. He had penned a shelf of books and articles and the very first had been about India: *Indian Policy and English Justice*, and *The Bankruptcy of India*. But what good did they serve, his ideas falling mostly on ears deafened by self-interest? What annoyed him more than anything else was that even amongst some of his so-called fellow travellers there were those who, whilst supporting self-determination and nationalism everywhere, fell silent when it came to India. And so, India weighed upon his moral conscience as an Englishman and on his integrity as a socialist. 'But justice must and will be done and India will awaken and rise,' he said to a passing cloud as he returned resolutely to his desk. He folded the paper on which he had been writing and slipped it into his breast pocket. He looked at his watch: it was time to walk across to Krishna Varma's house in Highgate.

Hyndman walked down the steps of his house into Well Walk and turned left towards the Heath. There were many things he was glad about: the weather, the inauguration of India House and the fact that he had been born into this age, the *fin de siècle*, and *debut du nouveau.* A time of endings and new beginnings when 'Attitudes will have to change,' he said aloud, 'because events will make them change and we will make those events.' He crossed the East Heath Road and entered the woodlands of the Heath. Rights for workers, votes for women and home rule for the colonies – everything would have to be fought for, everything would have to be won through struggle, but of victory he had no doubt. There was much to be done and he had no time to waste on 'old cranks, humanitarians, vegetarians, anti-vivisectionists and anti-vaccinationists, arty-crafties and all the rest', as he called them, who, along with the anarchists, socialists, suffragettes and Sinn Féiners, were also products of this age. The Heath opened out into meadows where sheep grazed and the spire of St Michael's Highgate stood out against the blue, cloudless sky. Hyndman swung his cane in the direction of Krishna Varma's new house and smiled as he thought of the afternoon with pleasure. He checked his pocket to make sure his speech was still there, but even if it wasn't he knew what to say. He'd said it often enough, to Krishna Varma, to friends and on podiums all over the place.

Another person making her way to the same house in Highgate was Mrs Charlotte Despard. A familiar London figure, her dignified presence frequently graced the radical podiums of the time, and at aged sixty she had more energy than many a woman half her age. Novelist, philanthropist, reformer, suffragette, socialist, Sinn Féinist, she was a tireless campaigner for the causes she espoused. Sitting upright in the Hansom cab that was climbing Highgate Hill, she noticed Hyndman waiting to cross the road and called for the cab to stop.

'Ah Charlotte, how very good to see you. It is only a short way from here.'

'Then I shall walk with you, Henry,' said Mrs Despard alighting from the cab.

In the house in Cromwell Avenue, there was an air of festivity and urgency. A number of Indians and some English well-wishers had gathered, and animated discussions could be heard in little pockets everywhere: in Hindi, Gujarati, Bengali, Tamil and English. Students had come from all parts of the country, as well as from Paris, Berlin and India, some of whom were staying in the house. The gathering of so many Indians under one roof where they could meet and talk freely, be themselves and temporarily relax from English formality and scrutiny, created the air of festivity. The urgency was inherent in the momentous occasion.

Shyamji was proudly showing Dadabhai Naoroji and Lajpat Rai around the building.

'It is a great honour that you do us, Dadabhaiji, with your presence at this opening.' Shyamji opened the door into a large room with bookshelves and tables flooded with afternoon sunlight. 'The lecture hall, library and reading room are all on the same floor, thus providing every facility for study and intercommunication.' Shyamji's voice took on a buoyant tone, 'The library will be known as the Hyndman Library, and we have already been donated a large number of books.'

'How many students can you accommodate here?' asked Dadabhai.

'Twenty-five at present, but arrangements will ultimately be made to build so that we shall be able to take in fifty students.'

'The students will be able to meet freely, discuss their concerns and be Indians together,' said Madame Cama, joining the party.

'Ah Bhiku, my dear, I didn't see you,' observed Dadabhai as she came towards them.

'To provide recreation there is ample space for tennis courts, gymnasium, etc. The management is in the hands of Indians only and the domestic arrangements are similar to those of Ruskin College, Oxford ...'

'I am very impressed, Shyamji, and wish you every success.'

'The success will be for all of us,' replied Lajpat Rai. 'The success will be for India.'

'Well said! Well said!' retorted Shyamji. Dadabhai nodded.

'And did you know, Sir,' Shyamji was ending the tour, 'that the borough of Hornsey is the healthiest in London, with the very lowest mortality rate? That's official.'

Dadabhai Naoroji occupied the place of honour at the gathering. His chair was at the centre of the podium and he looked around him with a host of feelings. He was glad he was not going to speak. His place was owing to his reputation: 'The grand old man of India', an acknowledged elder statesman, and a trailblazer and standard-bearer for the cause of India. The first Indian to be made a professor, the first Indian to be elected to the House of Commons, twice president of the Indian National Congress ... he had had much success. In three months he would be eighty and could count a lifetime of dedication to the cause. But although much had been achieved and more people were prepared to speak out for the plight of India, the actual suffering of the people of India, the bleeding of the economy, continued unabated. This was not what he had hoped for, what he had worked for, what he had expected.

'Nothing is more dear to the heart of England,' he'd once said, 'than India's welfare, and if we only speak out loud enough, persistently enough to reach out to that busy heart, we shall not speak in vain.' He'd believed in what he'd said wholeheartedly when he said it. Now, however, he was no longer sure. The partition of Bengal a few months earlier had left him deeply disillusioned with the British claim of 'fairness and honour'.

He bowed as Krishna Varma introduced him and then folded his hands together to acknowledge the applause. With the establishment of India House there would be competition for his own Indian Association. Maybe now new ways were required and as he looked around at all the faces it warmed his heart to know that the struggle to which he had devoted his life, his beloved India, would continue.

The next on the podium to bow and to receive applause was Mr Quelch, editor of *Justice*, the journal of the Social Democratic Federation, as representative of the working men of Britain.

Indeed, thought Dadabhai as he clapped his hands, he had met very many noble-minded Englishmen and women, but sadly they were not running the country. Neither was the bleeding of India providing any comfort to the working men of Britain who had been his constituents when he was MP for Finsbury. He remembered his election and the flare-up of the colour debate, and he wondered if this sense of racial superiority did not supersede their sense of justice and fair play. How else could the anomalies be explained?

Mrs Despard was now taking the applause as a 'representative of the women of England'. Dadabhai turned to look at her, a familiar figure at radical gatherings; she was a remarkable woman, an admirable woman. As usual a black lace mantilla crowned her head, her simple Edward Carpenter sandals peeped out from her ample black skirt, but more than anything she seemed to exude an aura of dignity and saintliness. Dadabhai was pleased she had espoused the cause of India, where she had once lived. Once, he recalled, she'd told him of Mazzini's view on Indian Independence and when he'd looked somewhat taken aback, she had said simply, 'Oh! Didn't you know? I converse with his spirit regularly through my planchette.'

Krishna Varma returned to his seat by Dadabhai's side as Mr Hyndman rose from his and started to read his address:

'It gives me great pleasure to come here today to open this remarkable and admirable experiment known henceforth as India House. As things stand today, loyalty to Great Britain means treachery to India. From England itself there is nothing to be hoped. Years ago I believed that when the frightful injustice that was being committed was made known and the wholesale wrongs done were exposed we should at once endeavour to change the system.'

Dadabhai nodded.

'We love freedom very much for ourselves and for all who are not directly under our rule. This is why I rejoice at the new feeling, which is growing up among you since the great victories of the Japanese. They are Asiatic, as you are. They, too, were spoken of with contempt, as you are. Yet the despised "yellow monkeys" have overthrown and trampled on the great bogey of Europe.'

A current of smiles ran through the room.

'Eschew your moderate men, for it is the immoderate men, the determined men, the fanatical men, who will work out the salvation of India.'

Instinctively, Dadabhai looked over towards Madame Cama on the far side of the podium. She met his look and smiled.

'The institution of India House means a great step in the direction of Indian growth and emancipation, and some of those who are here this afternoon may live to witness the first fruits of its triumphant success.

'I announce that India House is open.'

The applause was resounding and Krishanvarma so elated that his voice failed him. It was left to Madame Cama to bring the meeting to a close.

'It gives me great pleasure to announce that Sardar Rana of Paris has generously offered three more lectureships.'

The arrival of refreshments concluded the afternoon, and as Hyndman bit into a samosa, Krishna Varma observed, 'You know, Henry, my staff have become quite partial to Indian food. There might be only a handful of Indian restaurants around at the present time, but mark my words, a day will come when there will be an Indian restaurant in every English city.'

Everyone laughed heartily at the idea.

Later that evening, Shyamji went out for a long walk through Waterlow Park to digest the full implications of the day. He looked out over London in the direction of Whitehall and The India Office as he considered the idea that henceforth he might never be able to return to India again. It was the beginning of a lifetime of exile.

10.
1906: The India Office, Whitehall

Sir William Hutt Curzon Wyllie climbed up the grand marble VIP staircase, his feet sinking into the pile of the red carpet. Around him, the busts and portraits of the great and the good of the India Office past looked down imperiously from their pedestals and gilt frames. Viceroys, generals and administrators: the long and noble tradition of which he was a part. It was now some five years since he had returned from India to take up his position at the India Office, and these were all now familiar faces. As he climbed the stairs to his first-floor office he was pleased to see them again; he had been out of London for ten days, playing host to some visiting Indian princes.

His rooms adjoined those of Lord Morley, the Secretary of State for India to whom he had been appointed Political ADC, and as he stepped into them he smiled, glad to be back in London and the routine of work. His secretary came in with matters to be attended to and the daily files with which he needed to catch up. There was the usual mix of things – correspondence, memos, appointments – and he started to sift through them, ably guided by his assistant. There were numerous letters from Indians to whom he had been of some assistance during their visit, including one from Kundan Lal Dhingra, whom he knew from India. Then there were the usual petitions, requests, invitations, and a list of new arrivals from India. His attention was drawn to a letter from a V. D. Savarkar:

'To the Secretary of State for India. London, 15-7-06
Dear Sir,
As I have lately come from India, I have great curiosity to hear the Budget speech on 20th inst. So I shall feel myself highly obliged if you will kindly take the troubles of sending two passes – one for me and one for one of my friends – to enable me to attend the sittings of the House of Commons on the occasion.

Hoping to be excused for the troubles I am,
Yours V. D. Savarkar'

Attached to it was another letter from the Special Department in Poona that read:

'SPECIAL DEPARTMENT. Poona, 14th. June 1906
My Dear Ritchie,
I send you a short account of a young man called Vinayak Damodhar Savarkar, who, I believe, will shortly be in England. You may like to know at the India Office who he is. He is not, of course, of any personal importance, but holds somewhat the same opinions as Damodhar Hari Chapekar, who was responsible for the murder of Rand in 1897. In short, he promises to be a firebrand.'

Sir Curzon Wyllie put the letter down and turned to his secretary. 'Ask him to come on Wednesday to collect the tickets and to give us the name of his friend.' He then looked again at the letter and the Highgate address. 'Isn't this the address of Krishanverma?'

'Yes, Sir. It is.'

'I thought as much. Has Sir William seen it?'

'Yes, Sir. As you know, Sir, Scotland Yard has been keeping a watch on the house. It is Krishna Varma's establishment. His new hostel for Indian students.'

'Yes,' retorted Sir Curzon Wyllie thoughtfully. 'A hostel for Indian students is a good idea, but I am not so sure that Krishna Varma is the best man to run it. I would like to see the Scotland Yard file again.'

Later that evening, back home in Onslow Square, he found himself thinking about India House. He remembered he had once suggested that the India Office should sponsor a hostel or club that served Indian food and made Indian students feel at home. A lifetime of service in India had made him feel close to the land and its people. He even sympathised sometimes with their aspirations and the attitude of some of his own compatriots often made him feel ashamed.

He did not wholly agree with Sir William Lee Warner: 'Western education for the natives was a bad idea. It has filled them with half-baked delusions and they shout "Liberty, Equality, Self-government". Bah! They are utterly incapable. And they know it. What was there before we came – heathenism and barbarism.'

His own view was that Indians were a lot more intelligent than they were given credit for. Maybe a lot more intelligent even than was good for them. At least under the present circumstances.

11.
1976: The Monsoon Flood

It wasn't until 1976 that Madan Lal would reappear in my life. He did it in a dramatic way, and from then onwards would stay – and his story would entangle with my own.

For the previous eight years I had been living mostly in India with long visits to Europe. In 1975, with my husband and daughter, I was in the process of making a long-term move when the Emergency was declared and we were advised to postpone our return. This was a shock. Most of our luggage had already been shipped. We were dismayed and as we tried to find a new focus and purpose we moved into a collective.

I had joined an Anti-Emergency group, a broad front of organisations including the Indian Workers' Association, agitating about Emergency rule and oppression in India.

'Brothers and sisters! Comrades and friends!' The speakers would say, 'Make no mistake. Our struggle against oppression in India is the self-same struggle as the struggle against racism here.'

And it was at one of their meetings that my name was connected and I remembered Amrita, as once again someone said: 'Are you from the family of Madan Lal Dhingra? Great Patriot! Great Martyr! Supreme sacrifice! Our duty to remember!'

An elderly man in a red turban came towards me with folded hands and bowed low. I flinched, imagining that he intended to touch my feet.

'What are you doing?' I protested. 'Please, please, I'm ... nobody.'

'No. You are descended from Him. It is the same blood. This is my honour to meet you.'

And then I was asked: 'Do you have a photograph?'

I shook my head, which was in a whirl. I had said I was a nobody and I felt like a nobody, and yet here was this man looking at me, his eyes slightly moist, his hands roughened from years of work in the foundries in the north. I was moved. And confused. I felt caught out, I felt saved.

I thought of what Madan Lal had done. He had risen above himself, sacrificed his life for what he thought was the greater good. What was his story? Maybe finding it would make me a somebody again? Yes, I would find his story, make that my purpose.

I now had a quest, a focus and a task. And when I would walk the streets to protest and leaflet about repression in India, I would remember that Madan Lal had protested in the same streets, in the same city, for the same reason, seventy years earlier. And, of course, the double irony was not lost on me – that it was the very same repressive colonial legislation of that time that was now being used by Independent India. Both times to quell 'internal disturbances'.

I started my research with a visit to the India Office Library and took the bus to Waterloo. On reaching The Cut, I stopped to look at the Old Vic theatre and then I remembered that my last audition had been around there, a cold memory that made me shiver slightly. That fateful audition that had made me run away from the UK.

The director had said, 'That was marvellous darling. Really. But what are we going to do with you?'

'What do you mean?' I'd replied.

'Well now. Could you play Cordelia, Ophelia, Desdemona or Miranda?'

Taking that to mean that the colour of my skin precluded all that, I didn't reply. I just wanted to run away. And I did. As my French visa was still valid, I took the night ferry and went home – to Paris. To go home I needed a visa. I left London and abandoned my acting career.

I was troubled by the memory and I quickened my pace towards Blackfriars Road where the India Office was located and where, I had been told: 'You will find all the documents, right from the very first letter from the East India Company.'

In the library I wrote out a request slip for what I thought was a police log of arrests for July 1909, hoping this way to find Madan Lal. But I'd made a mistake. At the desk an immense volume awaited me with lists of names, and lists of ships, and I felt increasingly irritated at my mistake. But I suddenly realised that these were, in fact, arrests. Arrests in the form of deportations. Looking down the list at all these Indian names I felt a dull pain that unsettled and the overwhelmed me. I left the book, walked out of the library and down The Cut. I remembered my mother having said something about the assassination being in protest at deportations. I had a sense of a feeling that my uncle Madan Lal would have known.

A few months later, whilst I was buried in libraries, came the news that all the possessions we had left with friends in India had been either washed away or irretrievably damaged in a monsoon flood. I closed my eyes and imagined my little blue Air India attaché case, which I'd had since I was sixteen and which contained all my papers, photos and mementos, being washed down the river, knocked, bounced, beaten and drowned.

With my external life steadily crumbling, my husband finding companionship elsewhere, Madan Lal assumed an almost reassuring presence – and brought a sharpened focus and resolve. Yes, I would find his photograph and tell his story, and through that connect back to India.

Then there came a letter from my father: 'Uncle Madan Lal's body is being returned to India. Call Natwar Singh at the Indian High Commission and you will be able to accompany the coffin. They are expecting your call.'

My mother, who was in India at the time also sent me a cable telling me to come, that we would be travelling with the cortège through the whole of the Punjab up to Amritsar. 'You will see the Golden Temple. Come quickly.'

But I didn't go. I couldn't go. There was little time to plan the trip and little encouragement to undertake it. Could I justify going during the Emergency? the 'collective' asked. Was it not ideologically unsound? In my moves and labels and roles I had lost my own agency.

So I stayed and felt cheated as though I had been abandoned. An old familiar feeling.

It was the end of his exile and the beginning of mine. My focus and resolve disintegrated. They had taken him away and left me behind – and in England, too, the place that had killed him and rejected me. And I had failed to find the photograph. Just another uncomfortable feeling to sink down into my dark well of 'Partition'.

Much else crumbling, the family partitioning everywhere ... the well water rising uncomfortably. My mother's carefully guarded secret, that her marriage was over, that my father had another family, was discovered by a cousin, who announced it as a tasty item to be passed around with tea at a family gathering with my mother present. I wasn't there but I knew that scene. I felt for my mother. I felt for my father. I felt Partition and remembered the same cousin's letter of twenty years' earlier: 'you are not family'.

My sister's marriage had also ended and like my mother she, too, was constantly moving between visits to the Jungian Institute in Zurich, father in Paris, mother and sister in London, her spiritual guru in India and her sons in Venezuela, where she also had a shop to finance herself.

On one of her transits through London from India to Venezuela, I was helping her pack two large suitcases with piles of silk saris and Indian nik-naks for her shop, and books to wedge in between.

'With all these books won't you be over weight?' I asked

'No. Between Europe and India weight counts. But to the Americas they allow two cases whatever the weight.'

I handed her a pile of books, the top one entitled, *L'Abandon à la providence divine.*

She lifted it out and asked: *'Tu connais?'*

I shook my head. She looked at me, interrupting the packing, and started to rummage through her handbag: 'Look, I was going to talk to you after finishing the packing, but I'll do it now.' She continued to rummage as she spoke, eventually finding a card that she then brandished about as emphasis: 'Don't get pushed around in this collective like Mummy gets pushed around by the family in India. Don't let anybody tell you it's your fault. It isn't. You need all the support you can get. Mummy's lost, Daddy's not around and I can't help.' She then handed me the card, 'So, here, I've arranged for Giles, a friend from the Jungian Institute to see you for the next three months. Ring him up.' She handed me the card.

'Things that go wrong,' said Giles at one of our early meetings 'are trying to put something right.'

By the end of the decade the most significant and precious element in my personal scaffold had collapsed completely with the sudden death of my beloved father. I was angry. I was hurt. I was distraught. I was lost. I discovered, too, that heartache is a real, intense, physical pain. And also that it leaves a scar tissue.

I remembered a story from the Mahabharata:

One day the exiled Pandava brothers, parched and exhausted, arrived at a lake and ran to the water. The guardian of the lake warned them not to drink till they had answered his question. They took no heed and one by one fell unconscious. Yudhishtra arrived and saw his four brothers lying there.

The guardian of the lake repeated his injunction and question: 'What is the most extraordinary thing in life? Answer before you drink.'

Yudhishtra replied: 'It is, that though each of us knows that we must die, we behave as though we were immortal.'

And I thought of Sita, from the Ramayana, daughter of the Earth, the devoted wife, exiled, abducted, abandoned, rejected, then exiled again to bring up her sons alone, who finally appeals to her mother, the Earth, to take her home – and a chasm opens up and she sinks happily into its embrace. Nothing could hurt her any more.

But for me there was no comforting chasm. Just a well of pain, of Partition: full of fears and unformulated questions.

In between my moments of despair, images would float across my mind: My father disappearing in the cloud of steam as the train pulled away from the Gare du Nord. Meetings in London and Paris, in Delhi, his care, his concerns, his love, his wise words his goodness: 'You need to become a person in your own right. It's very important.'

It was a year since I'd seen my father. We'd met in Paris at UNESCO. We'd lunched, strolled in the Peace Gardens, then lounged in the large armchairs overlooking them. He'd said: 'You know darling, if I was to do things again, I wouldn't send you away. I'd keep you close to me.' And in one of his last letters he had written, 'When you become what you truly know yourself to be, all your relationships will be much easier.'

My heart felt broken, my father was gone, my marriage had fizzled out. I no longer had a profession. I had no country to belong to. No home to go to. And I was in England, the place that rejected me and from where I had so often tried to run away. I felt a failure. I had failed. In every way. As a mother. As a wife. Failed my father, failed myself, failed Madan Lal. And I felt guilty.

I was in a deep, dark pit and could see no light. Then there came a telephone call from Ana, a dear friend in Spain, who knew the family in India and the challenges in my life, to say that our meditation teacher Goenka was coming to France the following month to lead a retreat and who to get in touch with to attend.

'Go, Leena. Nothing like Vipassana to pump out pain.'

I arrived at the retreat a tearful heap and then spent ten days in perfect peace. But when it was time to leave, the tears started to gather up again.

'Goenkaji,' I asked 'How can I go out into the world now that my father is no longer there?'

'But *beti* (daughter),' he replied with a smile and pointing to himself,' your Dhamma father is still here. Nothing to fear.'

And I felt an energy, like a shower of benevolence flowing down from my head through my body to the tips of my toes. Nothing to fear? I tried to digest that idea.

Back in London, I enrolled as a mature student, in my third profession, to become a teacher so as to work and look after my darling daughter.

When I box-filed my research on Madan Lal, I recalled the connection I had made, that I hadn't found the photograph and put it away with the feeling of unfinished business.

12.

1906: MADAN LAL IN LONDON

Kundan Lal Dhingra had taken the train to Tilbury to meet his brother off the ship. He was the eldest of the Dhingra brothers, a businessman with a flourishing import and export trade in textiles. He had been in London for three months. His work was now almost finished and, having settled Madan in London, he would return to India in a few weeks. Business had gone well, the weather was fine and he was going to enjoy the relaxing experience of introducing his brother to London.

Harish noticed the meticulously dressed Indian gentleman with an umbrella carefully replacing his watch in its special pocket.

'I have seen your brother.'

'How do you know? We don't look alike.'

Harish smiled.

They travelled back to London together. On the way, the blue sky turned grey and it started to rain.

'Look, rain!' exclaimed Harish. 'Is this their rainy season?'

Madan laughed. 'They don't have a rainy season.'

'That's right,' explained Kundan. 'Their rainy season is spread throughout the year. In England you cannot plan an outdoor activity such as a game of tennis a month in advance. The weather is too unpredictable. It always has to be 'weather permitting'.

As Harish tried to grapple with the idea, the rain stopped as suddenly as it had begun and the sky started to curdle into clouds behind which patches of blue emerged.

In London they took their separate cabs and arranged to meet the following day for a walk around London. 'Weather permitting!' Kundan reminded them as they drove away.

Kundan had found lodgings for Madan in Gower Street. Three stone steps led to the porch and a polished front door. Madan looked along the line of railings.

'Look,' Kundan pointed down the street. 'University College. That's where Behari went. And he worked opposite in that red building – that's the hospital. We can take a stroll down there afterwards. We need to make an appointment for your interview. Of course, it's a great help that Behari attended University College and was such a good student. His achievement stands to your benefit, you know. It's a good recommendation. That is family: we help one another and stay as one. The bathroom has modern plumbing. Look around while I see to the rest of the luggage.'

Madan looked around his lodgings: two interconnecting rooms and a bathroom. He liked it. He also liked the idea that soon he would be on his own, independent and free.

The next morning Kundan took Madan to Mr Pickett, a gentleman's outfitters in New Bond Street. Madan was delighted. He had heard about the place and had always admired his brother's suits. He went around the shop feeling the different materials.

'Your brother, Dr Mohan Lal, had one made out of this when he was here earlier in the year,' said Mr Pickett. 'He told me it gets colder where he is than it does here.'

'Oh yes,' replied Kundan. 'Kashmir can be very cold, but there's less rain. In fact, Mr Pickett, the first thing I did on Madan's arrival was to take him to Gamages to purchase an umbrella. It was a warm summer's day, with a bright blue sky. Like today.'

'Quite right, too. Very wise of you. I'm sure, Sir, you've been told about the unpredictability of our weather.'

'Indeed, I have. When our brother Behari first came back, he told us that in England you sometimes had all the seasons in a day: hot, cold and rain.'

'Very well put, Sir,' said Mr Pickett, and they all laughed.

Madan chose some material for a suit. Kundan, who had been sitting, now rose and started to pace around the shop. 'Next year, Mr Pickett, our youngest brother, Bhajan, will be coming to study, and then you will have made outfits for all seven brothers.'

'And it has been a great privilege,' smiled Mr Pickett taking Madan's measurements.

'The privilege has been ours, entirely ours, to wear such fine clothes.'

As they discussed the cut, design and accessories, Madan could feel his brother's eyes observing him. He could almost guess what he was thinking.

'Madan is fond of the latest fashions, but I have told him that students must study, not follow fashions.'

'I'm sure he'll do that as well,' observed Mr Pickett. 'Where will you be studying, Sir?'

'He'll go to the same college as our brother Behari, that is, University College. It is a great help that Behari has been to the same college in getting Madan admission.'

Madan was looking at cravats and wishing that his brother wouldn't go on so. When Mr Pickett left the room, Kundan gave his brother instructions in Punjabi.

'You must take full advantage of your time here. Meet the right people. That's also part of your education. Sir William Curzon Wyllie at the India Office will help you with the right introductions. I will take you to see him.'

Madan was holding up some fine cashmere cloth and admiring its fall. Kundan watched him and wondered how, with his fastidious tastes, Madan had been able to put up with the harsh life of a ship's stoker. He didn't say anything, but to himself he admitted a reluctant admiration, now that the interlude was over and Madan was back on course, so to speak.

A man came into the shop demanding attention. Mr Pickett asked him to kindly take a seat, saying that he had nearly finished with his present customers and would attend to him soon.

'Are you asking me to wait while you serve these coolies?'

The new customer smiled sardonically.

'Really, Sir ... I must ...' began Mr Pickett, and then turned to Kundan to apologise.

'Make me an appointment now. I'm in a hurry,' said the customer.

'Never mind, Mr Pickett. It's all right. We understand,' replied Kundan softly as Mr Pickett went to get his big appointment book.

'It is not all right and we do not understand,' observed Madan.

Mr Pickett quickly drew the customer's attention to the appointment book. Kundan walked across to Madan to prevent a further outburst. 'There is never any need to answer rudeness with rudeness,' he said to him in Punjabi.

'And there is no need to accept insults,' Madan replied.

Later, Mr Pickett could not apologise enough. If his assistant had been in attendance, this would never have happened. 'Do forgive me, Sir. That was an outrage. I really am most terribly sorry.'

'Don't apologise, Mr Pickett. It was not your fault.'

Madan had been trying on a jacket. He looked at himself in the mirror. 'A coolie!' he said to himself under his breath.

They had arranged to meet Harish in Trafalgar Square. As they walked towards it Madan was in a sombre mood. Kundan tried to draw his attention to the buildings and the statues along the way.

'There's lots to see in London for budding civil engineers,' said Kundan as they located Harish. 'Lots of new developments and constructions. And the city is full of delightful parks and gardens. Come, follow me.'

As they walked he suggested a slight detour to the India Office.

'Come on up.' Kundan stood facing a building. 'This is the India Office and you can come in from the street here.' He pointed to a busy street at the end of the road. 'That's Whitehall.' I consulted Sir Curzon Wyllie about courses of study for you. He met Father in Hissar; Sir Dunlop Smith introduced them. He was very helpful.'

They were retracing their steps. Kundan pointed with his umbrella. 'I'm now going to take you down to the river where we can see the Houses of Parliament and Westminster Abbey. Come.'

It was a very fine day. London glowed and the young men were seduced.

'Look! Westminster Bridge,' Kundan pointed with his umbrella. 'If Bhajan was here he would surely break into Wordsworth, wouldn't he?'

Madan nodded as he looked across at the view the poet had described as beyond compare, and Kundan explained to Harish about their younger brother's love of poetry. 'Persian poetry, too.' Madan found himself thinking of his brother Bhajan and said 'Yes, I'll bring him here when he comes.'

The windows of the Houses of Parliament glistened in the sun.

'Do you think this Liberal government will change anything for us?' Madan heard Harish say and winced, anticipating his brother's reply.

'I have heard from reliable sources that they are planning some representation for Indians. And that will be a good thing.'

'But Queen Victoria promised that in the Great Proclamation of 1858, and that was nearly fifty years ago!'

'It will happen now,' Kundan replied confidently. 'Come, let's go on.'

They continued their stroll through the Inns of Courts where, Kundan pointed out, their brothers Chaman and Chunni had studied and where Bhajan would be studying the following year. Then they walked up the newly built Kingsway.

'I have seen so many changes and new developments over the years,' he pointed down Kingsway to the Aldwych. 'Nothing of this was here when I first arrived in London.' He smiled with pride.

15.

1906: THE HOUSE IN HIGHGATE

By the end of October Madan had established a routine, attending classes at the university and meeting up with other Indian students to compare notes about life in England and developments in India. For three months he had been on his own and was enjoying the freedom to follow his own impulses, to dream and to discover. This was something he had often longed for and it seemed paradoxical that he should find it in London where everything was so different. Sometimes he went to places with his friends, but often he went around on his own, walking whenever he could, looking at the buildings, monuments, exhibitions, museums, churches, parks, gardens and funfairs. Walking also had the added attraction of bringing you suddenly upon a street meeting or demonstration. London was full of dissenters, it seemed, and like other young Indians he visited Hyde Park, threading through the crowds and listening to the soap-box speeches at Speaker's Corner. It was there one Sunday afternoon that he came across a copy of *The Indian Sociologist* and found the address of India House. He recalled Basu, his luggage packed, ready to disembark, telling them to remember to find out about India House.

One evening he and some friends attended the Alhambra Music Hall in Leicester Square and had been curious to visit a pub, but none of them could pluck up the courage to enter. Madan observed that so much of the social life seemed to be centred on drinking and wondered what his father would make of this if he knew.

One bright October morning Madan awoke, drew the curtains and looked out into a mellow, powder-blue sky, the same blue as the turban his mother had given him when he left Amritsar. He decided that he would wear it and visit India House that day. As he got ready, he thought of his mother and the household settling down to lunch and had the sense that he was fulfilling a prior engagement. On his way he would call at Harish's lodgings and persuade Harish to accompany him.

'Where are you going in formal dress?' Harish asked on seeing Madan with his turban.

'India House. Will you come?'

'That's the place Basu spoke of, isn't it?'

'Yes. I have the address.'

'I'll come. But you haven't answered my question about why so formal?'

'I felt like it. And its nearly Divali!' Madan laughed.

Harish wanted to go by Underground, but Madan suggested the tram and showed him the map that he had consulted earlier in the morning.

'See here? We can get off at Waterlow Park and it will be a short walk.'

As they fell into step, Madan said: 'I was reminded of Basu last week, you know. I went to visit the Indian Sailors' Home in the East End.'

'You're always going somewhere; what about your studies?'

'I do that as well,' Madan replied. 'In any case, I said I would visit again, to help with writing letters, you know. Some of them are finding it difficult.'

'Did you meet anyone you knew or who knew someone from your old ship?'

'No. There are so many ships. But there is a great deal of poverty down there. Not just the Indians, but lots of poor white people.'

'Well, they're no concern of ours,' retorted Harish, taking the paper from Madan and leafing through it. Madan looked around the tram and caught the odd glances of people looking at him. He had noticed that when he wore a turban it drew rather more respectful glances than otherwise.

'I was thinking,' he said to Harish in Hindi. 'They grow old and sick just like we do, but have you observed that in India we never see the white man either old or sick or poor?'

Harish looked up from the paper and nodded thoughtfully.

Cromwell Avenue was a wide, tree-lined road with large houses on either side. The leaves on the trees shimmered copper and gold. They found the house and stopped to look at it and each other before climbing the steps to the raised front door. Madan felt that he was embarking on a mysterious adventure as he wiped his feet on the mat. Harish leant across him and rang the bell.

They were a bit surprised to find that an English maid opened the door. In the hall she took their coats and cards and led them to wait in the dining room.

'Can you smell it?' whispered Madan.

'What?' replied Harish.

'India!' retorted Madan. 'Can't you smell the spices and sandalwood lacing the polish and oak?'

Harish took a deep breath and smiled.

In the dining room they let out a little gasp as three banners, gold on red, greeted them. Over the fireplace was written 'BANDE MATARAM' with 'INDIA HOME RULE SOCIETY' and 'INDIA HOUSE' on either side. Madan placed his hand on his heart, faced the banner above the fireplace and declared, '*Bande Mataram*'.

'*Bande Mataram!*' came a reply. A young Indian was entering the room. 'Welcome, my brother, welcome. I am Vinayak Savarkar.' Madan, slightly thrown, quickly regained his composure.

Savarkar was slightly built with a high forehead and prominent cheekbones. He was around the same age as Madan and Harish, twenty-two or twenty-three, but there was an aura of calm determination about him that made him appear larger and older than he was. 'Yes. You are most welcome, my brothers,' he said warmly. 'I have come to take you upstairs. We are all gathered in the library.'

'The library? You have a library here?'

'Yes, and it is well stocked. Many well-wishers have given us books. We have some books in our library that are proscribed in India. All Indians should read them to learn the truth about this Raj of the *Angrez*.'

As they climbed the stairs Savarkar asked them questions to which Harish replied eagerly, sometimes breaking into Marathi, their shared language.

'So Basu told you about India House, did he?'

'Do you know him?' asked Madan.

'I have heard of him.'

'Are you the Savarkar from Fergusson College?' asked Harish. Savarkar smiled and Harish threw Madan an earnest look.

The library door was ajar. Draped over the fireplace on the facing wall was a flag, a tricolour with '*Bande Mataram*' written across the central orange band.

'What is that?'

'That is the flag of Free India,' replied Savarkar. 'Madame Cama is mostly responsible for it. The green band is the colour of the Muslims and the eight stars in it represent the eight provinces of India. This middle band of saffron is the colour of the Buddhists and the Sikhs, and it has the *Bande Mataram* in it. And the red band is the colour of the Hindus. It has the orb and crescent of Islam in it.'

'Madame Cama? Is she here? Basu told us about her.'

'She lives in Paris and frequently comes to London and to this house. You are sure to meet her, but another time.'

The library was awash with sunlight and looked well stocked. There was a large table in the middle and a smaller one in the bay. The middle-aged man with a beard, Madan guessed, must be Shyamji Krishna Varma. The other three were young men, two Indians and an Englishman. After the introductions he found that the 'Englishman' was an Irishman. The two Indians were Bapat and Bhai Parmanand. Bapat, as a student in Edinburgh, had produced a pamphlet about British Rule in India for which he had to forfeit his scholarship as its tone displeased the authorities. He had now become a protégé of Shyamji. After introductions and an invitation to stay to lunch they resumed their discussion – about an article on 'Indian Home Rule' from *The Gaelic American*.

'The cause of India and the cause of Ireland are one,' said the young Irishman. 'We were their first colony, where they sharpened their teeth. You must learn from our experience. It's not seats in their Parliament you want; that will never do. It's Independence.'

Madan smiled – at the idea and utter simplicity of it. He looked across at Harish and caught Savarkar looking at him; they exchanged a brief acknowledgement.

'Of course, of course,' said Shyamji. 'But we may need to take things step by step. The important thing is to be clear about the goal. This government is not going to make any concessions. The sooner that becomes obvious to people, the better.'

'We need to work on two fronts. Propaganda at home and building allies over here.'

'But the battle will have to be fought in India.'

The discussions covered a wide range of topics. Madan felt that they were being both included and carefully scrutinised, which made him self-conscious. After lunch he was ready to leave. Shyamji invited them to come again, to bring other Indian students and friends. All Indians were welcome, and there was always Indian food.

'Their Lord Macaulay cursed India with their system of education in which the old idea of values has been taken away, and the Western idea of values is alien to us. They are not an expression of who we are. We have to re-educate ourselves,' said Shyamji as he accompanied then into the hall. 'Here, you must take some copies of *The Indian Sociologist* and give them to your Indian friends.'

As he handed Madan the papers he remarked on his suit. 'That is a fine suit. Very fine tailoring.'

'Er ... yes. He's the family tailor.'

As they came down the steps, Madan said, 'There's still three-quarters of an hour of daylight. Let's walk back part of the way.'

Harish agreed and they both fell into a comfortable stride until they reached the Archway Road.

'Tell me about this Savarkar and that college.'

'He was at Fergusson College in Poona and got thrown out because he organised a boycott campaign and made a big bonfire of British goods. He's come on a scholarship from Krishna Varma.

He has to pledge that he will never work for the government in any capacity but must work for national unity.'

Back in his room Madan thought again of Free India and what it might be like. In Free India they certainly wouldn't wear these stiff Edwardian clothes, but he had to admit that he also quite enjoyed wearing them. He'd realised that when he'd come back from sea, his hands hardened from stoking and his skin parched by coal dust. He'd been away nine months. Then he'd come back, had a bath followed by an oil massage and stepped into his suit. He'd admired the cut in the mirror. And when he stepped out he knew that none of his fellow seaman would have recognised him. He looked such a sahib. Shyamji is right. Our heads are full of alien ideas. Even this concept of fashion was an alien idea. In India the sari and *dhoti* have remained unchanged for thousands of years. All this is but vanity and our heads have been filled with it – through 'education'.

His vision of a Free India was an India free of the white man. An India in which an Indian could breathe, where you didn't have to suffer the white man's arrogance and the continual petty reminders of an Indian's subjugation.

'Power makes people arrogant,' Baoji used to say. 'So the wise man does not seek power but service.'

He pulled out a paper from his pocket and went to his desk. Like other members of his family, Madan kept a notebook. It was full of quotations of various kinds: poems, sayings, extracts from books, in English, Urdu and Persian. But now he set it to one side and picked up another, empty notebook. He opened it and on the first page wrote:

London, November 1906. I visited India House today and I feel exhilarated. I will go there again. We discussed so many things. All are committed to India's total freedom. Krishna Varma, who was a dewan, has set the place up and there are scholarship-holders. One of them, Vinayak Savarkar, has been in the struggle since his teens.

He has such a focused clarity in his face. There was also Bhai Parmanand, an Arya Samaji like Krishna Varma himself. He spoke of Divali, about the long exile. 'Sita,' he said, 'is India, our Mother, our sacred earth. Ravana is British imperialism who has abducted and imprisoned Sita. Our exile can only end and our real Divali be celebrated when Sita is delivered from Ravana.'

I wonder what father would think of all this.

14.
1985: THE PHOTOGRAPH

My mother, an eternal optimist for whom the glass was always 'half full' used to say:

'And even if is empty. Why cry? It can only fill again.'

By the mid-1980s and after a rocky uphill climb I had reached a resting point. I had regained possession of my old flat, done well in my studies, found a job at the local community education centre, joined a writers' group and was working on my first book. The glass was filling.

It was ten years since the Emergency had left us 'stranded' in London and never before had I lived continuously in one city for so many years. In providing stability for my daughter, I'd inadvertently provided it for myself as well. And also for my mother.

My mother still travelled to India, where there were needy people she was helping, and where she was still trying to build a house, and to Venezuela to visit my sister and her grandsons. But London was her resting point, where she paid her taxes and had a small place of her own – where often, returning emotionally frayed from India, she could heal and regain her composure.

But I also remained a product of my conditioning, the partitioned, exiled self, longing to belong and still nursing the feeling that I should be somewhere else: that I wasn't where I was supposed to be.

Whilst studying I continued to entertain the idea of returning home to India, even of teaching in my old school, Rishi Valley, which remained a joyful highlight I wanted my daughter to experience. I visited the school and made connections, as well as a tape recording for her of the sounds around, the birds, the peacocks, the school assembly, the music ...

But then she asked: 'But Mummy, as a blind person in India will I be able to have the kind of independent life like I can here?'

In my best, reassuring, grown-up tone of voice, I explained India would give her a wider perspective, richer experience, depth of understanding to deal with life and its uncertainties.

She listened and then said: 'I think I'd really rather stay here where I know what to expect.'

I was dismayed and but also somewhat impressed she was so definite and clear.

One autumn half-term, when my daughter was away visiting her father and my mother was getting ready for her impending trip to India, I decided to go and see the film *Heat and Dust*, which was playing at a local cinema. To my surprise my mother asked to come along. She was short-sighted, never wore glasses and did not generally go to the movies. But in this case she knew the book, had met the author in Delhi and had even dined at her house in the early 1960s as the author's architect-husband was designing a house mother planned on building.

We sat near the front row and she clearly saw quite a bit. While watching a lavish dinner in the nawab's house, she whispered, 'From what I have been told, your grandfather entertained much more lavishly than that.'

Walking home, she said: 'You see that road, Fitzjohn's Avenue? Your father would never walk down that road.'

'Why?'

'Because *his* father died there. And he remembered running down that road to fetch the doctor.'

'I never knew that my grandfather died in London,' I said. But I understood my father's response. I had the same resistance to visiting Paris, the city which had taken him from me.

'Your father was very reserved. He never spoke about himself. He was such a good man, such a gentle, kind man. But, you see, I never understood him. And then when I was in Paris, I read this book called *How to be an Alien*, which described English eccentricities and as I read it, I recognised your father and then,' she stopped for effect, 'it suddenly dawned on me that I hadn't married an Indian at all, I'd married an Englishman! So ... no wonder I couldn't understand him!' My mother chuckled. 'We had such different upbringings. I grew up in a big extended family and we would go to the village and have village life. He was brought up in a princely state, had an English governess and such English ways. These were all strange to me. And yet, he could never live in England.'

'Why?'

'I don't know. He said his English education had instilled him with so much fear that he couldn't live here.'

I understood that, too. Sad, I thought. Had he been able to, we would have been more settled. Our family might have survived. Walking on, I was half-tempted to ask my mother about her marriage but half of me also didn't need to know.

'But, of course, at heart he was a true Indian. A true bhakta. Deeply spiritual.'

Images of my father flashed through my mind, His so very English ways, his offbeat friends, his humour, his laughter, the twinkle in his eye, his gentleness. My mother continued talking: 'I must say, though, he came from a most extraordinary family.' She looked at me, '*Your* family. Much more interesting than mine.'

'But I only really knew yours. And they didn't treat you well.'

My mother launched in to another story. 'Imagine Madan Lal!' she continued, 'All those years ago. Standing up like that against the might of the big British Empire! All on his own. So young. What courage!' She walked on. 'And then your grandfather, Sir Behari Lal. Now, you see, he wasn't a toady like my grandfather was.'

'What's a toady?'

'A *chamcha*. A sycophant. My grandfather was considered a toady and when the nationalist *morchas* would pass outside his house they'd all stop, beat their breasts and shout 'Toady *baccha hai hai*, toady *bacha hai hai*.'

My mother stopped to demonstrate the gesture, beating her chest and then her head in rhythm to the chant.

'But your grandfather was quite different. He genuinely admired the British. He saw them as a modernizing influence and he himself had modern ideas: he believed in women's equality, social welfare and education for all. He even sent your Aunty Shukla to Oxford in the 1920s, which was very unusual in those days. And then, of course, there was Bhajan Lal. You know about him, don't you?'

'No, I don't. Who was he?'

'Well now, he was the youngest of the brothers, and he was here in London at the same time as Madan Lal when everything happened. Later, he became a Sufi *pir* and has a *mazaar* in Lyallpur, which is now in Pakistan.'

'What does that mean?'

'He became a Sufi mystic. He's regarded as a holy man, and the *mazaar* is where he is buried. His tomb. People go there to pray or to make wishes. Your father told me, but I never met him.'

'So each of them took a completely different path.'

As we walk along, my mother in her reverie, I am in mine: sixteen years old walking with my father to the Champs Élysées for our Sunday lunch at the Snack Bar des Élysées. My father is striding along silently, I'm tripping alongside, wanting to engage and say something ... significant. I say:

'Papa. What does it mean for me to be a Hindu?'

'Well, darling, there are certain concepts, like *dharma*, *karma*, *moksha* and others which we can discuss, but most of all it means that you must find and follow your *swadharma*, which is to say the path of your true nature. And it must be your way, not Mummy's way or my way or anybody else's way but your own way.'

It had felt like a conundrum. I thought I'd understand when I was grown up. But now as I remembered it, walking down the hill with my mother, I was still trying to grapple with the idea – my own way? My true nature?

Suddenly my mother stopped.

'What is it? What's wrong?'

We had stopped at the road parallel to ours and my mother indicated it with her chin as we walked past it.

'Diane is living there now.'

'I know that.'

'I saw her moving in last week, and I told her – It makes me so happy to know that my Leena will have a friend nearby.'

A wave of irritation swept over me. Living with my mother sometimes made me feel trapped in an old child-self. But my daughter adored having her storytelling grandmother around and I was resigned to the reality. I looked at my mother with a frown. She returned my look with a knowing glint. I would soon learn that it was a prescient comment. As indeed was the whole of our conversation during our walk home from the cinema that day.

A few weeks after my mother left, I came home from work to find a large A3 packet from my cousin Prem in Canada. He and his wife Peggy had passed through London in the summer, so I imagined it was some sort of gift and wondered what I might send them in return.

But the contents were a complete surprise: newspaper cuttings from 1976 from the Indian press of Madan Lal's return to and a hero's welcome in India. All front-page news. '*Comet in the revolutionary sky*' read one of the headlines. There were also two separate envelopes. One said: 'Madan Lal', the other: 'Our grandfather'. I opened the first and found myself pulling out a photograph – the photograph of Madan Lal and a folded, typewritten page on headed paper of 'Centre de L'Inde Libre' entitled 'Statement of Madan Lal Dhingra, Revolutionary Martyr who died for the country on 17 Aug. 1909'. The document was authenticated by Madhava Rao and addressed to 'The family of Madan Lal Dhingra'.

I was transfixed. It was almost too much to take in. Madan Lal Dhingra, my great uncle who looked like my father. Oh my God! And suddenly my mother's 'this man we met in Paris' now had a name: Madhava Rao.

I leant back in my chair, open-mouthed, closed my eyes and conjured up what must have been an extraordinary meeting. There must have been a gathering of Indians in Paris to celebrate the advent of Indian Independence on 15 August 1947. Could it have been at UNESCO, where my father was working? Or could there have been the skeleton of an Indian embassy to come?

Does Madhava Rao, from the 'Centre de L'Inde Libre', who has been living in Paris these last thirty-seven years, see a man across the room who looks just like his friend ... Could it be?' Does his mouth gape like mine? Does he do a doubletake? Or a sharp intake of breath? Maybe he asks, 'Who is that man?'

'That's Baldoon Dhingra. He works at UNESCO. Press Officer for Asia.'

'Dhingra, you say. His name is Dhingra? But of course. It must be.'

And he walks over, almost in a dream. I see the rest of the scene at a distance as Madhava Rao puts his hand on his heart and my father, takes a step back, looks at him in amazement and delight, then looks around for my mother to include her in this momentous meeting. Madhava Rao also signalled to a friend of his to come and join them and Sardar Rana walks over.

My camera-eye views the scene from a distance, unable and unwilling to intrude – and foist any interpretation on this moment.

But I wished I'd known earlier and had asked my father.

In the second envelope was a photograph of my grandparents, my grandfather's death certificate and obituary from *The Times*: London, 3 July 1936 ... 'Sir Behari Lal Dhingra, who died in Hampstead yesterday'. That photograph was familiar as it used to live in our Paris flat and the death certificate gave the exact address in Fitzjohn's Avenue: 108.

Was this all a coincidence? Was it unfinished business? It certainly felt like a meaningful moment. Ten years earlier I'd searched for a photograph and now, without my having done anything, it had been delivered to my door. Ten years earlier I had imagined that the search for Madan Lal might reconnect me to India. Maybe now? But how? I was a single mother with a full-time job and little leisure.

My cousin Prem's letter explained that on a visit to India he had taken some documents and knowing my interest in Madan Lal had sent them to me. That my father had posted them from Paris, to his father, and he had retrieved them from the metal *Godrej* cupboard in the cottage in Simla.

'*We met this man in Paris ...*'

Another scene. Madhava Rao invites my father to visit him at his home, 52 Rue La Fayette, to give him the photograph.

'To whom should I make it out?' he asks. 'You have an unusual name, how do I spell it?'

'Make it out to – the members of the family. I will send it to my elder brother in India. He will be happy to receive it and I will be back there myself next month.'

Dear Daddy. How could you have imagined that you would never return? Never see Lahore again nor your house in Model Town, which your wife sold her wedding jewellery to build and so fulfil her dream. You never spoke about the past and I never asked.

My mother never forgot, and the past was always present:

'Never in my wildest dreams did I ever imagine that we would ever leave Lahore. Why? We all lived to together with so much love. It was simply not possible to imagine.'

I lightly touch the photograph and think of my father touching it, too, and my uncle in Simla, and my cousin Prem and Madhava Rao ... and who else. Fingerprints over time. It felt just right that it should come back to me from within the family.

And, that it should connect me back to my father and to Paris unleashed a host of emotions and images. Too many to absorb.

Coincidence? Meaning? Message? I recalled how, years ago, I had imagined finding Madan Lal's story connecting me to India and my place there. The end of my exile?

I started to daydream about it, watch it waft through in my daily activities or walk to work. And I remembered the box file that I'd put away. But where?

'Well, I think it's significant,' said Diane when I told her during our walk on the Heath. 'In fact, I seem to remember that when we first met at that Anti-Indian Emergency meeting in Red Lion Square you asked Manu if he knew where you might find a photograph.'

'Did I? Really? I don't remember at all.' I walked along trying to remember and said: 'It was a bit of a hazy time, that. But I was looking for the photograph then.'

'And now you have it.'

We had reached the top of Kite Hill and stopped to look over the view of London.

Then, that winter in Delhi, sitting in the garden of Romila, my historian aunt, soaking in the winter sun after lunch, I mentioned my initial research into Madan Lal, the little I knew, that I'd been sent a photograph and wondered if it was something I should pursue?

'You know,' she said as she poured the tea, 'when you start to find out about your family history, you start to find out about yourself.'

'Really?' I replied.

'The first thing you need to do,' she continued, handing me my cup, 'is to go to the Public Record Office. It's in Chancery Lane. There you will find the Trial Deposition. That's where you start. And for the Indian part, you go to Hardwar. There you will need to find your *panda*, the priests who keep the genealogies of families.

'Did you say his younger brother became a Sufi *pir*?'

'That's what I've been told.'

'What was his name?'

'Bhajan Lal. Strange, isn't it?'

'Well. It's the same impulse, you know,' said my aunt.

'What do you mean?'

'The revolutionary and the mystic. The search for utopia. The utopia without and the utopia within.' She smiled. 'Is the tea all right?'

Driving back, more voices floated through my head:

'When you start to find out about your family history, you'll start to find out about yourself.'
'Become what you truly know yourself to be. Find your own way.'

A few months later, with three days of 'time off in lieu' from the community education centre, I climbed the steps out of Chancery Lane station, rhythmically repeating my aunt's instructions in my head and translating them into French and Hindi and then back into English.

'*La première chose à faire, c'est d'aller à la Public Record Office à Chancery Lane ...*'

'*Sab se pehle tum ko Public Record Office jana padega, Chancery Lane main hai.*'

'*The first thing you need to do is go to the Public Record Office in Chancery Lane ...*'

I recognised that this simultaneous translation business was a habit of nervousness. But why was I feeling nervous? Or was it something else. Excitement? Anticipation?

I walked down towards a magnificent, Gothic-style building with its crowns of cupolas and instead of going in I crossed the road to admire it. Then I decided I needed some new notebooks and pencils and pens. There were a couple of legal stationers nearby, so I walked into the first and after a spell of indecisive deliberation I picked out a green spiral A4 book and another smaller blue one called 'Notebook'. With these, I entered the building.

I had filled out my requisition slips and was waiting and trying to harness my thoughts. I opened my blue Notebook and stared at the blank page. As I sat quietly waiting, I suddenly remembered and was transported:

Another time, another hall with desks, another age. Sixteen years old, I am sitting my French 'A' level exam. The book was Jean Anouilh's *Antigone*, the question:

'With whom do your sympathies lie? With Creon or Antigone?'

My ever-so-certain sixteen-year-old self wrote with great aplomb that my sympathies certainly lay with Creon. After all, I argued, was it not much easier to rebel, to refuse, to say no and to hell with it, and was it not much more difficult and did it not require greater courage to balance realities, accept compromises and fulfil responsibilities?

Then, as I sat there, all those years later, I wondered that I should remember that incident. Now that I was setting out to meet the rebel of the family, could I really say that it was such an easy choice?

'Forgive me, Uncle Madan. I am sorry,' I murmured.

A box tied with dusty tape was placed on my table. Alongside was a thick book recording the trials of 1909. I stared at them for a while and then started to unwind the tape, wondering if I was the first member of the family to do this.

I lifted the lid off and then looked at the bundles of papers inside, also wrapped in grubby tape. I pulled out one bundle and flicked through a pile of wide, slanting handwriting on lined foolscap and occasional typed sheets. I read:

'My name is Mary Harris, I am married and live at 108 Ledbury Road, Bayswater. The man Dhingra lodged with me ... was very regular in his habits ... very steady ... quiet in manner ...'

Suddenly for an instant, I saw him. My heart started to pound. I put the papers back. I didn't want to read them there. I quickly located the trial pages in the thick, bound book, selected a few items from the box and took them over to the photocopying counter, which I had stared at absently while I had been waiting.

'Would you like to collect them or would you like them posted to you?'

'Posted to me, please.'

Back home I wondered about why I had remembered *Antigone*. Yes, Antigone and her need to bury her brother's body. She had needed to put it to rest properly. She needed to pay it respect. She needed to do this. And she did.

And I wondered about my own search. What was it I needed to do? Was it for him? Was it for me?

I took the photograph from its envelope, propped it on my desk; alongside it, I placed my green spiral book, the 'Notebook' and my applications for funding. Then I lit a candle and I looked at the flames: red, yellow and saffron.

'*Saffron is for fire – the purifier, the colour of renunciation. That is why our yogis wear it and we call it* jogia.' And mentally I made the request that I should get the funding – if it was something I needed to do.

15.

1906: LONDON – SAVARKAR

*'I saw a certain amount of Savarkar and was more than ever struck
by his extraordinary personal magnetism. There was an intensity
of faith in the man and a curious single-minded recklessness,
which were deeply attractive to me. The place in which he was
living brought out both his refinement and also his lack of human
sympathy, both characteristic of the high caste Brahmin ... He was
wrapped in his visions. What was his vision then? I cannot say,
but I believe it was that India was a volcano, which had erupted
violently during the Mutiny and which could be made to erupt
again, and that every act of terrorism or violence would beget
further violence and further terrorism, until Indians regained their
manliness and their mother country her freedom. All the sufferings
involved were but a fitting sacrifice to her.'*
(David Garnett, *The Golden Echo*)

Shyamji Krishna Varma had given Madan and Harish a selection
of back issues of *The Indian Sociologist* and they circulated these

amongst their friends and other compatriots. The most recent issue announced a competition with a prize of £50 for an essay on: 'The best form of government for India'. Readers of the journal met in groups and discussed the possibilities of affecting change by constitutional means, demanding Home Rule like the Irish, Dominion status like Canada and Australia, new forms of power sharing – or even Independence. They had all been brought up on English history, prose and poetry, the blessings and advantages of being part of the British Empire and the importance of loyalty, so some of their ideas were challenging, to say the least.

Shyamji's India House was not the only organisation vying for the time and attention of the Indian students. There was also the much older London India society, formed in 1872 by Dadabhai Naoroji who remained its president. Dadabhai was the first Indian to become an MP. His book, *Poverty and Un-British Rule*, which set out the facts and figures of the drain of India's wealth, was mandatory reading. Madan visited the London Indian Society as well as India house.

'We have become a nation of beggars and petitioners,' Shyamji would say. 'This style of mendicant politics does nothing.' And he would reiterate the advice of his friend H. M. Hyndman that 'Indians must learn to rely upon themselves and organise themselves apart from their foreign masters for their final emancipation.' Englishmen and their agendas had for too long dominated the Congress committee. Now, the spirit of the time, of nationalism, demanded defiance and self-assertion. 'We must learn and take courage from the Russians and the Irish.'

'Vinayak was asking about you,' Harish said to Madan one day.

Madan was pleased that he should be remembered. The following week, when he went to Gray's Inn to collect some information for his brother Bhajan, he bumped into Vinayak Savarkar. They were both surprised and pleased.

'I don't believe in coincidences. Things happen as they should,' remarked Vinayak as they walked along together. 'I have a few errands to do, but this evening there is the meeting of the Home Rule Society and it should be interesting. Why don't you come?'

'Yes,' replied Madan, feeling somewhat flattered. 'I'd like to come.'

'So your brother will be coming to study at Gray's Inn?

'Yes. Later.'

'How many brothers do you have?'

'Six.'

'And how many of them are already lawyers?

'Two. And two doctors. I have decided that I will never work for the government.'

'Harish tells me you went away to sea.'

'That's right. I ran away. I wanted to see the world.'

'And did you?'

'As much as I could, or did. I was on a ship carrying opium from India to China. Another time we were almost boarded by the Japanese.'

'What did you run away from?'

'I just … I wanted to see the world. Other places; other ways of being.'

'I know the feeling. But a slave has nowhere to run to. If our Motherland is enslaved are we not slaves? A subject race.'

'No,' Madan replied indignantly. Vinayak looked at him and smiled.

Vinayak Savarkar had noticed Madan Lal the first time he came to India House. Madan felt that Vinayak emanated a power, a groundedness, something that he recognised and found comforting.

'Harish told me he is helping you with a book?'

'Yes. It's about the First Indian War of Independence in 1857. It was not just a mutiny. It was a national uprising against the enslavement of our Motherland. In the British Museum they have all the documents. My book is a guide to action for the present, taking inspiration from the past. The book is just part of the plan.'

'The plan?'

'Yes. Harish is helping me with the first draft of the translation as I go along, so that we don't waste any time. I have already translated the *Autobiography of Mazzini* into Marathi. That is also a guide for how to go about setting up the conditions and organisation to dislodge a predatory power. You must try to read it.'

'Yes. I would like to.'

'I was fourteen years old when I swore on the altar of the Goddess that I would henceforth devote the rest of my life to the service of the Motherland. It was when they hanged the Chapekar brothers. I witnessed this, and at once I knew my destiny and why I was born at this time. A country in chains is a country in pain. It cannot contribute anything to world peace, progress or prosperity.'

They walked on in silence for a while. Vinayak knew that Madan was digesting what he'd said. He knew the signs because for some years he'd been persuading people through the use of 'truth and logic', as he called it. Though aged only twenty-two, he already had an organisation behind him in which many of the people, though older than himself, had chosen him as their leader.

'What will you do if you do not work for the Government?'

'I'll try to find work in one of the independent states. Two of my brothers work in them: in Kashmir and Jind.'

'That is very good. The native states will be important in the plan.'

'What is this plan? You mentioned it earlier?'

'Yes, the plan for the liberation of India.' Vinayak said this as though stating the obvious, and on seeing Madan's face he smiled. 'You will hear about it. In time.' Suddenly Savarkar stopped walking and looking at Madan said, 'Would you like to come to the House of Commons with me and hear the Indian Budget?'

'Yes. I would,' Madan replied.

'It will be very late at night and the place will be half empty. That's the measure of their concern.'

Kier Hardie, House of Commons: Indian Budget

'The average income per head of an Indian is a mere £1 and yet £30,000,000 is taken out of the country annually for which there is no return and in addition, last year alone, £22,000,000 was spent to keep in existence the most expensive army in the world, armies which can be used against the people.'

16.

1907: London, India House

When Shyamji Krishna Varma, together with his friend Hyndman, had first conceived of the 'remarkable and admirable experiment known henceforth as India House', he had assumed that the Indian students he would gather around him would quite naturally come under the tutelage of their elders, namely himself and his friends. Certainly, this was what he expected from the holders of lectureships and fellowships that he had been instrumental in establishing. It was the time-honoured Indian tradition of teacher and pupil, the guru and disciple.

But Krishna Varma had been out of India for nearly a decade and was not wholly aware of how much everything had changed. How much India had changed; Lord Curzon's legacy had seen to that. A new mood had set in and although Krishna Varma knew about developments in some detail, they were not something he had experienced at first hand. It was a point that his protégés never tired of mentioning. But he had not thought that he would find himself leaving his own house in protest. As he climbed down the steps he could sense that he was being watched, not only by the innocent-looking man seemingly checking an address, but also from the library, where he had been sitting five minutes previously before he had stormed out and slammed the door.

'You should be delighting in this new mood, as indeed I do,' his friend Hyndman had said to him earlier. 'You know as well as I do that there is nothing to be expected from this Congress committee until it changes, which it undoubtedly will. India has come of age. It has entered into the spirit of the time, it is part of the *zeitgeist*, so to speak – although I do not like to use German words – and these young men are living proof of it.'

Shyamji made his way down towards Waterlow Park. A walk always changed his mood, settled his thoughts and calmed his spirit.

Through the library window, Chatto watched him go and then turned to the room that still resonated with voices.

The argument had been about holding a meeting at India House to commemorate the fiftieth anniversary of the 1857 uprising. Shyamji tried to impress on his young protégés that it would not be appropriate.

'I came to England nine years ago, and I bided my time. You have to gauge the time for things, the right time.'

Bapat interrupted him. 'Time, time, time! With all due respect, I believe you have been away from India too long.'

Shyamji was stung by this remark and raised his voice. 'I am well informed about developments in India. I am in close contact with both events and people. I had a letter from Tilak only last week. Lajpat Rai was here a few months ago. People are constantly coming and there are letters to *The Indian Sociologist*.' He turned to Madame Cama for support. 'Is that not right, Bhiku?'

'Come, come, friends!' Madame Cama intervened. 'There is no need to argue. We share the same aims, the same goal – the desire for self-determination.'

'That's just it. Do we?' said Savarkar. Everyone turned to look at him as he in turn looked at each of them. 'Think about it. Self-determination, under Home Rule, within the aegis of the Empire!' He shook his head. 'It just doesn't add up. The demand can only be for freedom. Nothing less.'

'Come, Vinayak,' interceded Madame Cama, 'I don't think that Shyamji sees Home Rule as an end in itself.'

Chatto interrupted, 'We must state our goal from the beginning. We must keep our eyes on the prize.'

'Exactly!' echoed Bapat.

Savarkar rose and walked over to where Madame Cama and Madan were stitching stars on to the flag. 'Bhikuji, why are you protecting him? You yourself are in total agreement with the Free India Society.'

'Of course I am, and I am not protecting anybody, Vinayak. I'm simply trying to tell you that this is a needless argument.'

'Bhiku is right,' retorted Shyamji, also rising from his chair. 'There is no real disagreement. But we need to take things step by step. A lot of things are happening at the moment which will help our cause, and the government needs to know what we feel.'

'The government knows very well what we feel. It papers the walls with our petitions.'

'You are deliberately misunderstanding me. What I am trying to impress upon you is that we need to ride on the tide of changing awareness. It is happening all around us, the suffragettes, the Labour movement, Sinn Féin. Times are changing.'

'Times don't change by themselves. We make them change. We are the time,' sighed Chatto.

Madan found himself nodding in agreement.

'And that is why the meeting should be held here. After all, this is India House, is it not?' Savarkar walked over and faced

Shyamji and they both stared at each other. 'You contradict yourself. You write one thing, but you don't act accordingly. You are inconsistent, Sir! It makes no sense. I don't understand why the meeting can't be held here.'

'You do not understand. Or else you are simply not willing to listen. Care needs to be exercised. We do not want to draw notice to ourselves too hastily or unnecessarily. There is no reason for it yet.' Shyamji turned again to Madame Cama. 'Bhiku!'

But she didn't have time to say anything as Bapat got up and threw his arms in the air.

'No reason for it? What are you saying?! Bengal has been partitioned, arbitrary arrests are taking place, new legislation is being enforced. All this is happening – how you can say such a thing? We need to mobilise and train.'

'Come, friends, comrades, please, please, there is no need for this.' Madame Cama put down her sewing and stood up.

Krishna Varma raised his voice and swung round to face Bapat.

'Who do you think you are saying this to? You do not have to tell me! Who did you write to for help and guidance to write your pamphlet? Who gave you the information? Who set up the scholarships of which you are such worthy recipients?'

'Please, let us lower our voices,' pleaded Madame Cama. 'Shyamji, none of this diminishes the important work you have done.'

Shyamji raised his voice higher. 'Bepin Chandra Pal will be arriving on the fellowships I have now set up with Rana. Why do you think I set them up – these scholarships and fellowships? With my own money.'

'Money is just money,' said Savarkar. 'We all must serve the cause, in whatever way we can.'

'Quite right,' said Madame Cama. 'And arguments will not serve the cause. Come come, we must discuss calmly about holding a meeting ...'

'Some of us,' announced Bapat's voice over hers, 'have taken *diksha*, have vowed to sacrifice our lives.'

'Of the twenty-three residents of India House, the great majority would support the meeting being held here. I have spoken to them,' said Savarkar.

'You have spoken to them? I see. And by what right?' said Shyamji. Then, without waiting for a reply, he turned to Bapat. 'As far as *diksha* is concerned, I would remind you that I am the executor of Swami Dayanandji's will.'

'That was more than twenty years ago,' said Savarkar quietly. 'It has taken a long time for you to take up your duties.'

'Vinayak!' Madame Cama's voice was reproachful.

Krishna Varma was furious. 'Forgive me, Bhiku, but let me make one thing clear. Whoever you speak to or don't speak to, this is still my house. As long as I run it, it is I who will decide what meetings are held or not held here.'

Savarkar looked at him and then put his hands together, saying, 'Pardon me for my confusion, Sir! But I thought this was India House?'

Shyamji stormed out of the room.

'Really, Vinayak! I think the remark about Swami Dayanand was misplaced.'

'The truth is never comfortable for those who don't wish to see it. But truth must be our guide.'

'Shyamji himself admitted that he only left India so as to get away from a life of pinpricks and servility. He was never outspoken in India. Even here he seeks the approbation of his white socialist friends,' said Bapat.

'You cannot hold these things against him. Many people are quiet in India. Sometimes you have to leave to learn the truth.'

'Do you think that maybe Shyamji, like Dadabhai, still believes that reforms will come from the government?'

Madan's suggestion was greeted with much mirth.

Chatto immediately placed his hand on his heart in a melodramatic gesture 'Ah! England's busy, but essentially good, heart.'

'There is no need to mock Dadabhai,' said Madame Cama, her voice grave. 'He has been a guide and an inspiration to us all, and has worked for the cause unflinchingly.'

'Yes, but we have also all been conditioned to believe in British Fair Play. Did we not all have to learn the 'Ten Great Blessings of British Rule at school?'

Chatto laughed. 'Ah yes! Didn't we just! The ten great blessings! *Post* and *Telegraph*! Thank you! Thank you!' He made an elaborate bow that both Madan and Bapat returned before starting a little dance around the room.

'Law and Order! Thank you, thank you!'

'Roads and Railways –'

'Thank you, thank you!'

'Deportation!'

'Thank you, thank you!'

'*Bas bas*! Enough!' said Madame Cama, and they all stopped.

Vinayak, who had been looking out of the window, came back into the middle of the room.

'We have less than two weeks. We will find a place. The meeting will go ahead.'

17.

1988–89 INDIA HOUSE: *SEE S FOR SEDITION*

I started my research at the School of Oriental and African Studies and felt a definite lightness in my step as I climbed to the door and made my way down its corridors.

'Call me Ken, there's no need for formalities,' said the professor as he ushered me into the room and indicated a chair. 'I'm so glad you wrote to me.' I noted a neat pile of books on the floor and guessed they had previously occupied the chair I now sat on. 'Remind me again, what relation are you to *the* Dhingra?'

'He was my father's uncle, my grandfather's younger brother. But I don't know anything about him.' I noted the slight defensiveness in my tone. Nonetheless, the professor smiled and I felt reassured. 'The story goes that my grandfather never allowed his name to be mentioned in the house.'

'Ah-ha!' the professor raised his eyebrows and jabbed the air with his index finger, just like my father used to do when he told me Sherlock Holmes stories. 'Have you heard of the debates between Wilberforce and Huxley?'

'No.'

'Well, amongst other things, it's about elder sons and younger sons. One following the route of tradition, working within the status quo, and the other following the route of change – revolt. I've found that it often applies. Did you say something about making a television programme?'

'I hope so. I've applied for some development money to research the idea for a television programme. But I need to find a focus. I thought about a London story of the struggle for freedom. Buried and forgotten in the bricks and buildings of the city.'

A very fascinating story it is, too,' said the professor, sitting down behind a desk piled high with folders and files 'They were called "The India House Group" and achieved a lot of notoriety. They spread propaganda among the Indian soldiers during the First World War among other things. In fact ...' He rose from his chair and started to scour the shelves behind him. 'There's a thesis about the young Indian revolutionaries abroad. I have the reference somewhere, if I could just lay my hands on it.' As I wondered just how it could be possible to locate anything in this room, Ken found it. 'Ah ... here we are.' He opened a file and passed it across the table. 'Here, take the reference. You'll be able to find it at Senate House.'

I opened the green spiral notebook and wrote down the reference.

'You know about the exhumation, of course?'

'Yes. I do. I could have ...' I stopped myself, 'My mother was in India and she accompanied the coffin when it was taken in a cortège in the Punjab and told me about it. Later, I got some newspaper cuttings.'

'They must have been from Indian newspapers. You wouldn't have got any newspaper cuttings from here. They served a "D" notice, you see.'

'What's that?'

'The government issues a "D" notice when it doesn't want something to be reported in the press. It means that they deemed it politically sensitive information. Though it does seem somewhat strange after all these years.'

I wrote, *'D notice? Wilberforce and Huxley'*, and said: 'I remember reading that they were greatly influenced by Mazzini.'

'Quite so, quite so. Mazzini was a most important influence. He liberated Italy from the Austrians. At the time, the end of the last century, the British had this theory, the Climatic Theory, which maintained that people born in warmer climates were more indolent, less disciplined, lacking in moral fibre, and thereby, a naturally subject people, whereas those born in colder climes were hardier, self-regulating, and naturally born rulers. This, then, formed a moral justification for colonialism. Now Mazzini, you see, turned this theory on its head, because under his influence Italy was united and threw off Austrian rule. Because the Climatic Theory applied to the Italians, as well, the events in Italy were seen as a parallel to India and there is no doubt that Mazzini's ideas would have influenced the young men of India House. In fact, I'm sure they did – as, indeed, did the Japanese victory.'

To my questioning look, he replied: 'The Japanese defeated the Russians in a naval war sometime around 1904–1905. This sent shock waves across Europe because people couldn't believe that an Asiatic power could defeat a European power. But it was a time of changes and upheavals, activity and agitation, with the trades union movement, the suffragettes, upheavals in Russia and, of course, the Irish. Sinn Féin were in contact with the Indian revolutionaries. The Irish connection was quite important, really. I think they even called themselves the Indian Sinn Féinists. You might also like to look at some contemporary material. H. M.

Hyndman, for instance, had close connections with India House.'
He spelt out the name for me.

'Did he by any chance live in Hampstead?' I asked as I wrote
it down.

'You might also look at W. S. Blunt's diaries and David Garnett's
autobiography. He also had some connection with the group,
particularly with Savarkar. Now that's another very interesting
story indeed: Savarkar. And, of course, you must remember that
individuals also wrote their own accounts, and members of the
group did that as well. You will find material at the India Office
Library, and in our own library downstairs. I'd be happy to sign
any forms you might need to get a researcher's ticket.'

When I left we exchanged books: I gave him a signed copy of
my novel and he gave me a signed copy of his book, *Race, Sex and
Class under the Raj*.

The 'researcher' was a comforting persona, I thought, as I
climbed down the steps of SOAS. It gave me distance. As I walked
down Gower Street towards University College, it occurred to me
that both Great Uncle Madan and my grandfather had walked this
very same way as they had both studied there.

I had arranged to meet Martin at the India Office Library and
made my way to Russell Square to catch the bus to Waterloo. As
I walked down The Cut towards Blackfriars Road, entered the
building through the glass doors and went up in the lift, I tried to
sense the difference in my feelings from my first visit when I had
mistakenly requisitioned a log of deportations and had to rush
out of the library. That time, the research had become entangled
with the crisis of my own life falling apart. Now I was a bona fide

researcher. Detached. In search of 'facts'. And this time I had help. Martin Moir, ever punctual, was there waiting for me.

'How can I find out about India House?' I asked

I was guided to the Index. It said: *'For "India House" see "S" for Sedition.'* And there was the address: *65 Cromwell Avenue, N,* which I copied into my green spiral notebook.

'There are two series of files you will find useful,' he whispered, 'the L/ P&S, which is the Political and Secret and the L/P&J, which is Public and Judicial. Every week the Secretary of State would receive a file of matters to which his officers felt his attention needed to be drawn.'

As he showed me the requisition slips and procedure, explained the time it would take. I nodded and made notes.

'You can also fill up the slips in advance, put into the request today to come at a later time, tomorrow say or even next week.'

I smiled. 'Yes. I think I'll do that. I can then come early and have the whole day.'

So I filled up some slips, put a date for the following week and left to catch to bus home.

Was it a family secret? I wondered on the bus home. Or was it a family shame? And was I doing the right thing in finding out about it? I thought of my grandfather: 'never allowed his name to be mentioned in the house'.

The bus pulled into its terminus. It was a lovely late afternoon and I decided to take my thoughts for a stroll on Hampstead Heath.

A few months earlier when I was applying for funding, my sister on her way through from India back to Venezuela had asked me: 'Do you think that if the dice had tumbled differently and you had found yourself living in India, France or Belgium, would you have been as interested in Uncle Madan Lal as you are now?'

'What do you mean?'

'Well, does your interest have something to do with being in England and caught up in this whole colonial-racism business?'

'I don't know. But the story is here, in this city. As indeed am I,' I'd replied.

I felt the weight of the 'business'. It was an obvious connection. And yet there was something else ...

I looked across to Highgate and wondered where India House might be. And then I thought that this would be a good visual for my film and imagined a commentary: 'In the "far off land" where my great uncle died, I now live. The freedom for which he sacrificed his young life made me a refugee. For along with Independence, came Partition, loss and uprootedness, for my family and countless others – as we lost our homes and our histories became mysteries.'

Histories and mysteries, I thought. *His*-story and *my*-story.

The arc of my walk took me down the tree-lined avenue on the Heath and into Well Walk, where I stopped in front of a tall house by the old well and looked up at the inscription on the blue plaque: 'Henry Mayers Hyndman lived here'. I was pleased I had got it right and as I walked on I wondered if Mr Hyndman might have met my Great Uncle Madan.

Arriving at Hampstead High Street, I cross the road and walk up an alley, Perrin's Court, which leads into Fitzjohn's Avenue, and look at the house in which my grandfather died and the road my father never took again. My grandfather, whom I'd only known from a photograph: a Victorian Indian gentleman, double-breasted, gold watch-and-chained, who'd employed English governesses for his children and had sent his daughter to Oxford – in the 1920s.

'*Your grandfather was very modern. He believed in women's education.*'

My story. Mystery, I thought. Lost stories. Buried in the city. Needing to be teased out. The point was to find the right questions. And what might they be?

Walking down the High Street I tried to imagine how the area might have looked in 1906 when Uncle Madan might have walked down it. Or in 1936 when my grandfather might have taken a stroll.

I stopped at Ryman's and bought a new folder – my planning folder – and a block of multicoloured Post-it notes.

That night I dreamed that I had accompanied the body, brought him home. Sitting between my mother and my aunt Danti in that '*open bus, the coffin covered with marigolds and roses ...*'

18.
10 MAY 1907: MARTYRS' MEMORIAL

On 10 May the meeting to commemorate the fiftieth anniversary of 1857 took place, without Shyamji, at a house in Goldsmith Avenue, Acton, renamed as 'Tilak House'. The freshly painted nameplate was placed above the door to mark the occasion.

Thirty-five people had squeezed into the front room. Stretched across the wall were two banners with the inscriptions: 'FREE INDIA SOCIETY' and 'REMEMBER THE MARTYRS OF 1857'.

The meeting opened with the national prayer. Everyone rose and placed their hands on their hearts.

Ek Dev; Ek Desh; Ek Bhasha
Ek Jath: Ek Jeev: Ek Asha
(*One God, One Land, One Language. One Creed,*
One Life, One Hope.)

Savarkar rose and read:

'Today is the 10th of May. It was on this day that in the ever-memorable year of 1857, the first campaign of the War of

Independence was opened by you, O Martyrs, on the battlefields of India. The Motherland, awakened to the sense of her degrading slavery, unsheathed her sword, burst forth the shackles and struck the first blow for her liberty and for her honour.

'This day therefore we dedicate, O Martyrs, to your inspiring memory. It was on this day that you raised a new flag to be upheld, a mission to be fulfilled, a vision to be realised, a nation to be born.

'But, O glorious Martyrs, in this pious struggle of your sons, help us by your inspiring presence. Whisper unto us how the Higher love of the Mother united the difference of casts and creeds, Brahmins and Shudras, Mohammedans and Hindus.

'Fifty years are past, but O restless hearts, we promise you with our hearts' blood that your diamond jubilee shall not pass without seeing your wishes fulfilled, without seeing the resurgent Ind making a triumphant entry into the world.

'For the bones of Bahadur Shah are crying vengeance from their grave. The spirit of Mangal Pandey for fulfilment of the sacred mission. The blood of the dauntless Laxmi is boiling with indignation. Kunwar Singh, Azim Ullah, Pir Ali Shah! And Tantia Tope who, on the gallows, prophesied:

'"You may hang me today, you may hang such as me every day, but thousands will rise in my place – your object will never be gained."

'Indians, these words must be fulfilled. Your blood, O Martyrs! shall be avenged. *Bande Mataram*!'

'*Bande Mataram*!' echoed the gathering as they raised their right hand. Madan, Harish and Madhava Rao were standing together, visibly moved.

Not long after, the meeting was interrupted with shocking news from India: two prominent leaders had been arrested.

'Lajpat Rai and Ajit Singh have been arrested and deported to Mandalay!'

'Lajpat Rai and Ajit Singh from Lahore?'

'What? What for?'

'There has been no trial and no charge.'

'Then under what law?'

'Some regulation of 1818.'

'But that's an obsolete law!'

'Not anymore!'

All agreed that meetings needed to be organised, support mobilised, leaflets distributed. Working parties were set up.

Madame Cama prepared to speak in Hyde Park.

'Our few square yards of free speech,' said Mr Hyndman.

'We don't even have a square inch in India,' she retorted.

Madan returned home late that night, exhausted but unable to sleep. Instead he spread out *The Indian Sociologist* on his desk and started to read. He read Shyamji's long editorial and then about the new Society for Political Missionaries. There was also a letter:

THE MEN WE WANT

What sort of men do we require for this society? Those who aspire to serve the country must believe in the profound truth that life has a mission. They should be called to the sacred task of uplifting and organising a fifth of the human race. We must possess a keen consciousness of our position as the trustees of the future of an ancient and civilised nation.

We want young men who should place the good of their country above every other consideration. They should abandon the craving for wealth, social rank and physical comfort. They should spurn all prospects of worldly advancement and dedicate their lives to the service of the Fatherland with a solemn sense of their responsibility. They should love nothing more than the cause; it should be to them in place of Father, Mother, brother and friend. They should eject the counsels of timid prudence ...

If such men appeal to the downtrodden masses of India, they would conquer the hearts of the multitudes of our people who pay inner homage to genuine character, but are not moved by mere rhetoric ... He who dares nothing can win nothing ...

The ideal of Renunciation is familiar to every Hindu child. Let such missionaries arise and save the country from despair and destruction.

Signed: ONE WHO IS PREPARED TO BE A POLITICAL MISSIONARY

19.

June/July 1907: London – Speakers' Corner

At Speakers' Corner, Madame Cama's appearance alone brought a crowd. Standing there on the podium with her sari and shawl, wielding her rolled-up umbrella, she presented an unusual sight. As she spoke, the young men from India House milled about amongst the crowd, variously handing out leaflets, looking for potential recruits and keeping a watch for the surveillance men. Madame Cama's voice, high and urgent, floated across.

'I was shocked to hear that one of us, Mr Lajpat Rai, a true patriot, was snatched away from hearth and home and became a prisoner. Men and women of India resent this atrocity. Make up your mind that the whole population should rather perish than live in such slavery.

'If we all speak bravely like Lajpat Rai, how many forts and prisons must the government build before it can deport or confine us all? We are 300 million strong. Hindus, Muslims, Parsees, Christians – we are Indians – let us all combine.

'Let us make his cause and his sufferings our own. Friends, show self-respect and stop the whole despotic administration by refusing to work for it in any capacity. Sever all connections with it. Tender resignations by the thousands every day. Remember, freedom is a conquest and never a bequest.'

In the House of Commons, at the same time that Madame Cama was speaking, Mr Rees asked Lord Morley, Secretary of State for India, whether his attention had been called to Mr Krishna Varma's paper, *The Indian Sociologist*:

'… in which it is said in an editorial article that if a man must be dubbed an ardent native rebel simply because he advises his countrymen to shake off an oppressive foreign yoke, we confess we are proud to be called such, and in which it is further said that there is a school of Indian patriots whose ideal is not only to have independence in government by ousting the English from that country but also to recover untold millions of money of which the Indian people have been unjustly deprived, which ideal involves the occupation of England by India until such claims are satisfied … since the editor claims that he is no British subject, the government will consider the propriety of moving the Public Prosecutor to proceed against this person in view of his ultimate expulsion as an undesirable alien who endeavours to debauch the loyal subject of His Majesty.'

After the questions in the House about him, Shyamji thought it prudent to leave for Paris. He sent word to his collaborator Rana, `a businessman settled in Paris, to find suitable accommodation there – and quickly packed. A meeting was held in the library. He informed the residents that Rana would come once a month from Paris to oversee things and left the day-to-day affairs in charge of Har Dayal. Many, however, thought that Savarkar was the leader.

Madan and Harish both moved into India House.

At the India Office, Whitehall, Sir William Lee Warner sat down at his desk and wrote:

Personal and confidential

20 VIII.07

Dear Sir Harold,

Some months ago I was consulted by Scotland Yard ... as to the possibility of an outrage being committed by the violent section of Indians in London. I made secret enquiries, which led to the conclusion that such an event was improbable. But I ascertained beyond doubt that large and excited meetings were held at 'Tilak House' in 78 Goldsmith Avenue, Acton, in which threats of assassination and other violence were indulged in ... there was talk of smuggling arms and bombs into India from Germany ... agents calling themselves swamis or lecturers in Indian philosophy were sent to America where they were in touch with the Irish American Party.

It was observed at Scotland Yard that they had no one in London capable of dealing with Indians, of distinguishing between Hindu and Mohammedan, harmless or dangerous agitators ...

I am told that an agent, passing himself as an anti-British student, could soon get into the confidence of the London organisation ...

Sir W. Lee Warner.

20.
1989: The India Office

Neatly laid on my desk were some labelled files, my green spiral A4 book, planning folder and blue notebook. My desk faced the window, with shelves to the right on which I had stuck multicoloured fluorescent Post-it notes: green for places to visit, yellow for people to contact, pink for references and books and blue for general memos. I sat back in my chair, looked out of the window and thought about the shape of my day. A rain-free day had been forecast. I unpeeled two green stickers marked, 'Transport Museum' and 'India House'. Yes, after a morning's reading/research I would visit them in the afternoon. I was looking up the route in my *A to Z* when the phone rang.

'Hello, Leena. It's Martin here. I hope I'm not calling too early, but I had this idea. In fact, I thought of it last night. You see, in the early 1960s when I first started work as an archivist, the India Office Library had not yet moved and was still in Whitehall, in the actual building of the old India Office. This would have been where the students like Madan Lal would have come, or been summoned, to visit any officials. So I thought you might find it interesting to visit. As you were saying, the stories are in the city's buildings.'

'Oh, thank you, Martin. Sounds wonderful.'

'It's now the Foreign and Commonwealth Office, but they sometimes do guided tours. So I called them this morning and there's one today. I realise it's short notice ...'

'No, no. I can be ready in ten minutes.'

Martin laughed. 'You can take a bit longer than that. Say I ring your doorbell in an hour and we can walk down to the 24, which will take us all the way there. And the visit will be over by lunchtime.

As I got ready I reflected on how fortuitous meeting Martin had been.

Not only did he know his way around the archives, he was also a historian working on issues relevant to my research and introduced me to interesting people and places.

'I thought a visit might throw up some ideas or images for your film,' he suggested as we walked to the bus.

'Definitely. Thank you. And very thoughtful of you.'

'I also thought it an interesting angle, of one family and three brothers ... three different paths or responses to British rule.'

'Yes,' I reply, 'three narratives.'

'After our tour I am going to meet my collaborator on a book, *The Great Indian Education Debate*. And this debate was about establishing the colonial narrative.'

I detected a slight breathless enthusiasm in Martin's tone as he continued.

'There was in fact a very long ideological battle between Anglicists and Orientalists, who thought that Indians should retain their own language and culture. In the old days, Warren Hastings was quite a Sanskrit scholar, whereas the Anglicists had a different view. And they prevailed ... you probably know about Macaulay and his famous "Minute on Indian Education".'

'Yes I do: "A single shelf of a good European library was worth the whole native literatures of India and Arabia."'

'Yes. That's it.'

'Thomas Babington Macaulay ... "form a class ... of persons, Indian in blood and colour, but English in taste, in opinions, in morals, and in intellect".

Martin laughed that I should know it by heart. 'Macaulay and Trevelyan's view was that the destiny of Indians was to become like Englishmen.'

'I don't know whether to laugh or cry!' I laughed. I knew that dichotomy. 'But they never could,' I noted the bristle in my tone, 'Race would always stop them, and racial and cultural superiority were at the heart of Empire. Weren't they?'

Martin nodded. 'Yes. And the Indians felt this acutely. There is a quote by C. N. Bose in Judith Brown's book *Modern India* that I think you might find illuminating, I'll copy it and put it through your door when I get home.'

As we get off the bus in Whitehall, I think about all the snippets of information in my head when, an old snippet, long-dangling, drops into my mind. 'Martin, let's see if you can enlighten me about this: some years ago I was at a dinner where there was this rather magnificent Quaker lady called Marjorie Sykes who'd known Tagore and Gandhi and lived most of her life in India.'

'Yes I know of her. She wrote a book about Rev C. F. Andrews, who worked with Gandhi.'

'She said something that evening which has stayed with me.'

Martin looked at me as I grappled with words. 'She said that during the first colonial categorisation exercise, maybe census or whatever it was, Bentwick, the Governor General, wrote to the authorities

– in Whitehall, maybe? – basically pointing out that some of the categories listed were not that rigidly delineated, one of them being Hindu and Muslim. He said that someone could be an observant Muslim in his profession and an observant Hindu at home, or vice versa, and therefore which aspect decided their categorisation. That struck me, especially with my own history of the violent demarcation of Partition and all that, so I've puzzled about it since.'

'Yes, it's correct. In fact, the historian Christopher Bayly has emphasised that it is almost impossible to detect the presence of any communal identity before 1860.'

As we walked, I calculated that 1860 was just two years after India was taken into the jurisdiction of the Crown, when Martin suddenly branched off, pointing to a building. 'There it is, the old India Office. The very heart of the colonial discourse.'

'Yes,' I said, looking at the building, and raising my eyes to take in the statue of Clive of India.

Martin was also looking at it, 'I'm sure Madan Lal and his comrades would have had something to say about it.'

'Yes. They might say "Clive of England", more likely. And maybe bristle a bit! And feel indignant. Like me.' I smiled. 'I could have a little scene to that effect.'

'Except, that it wasn't here then. It was placed here a few years later.'

'What a shame,' I say as we enter the building, 'So, nationalism, revolutionary violence, communal identities, even nonviolence maybe, are all part and parcel of the process and legacy of Empire.'

Inside the building are many staircases: formal staircases, VIP staircases and others ... marble, stone, carpeted. There are portraits of the various secretaries of state, busts of the illustrious and, inside, a magnificent internal courtyard where the durbar for visiting princes and dignitaries would be held. All around were Roman-style statues of military men and administrators, symbols of English might and invincibility.

The tour started and our small party trouped up what we were informed was the 'Naiad', or muses' staircase.

'As you can see,' our guide threw her arms around the room we had entered, 'there are two fireplaces, each with a baroque overmantle, so that visitors coming from warmer climes would be protected from the awfulness of the British weather. And the very curious chief feature of this room is that it has two doors side by side with different approaches leading to each door, so that if two Indian princes of equal rank arrived at the same time they could be ushered in simultaneously, without either having to wait for the other. Protocol, you see, was so very important.'

'Protocol Raj!' whispered Martin.

'Some of the features here,' continued the guide, 'came from East India House in Leadenhall Street in the City of London, the whole area of which has now been taken over by Lloyds. This chimney piece dates from 1730 and is a typical East India scene. You have the young Britannia seated by the sea receiving the tribute and trade of the East with allegorical figures representing the different countries: a camel representing Asia, a lion Africa and the river god or Neptune, the Thames, bringing all this trade from afar to Great Britain. The two figures on either side are what the Flemish sculptor took to represent Indian brahmins.' I looked around, wondering which staircase Madan Lal and the other students used when they came to visit. Clearly there was a hierarchy of staircases. What he might have thought of all these imperial busts and paintings and statues – all heaving superiority, self-righteousness and right to rule.

Out in the street we chat whilst making our way to the bus stop. Martin prepares to depart to meet his collaborator, and I to go to look at some more bricks and mortar, for my story: 'The House in Highgate.'

'Ah Yes. India House' says Martin, 'I remember: *see S for Sedition*. The revolutionary narrative.'

'That's right. And thanks to that Index I know the address: *Cromwell Avenue N.*'

'What about the Sufi narrative? Have you had any thoughts about that?'

'It's about transcending the other two maybe? The colonial narrative and the revolutionary narrative are bound through their reactiveness. Maybe the third narrative is the Indian narrative. Just as Gandhi and nonviolence, *ahimsa,* is deeply embedded in India and goes back a long way to Jainism and Mahavira who was a contemporary of the Buddha.'

'You said his name was Bhajan Lal?'

'Yes. That's right.'

'Do you know his Sufi name?'

'No, I don't. Do you think there might be some pointers in the India Office Records somewhere?'

'I'll see if there is anything I can find out. Do you think your family in India might know something?'

'Well, I'll ask when I am there. But I don't know much about my father's family. Of course, the Sufi narrative itself is something I could have found out through my father. When I was younger I visited some Sufis with him. He was into all that. There was a Vilayat Khan in Suresnes, just outside Paris and in Delhi, in the 1960s when he was working there, we used to drive in the evenings to see a Rehanna Tyebji who lived at the Gandhi Ashram. She was a Muslim /Hindu Sufi mystic.'

'Indian assimilation is well known. Syncretism is an important, central aspect of Indian civilisation. Speak to Zawahir about it.'

I made my way to Covent Garden to visit the transport museum, see the trams and the buses and get a sense of how my Uncle Madan might have travelled around the city.

I threaded my way through all the other visitors. I looked at old photographs and surveyed the trams. Suddenly I had this feeling and then – I saw him. He was wearing a grey flannel, double-breasted suit, a soft, blue turban, carrying a black umbrella, and under his arm was a rolled-up newspaper. I saw him as he swung on to the tram. He was so young that it surprised me. He could be my son. I stood there for a while and closed my eyes to capture the image and print it on to my mind's eye. I could feel my heart beating as I walked out and down Long Acre to Leicester Square station. Having consulted the *A to Z*, I planned my route: I would get off at Archway and then take a bus up the Archway Road, which I imagined is how Madan Lal might have travelled by tram. I would get off after the Archway bridge and turn into Cromwell Avenue.

I walked up towards the house, wondering what the people of that time would have thought about the Indians who made their way along this road to attend the regular Sunday meetings at number 65. The month before Madan Lal visited India House for the first time, Gandhi had come from South Africa and had stayed there. Later a historian friend of Martin's, Anthony Parel, would tell me that it was Madan Lal's violent action that fired Gandhi up to write *Hind Swaraj*, his famous exposition of nonviolence. Cross-connections, and colliding narratives, and passing time, I thought.

But these large, old trees must be the same ones that were standing here then. Silent witnesses who had seen people come and go, generations flit by. They knew. I stopped and touched one, running my fingers over its patches of rough and smooth bark. Yes, the trees knew. I wondered if Madan Lal or any of the other Indians might have touched these trees. Maybe on that night, the night he decided.

The house had a blue GLC plaque: '*Vinayak Damodhar Savarkar 1883–1966, Indian patriot and philosopher, lived here.*'

Why only Savarkar? I wondered. So many other patriots and philosophers lived and conspired in this house – Shyamji Krishna Varma, M. K. Gandhi, Har Dayal, Senpati Bapat, Madame Cama, Rana, Virendranath Chattopadhya, V. V. S. Aiyer, Madan Lal Dhingra, Bal Gangadhar Tilak, Lajpat Rai, Bepin Chandra Pal, Asaf Ali, Bhai Parmanand, Madhava Rao and many more. I knew little about most of them other than their names, but each had a story.

Later, as I sat on a bench in Waterlow Park looking at the sky and the trees, I found myself thinking that the people from India House might also have come and sat on the same bench. Possibly Uncle Madan and maybe Gandhiji – whose funeral I had attended just two weeks before leaving India, for Paris. My big sister and me. Two little girls, travelling alone. Refugees. Little Leena with her chubby cheeks and big tin of ghee and feeling so happy.

At the funeral, there had been a big fire and lots of people. I had been given a stick with candy floss … '*Budi Mai ki baal*' or 'old woman's hair', it was called.

'You'll remember this day,' my aunt Danti had said.

'What remember? She's only five!' scoffed my aunt Padma.

But I did remember. I remembered what they said and the sweet syrupy smell of the 'old woman's hair'.

True to his word, Martin had put an envelope through my letterbox. I pulled out the handwritten sheet and read it as I slowly went up the stairs and smiled at Martin's archivist training and meticulous reference:

"English education tells us that we live under tyrannies more numerous and more radically mischievous than those which produced the great political revolution of '89. It tells us that here in India, we have a social tyranny, a domestic tyranny, a tyranny of caste, a tyranny of custom, a religious tyranny, a clerical tyranny, a tyranny of thought over thought, of sentiment over sentiment. And it not only tells us all those tyrannies but makes us feel them with terrific intensity.'

C.N Bose's essay quoted in Judith M. Brown. Modern India; The Origins of an Asian Democracy *(Delhi, 1986) p. 147*

The quotation comes from C.N Bose's essay read in 1878 originally quoted in B.T McCulley, English Education and the origins of Indian Nationalism *(Columbia, 1940)*

21.

1908: BHAJAN ARRIVES IN LONDON

Madan took the train to Tilbury to meet his brother Bhajan. He was agitated. The power struggles at India House continued, but his loyalty remained with Vinayak. He wondered about the meeting with Bhajan and how much he would tell him. But by the time he arrived at the coast his head had cleared and he knew what to do.

'You smell of home,' Madan said as they embraced. On the way back to London in the train they talked quietly in Punjabi. Bhajan was excited to be in London and to see it for himself.

'I'll take you for a walk around London today,' said Madan.

Bhajan was delighted. 'Okay. I'm ready. Kundan Bhai told us about your walk.'

'Yes. But there is another London.'

'Really? Will you show me that as well?'

Later, as they were walking down the street together, Madan burst forth: 'Oh Bhajan! You can't imagine how exciting it is! Everything is changing! The entire world order. And we are part of it. We're living in the most exciting time. When I first came here I walked everywhere. Searching. For something I needed to understand.'

'Like what?'

'I didn't know. It changed. At first I wanted to understand their power. What it was. Where it came from. Then I wanted to know who I was, where I fitted in to things.'

They arrived at Westminster Bridge. Bhajan beamed a smile of recognition.

'This is it, isn't it?'

'What?' Madan was lost in his thoughts.

'Shh! Is this *"Earth has not anything to show so fair…?"*

Madan was laughing. 'When I first came here, I thought that when Bhajan comes he's sure to recite Wordsworth.' They admired the view.

'But you see,' continued Madan, 'I have also learned that in that beautiful building there they make decisions and pass laws that humiliate, oppress and rob us. I have been inside and I've heard them. In any case, who is he to say that there is nothing as fair as Westminster Bridge? What else has he seen? Has he been to the Himalayas?'

Bhajan was also laughing. 'It's a poem, Madan bhai. He's describing a feeling.'

'Well, I'm also describing a feeling. The world hath not seen anything so unjust as these – descendants of pirates and buccaneers, now so puffed up with self-conceit from strutting around the globe, looting and pillaging, drugging and destroying and doing what they like – by virtue of their superior might and weapons of destruction.'

'It's not as simple as that.'

'Isn't it? Thirty million pounds are taken out of India every year and the return is famine and plague. What a sorry plight we have been reduced to. And they can stand up in that House of theirs and declare that all the literatures of Arabia and Asia are worth less than a single shelf of good European books. We have read that shelf and more, whereas they probably haven't read anything.'

'What about Sir Edwin Arnold? His *Song Celestial* is a beautiful rendering of the *Bhagavat Gita*. You used to like it.'

'We read *our* texts in *their* translations. Look at us, Bhajan! Are we not fine examples of Macaulay's minute? What was it he said?' Madan assumed a mock-pompous Victorian stance: '"A class of persons Indian in blood and colour, but English in tastes, in opinions, in morals and in intellect." Imagine, we can eat with a knife and fork, play cricket, dance and recite Wordsworth. But what you'll soon find out is that however cultured, refined and capable we may be, all *they* see is colour. Coolies! And this conceit of colour they call – culture! The audacity! We were a great civilisation when they were running around in bearskins. Do you understand what I am saying?'

'Of course. I'm listening.'

'But do you *understand*? They have taken away our self-respect and we must wrench it back from them.'

'Self-respect can't be taken away. Father has not lost his self-respect, neither have our brothers, nor have you.'

'But we have lost our *selves*. Observe the statues we pass, statues of their heroes whom they chose to honour. You will see that it's all battles and generals – men of valour and violence.'

'I had already observed that.'

'That's what they respect; that's what they admire. Our subjugation is their prize and worthy of nothing but their contempt.'

They walked along the river for a while. Madan was in a dark mood.

'Well, you know, as Kabir said, just because I live next to thieves and murderers doesn't mean that I have to become one.'

But Madan was not in the mood to talk. Bhajan tried again. 'Where's that hostel you were telling me about? Did you say they served Indian food?'

'Indian everything. Would you like to go there? We can go now. We can walk a little way along here and then take a tram.' Madan was enthusiastic and Bhajan pleased.

'It's a lot more than a hostel, you know,' said Madan after a while.

'What do you mean?'

'Well,' Madan was thoughtful for a moment. Then he thought of India House and could no longer contain himself. 'Oh Bhajan! You cannot imagine what it's like. It's called India House. Imagine a place in England where you can be an Indian, a true Indian, as you cannot be, even in India. And we talk about freedom. You know that we even have a flag? The flag of Free India. I helped to sew it with my hands.'

Madan showed Bhajan his hands excitedly. 'You'll see it. It has three horizontal bands: green for the Muslims, orange for the Sikhs and Buddhists, and red for the Hindus. All the many people of India, all are included, just like our gods who have many heads on one.'

The brothers laughed.

'It was designed mostly by Madame Cama and some months ago she took it to the second Socialist International and unfurled it in public.

'Where was this?'

'In Stuttgart. People were there from all over the world. Freedom-loving people. That's what socialists are. I think we can learn from them when we are free. They helped us – Hyndman,

Jean Jaurès from France and Rosa Luxemburg from Germany. Madame Cama walked on to the stage, unfurled the flag and said: "This flag is of Indian Independence. Behold, it is born; it is already sanctified by the blood of martyred Indian youth; I call upon you to rise and salute it." They all rose. All of them. And they applauded her.'

'Really?!'

'Yes. "This flag is of Indian Independence. Behold, it is born" … I know Madame Cama's words by heart. I haven't described the flag fully but soon you'll see it and can salute it for yourself.'

They were approaching India House.

'You'll like it, Bhajan. I know you will. I've learned so much there. When I first came I was looking outside, trying to understand their power. Then I realised that what we needed to do was to look *inside*. We need to find our own way; we need to rediscover our own power.'

They had now arrived at India House. 'Come,' said Madan, 'you will now meet Vinayak. He is also my brother. We call him "*Tatya*", brother in Marathi.'

'That's the only way, Madan bhai. I understand that perfectly.'

'I knew you would – because you're my brother!'

22.

10 MAY 1908: 'MUTINY' CELEBRATION

The fifty-first anniversary of the 1857 'Mutiny' was celebrated at India House, Shyamji no longer being there to object. On 10 May 1908 a number of Indians could be seen making their way from different directions to the house in Cromwell Avenue. There was a sense of urgency and confidence in their step.

The neighbours and locals were used to seeing Indians in and around Highgate, but observed that there appeared to be more of them than usual. Or maybe the Indians were more noticeable because India had been in the news. The previous week, on the first of May, a bomb had had been thrown, two English ladies had been killed and Khudiram Bose, an eighteen-year-old Bengali youth, had been detained. The ladies were in fact Irish, but in India they became English.

Neighbours of the house in Cromwell Avenue, watering the geraniums, had long assumed that the regular gatherings that took place at India House every week were more than likely to be of a religious nature, having heard that Orientals tended to be very devout and fond of their pagan rituals. If any of them had entered the house that day they would have thought themselves proved right.

Inside there was a definite solemnity. Stretched above the mantelpiece was a banner: 'REMEMBER THE MARTYRS OF 1857'. Below it another banner: '*Om*. May the Goddess of Independence be pleased.' In front of the fireplace an 'altar' had been set out, with flowers, incense, candles and badges, with 'Remember the Martyrs of 1857'. There was also a red and black box with 'Donations to the Martyrs Fund', and the *parsaad* – the consecrated food, instead of being the usual sweets, was replaced by *chapattis*. *Chapattis* had been used to send messages during the 1857 uprising; the present *chapattis* would now be consecrated and offered around for all to share and remember.

On either side of the altar, like officiating priests, sat Savarkar and Madame Cama. As she rose, a hush fell upon the room and she spoke softly: 'Let us all rise for the National Prayer.' She placed her right hand on her heart. Everyone did the same and repeated after her: '*Ek Dev, Ek Desh, Ek Bhasha. Ek Jath, Ek Jeev, Ek Asha.*'

Madan smiled at Bhajan as they sat down. The two brothers were sitting together at the back of the room. Madan was now a resident of India House and had participated in the preparations for this commemoration; leaflets had been made, badges had been prepared and special invitations had been printed for the occasion. He had gone himself to Bhajan's lodgings to deliver his invitation, but hadn't been sure that his brother would attend. He'd been so pleased when he saw Bhajan arrive.

Bhajan, however, had other matters on his mind. 'I've had another letter from home,' Bhajan had said on arrival. 'You really must write to them, Madan bhai.'

'Oh, I will. I will. I promise you. It's just that, look ...' he indicated around the room with his arm, 'It's just that we've been so busy. Find a seat and save one for me, and I'll come and join you.'

The rooms had been opened out to include the hall, and the altar was so placed so that it could be seen from all angles. Bhajan found seats near the garden doors. They had a good view of everything and could also hear the birds.

'Freedom is coveted because it alone consists of peace of the soul.' Savarkar's voice reverberated through the room and Madan sat alert.

'Honour is greater than loss or gain. The forest of Independence is better than the cage, though of gold. Those who understood this principle, those who fulfilled their duty to their religion and country, those who lifted their swords for *swadharma* and *swaraj* and courted death, if not for victory, at least for duty, let their names be remembered and pronounced with reverence.' The names resounded like a prayer.

'As we sit here today,' Madame Cama looked around as she spoke, 'we are all aware of the recent events in India and the great suffering of our people. Our legitimate grievances and aspirations have been met with tyrannical repression and torture. Patriots are being arrested, deported, hanged, papers have been closed and printing presses seized. Repressive laws are being rushed through every day and all peaceful means of protest are being denied to us. Some of you say that as a woman I should object to violence. Three years ago, it was repugnant to me even to talk or hear a discussion about violence. If now we use force, it is because we are forced to use force.'

The audience murmured its agreement and Madame Cama raised her voice. 'Struggle for freedom calls for exceptional measures. In Mazzini's words I appeal to you: "Let us stop arguing with people who know our arguments by heart and do not heed them."

'John Morley is always talking about his Western institutions and English oak. We do not want his English Institutions. We want our own country back.' Everyone clapped and Madame Cama again raised her voice. 'No English oak is wanted in India. We have our own noble banyan tree and our beautiful lotus flower.'

Madan smiled at Bhajan. 'What is Morley's civilisation?' continued Madame Cama, a new edge of indignation in her tone. 'Persecution of women? For what? For asking for their human rights. What do I see all around in this country? Poverty, misery, robbery and despotism. I tell you all, resistance to tyranny is obedience to God. We are all Indians – India for Indians. *Bande Mataram.*'

'*Bande Mataram,*' rejoined the meeting, and in the background the record player started to play the song. Some joined in the singing, others wept to hear the National Hymn. Madame Cama sang as she lit the oil lamp, circled it around like an *arti* and placed it among the bowls of *chapattis*. Everyone came up to the altar, saluted the light and was given some *chapattis*, a badge and reminded to put a donation into the box.

'Reflect for a moment,' came Savarkar's voice, 'on what it means to be an Indian today. What we are willing and able to do to free our Motherland. What we are doing to prepare ourselves for the sacred cause it is our privilege to serve. The cause needs strength of character, energy, commitment, constancy, clarity, devotion. How are we developing these in our daily lives?'

The atmosphere was elated and became even more so when refreshments arrived.

Bhajan wandered out into the garden and Madan came out to join him.

'Wasn't the meeting wonderful?' Madan asked.

'Yes, it was,' replied Bhajan. 'Plenty to think about.'

'And plenty to do,' retorted Madan. 'Last year we couldn't even hold it here. Shyamji objected. You see there?' He pointed to a distant spot in the garden. 'We're going to put a miniature rifle range there. I suggested we apply as we had such trouble when we tried to enrol at shooting class. Not too keen on Indians, you see.' Madan frowned.

'Ah,' Bhajan replied quickly, 'so that's why I could never find you at your college.'

'What are you suggesting? That I don't go to college? I go when I need to and have the time. There is so much to do here. We have to prepare ourselves for the struggle. That is the most important thing.'

'That's true, but it isn't the only thing.' Bhajan stopped himself from saying more.

'But it is the central thing,' Madan replied defiantly.

The brothers strolled back towards the house. As they were the two youngest in the family, their stories had become intertwined. Madan was not even a year old when their mother was expecting Bhajan, her youngest child, and being tired and unwell she had been persuaded to let Madan stay with his elder sister and brother-in-law at the old family house in Sahiwal. When he returned home it took him a long time to settle down. Ammaji felt she had let him down and subsequently always tried to make it up to him and to protect him, and Bhajan had learned on his mother's knee to do the same.

'You must write home, Madan bhai. Why don't you write them a few lines now and I can send them off with my letter?'

'You know as well as I do that father would never be satisfied with that.' He felt tense as he thought about it. Then he thought of his mother and added, 'I'll write very soon.'

'You know,' he added as they returned to the house. 'Vinayak is so clear. When I listen to him he dispels my old confusion. You must come to our study meetings. It will really get you thinking about things. Such as what *does* it mean to be an Indian today? Why don't you come this Thursday? That's one of our topics. Come for dinner and then you can stay over. Will you?'

Bhajan thought about it for a moment, then said he would.

'Excellent!' exclaimed Madan delighted. 'Vinayak will be happy to see you.'

When Bhajan left to return home he was handed some leaflets and a copy of *The Indian Sociologist*. It was the April issue and contained an article about the organisation of Russian secret societies. There had been much discussion at the meeting about the Muzaffarpur bomb ... some critical, but mostly full of bravado in support. Bhajan was aware that though it had been meant for the brutal magistrate Kingsford, in the end it was two innocent ladies who had lost their lives. Kingsford survived and would just be crueller still. That was the trouble with bombs; they did not discriminate. Bhajan was aware that he had not raised this conversation with Madan. Maybe he should.

Madan, back in his room, sank into the armchair, exhausted. Bhajan had left him the letter from home, but he felt too weary to pull it out of his pocket. Instead, he stretched out his legs, closed his eyes and allowed the images of the day to appear and disappear.

'Honour is greater than loss or gain. The forest of Independence is better than the cage, though of gold.' He'd write that down in his book.

Sahiwal had forests around it, he remembered. It was a rustic village, quite different from the wealthy cosmopolitan world of his father's establishment in Amritsar. It had suites, stables and terraces where the sunlight made luminous patterns through the stone latticework and where at the end of the summer's day you'd throw down buckets of water to cool down the stones. The heat would steam out and sometimes it would even crack and hiss.

He was rushing across the terrace, the steam lapping his legs, barefoot, like the village boy from Sahiwal. He was lost and looking for his home and was told that this was his home, and then his village clothes were removed and he was wearing a shirt with a stiff collar, trousers and shoes that pinched and he was still running and running but it was a cage of gold – gold latticework – and he was trapped. But then suddenly there came a bird. It flew down from the sky and landed on the terrace. It was Vinayak, as a bird, and now they were two birds flying to the forest.

'Look, the forest of Independence.'

And the two birds landed: he and Vinayak, in the forest in Sahiwal.

Madan's head dropped over the arm of the chair and he awoke. For a moment, he didn't know where he was. It was a long moment, a strange feeling. He had to jog his memory. Ah yes, I'm Madan Lal; I'm in London. I'm a student. But what does that mean?

It was night. The house was quiet. Madan got up and went out of his room into the hall and down the stairs. There was enough light from the moon to see and his eyes were used to the dark.

In the hallway the floorboards creaked.

'Who is it?' came a voice. Madan was startled. He stepped into the dining room. Vinayak was sitting in a chair by the French windows, not far from where he and Bhajan had sat earlier in the day for the meeting.

'*Tatya*? You're still here.'

'And how is it you are still up?'

'I've been sleeping. I forgot to go to bed.'

'Yes, there's been a lot to do. There's been no time to think. I seem to have gone beyond tiredness.'

Madan came across and sat down beside his friend.

'The bomb was premature,' said Vinayak, voicing his thoughts. 'It is not yet the time for bombs. Bapat was always too impatient. I told him before he left. Take the manual by all means, but wait until we return.'

'And now it's happened.'

'Yes, it's done. It has forced our hand before we were ready. We needed more time to build up the organisation, to get proper military training. Mazzini first built up a network of secret societies. We have some, but not enough, and not yet everywhere.'

'But it is the government that has forced bomb-throwing on us.'

'That's as may be, but we should still act in our own time.'

'Swami Vivekananda said: "What our country wants now are muscles of iron and nerves of steel, gigantic wills that nothing can resist ... and which will accomplish their purpose even if it means going down to the bottom of the ocean and meeting death face to face."'

'Swami Vivekananda has put it well. We must work with extra diligence and vigilance.'

'Can anyone aspire to be a martyr?' Madan asked suddenly.

'Anyone can aspire, but not anyone can rise to the call. It demands the supreme sacrifice. For only then can the martyr fulfil his or her mission – to inspire others to rise to the call. Sacrifice means to make sacred. It is a sacred call, a sacred mission.'

'And how do you know if you can rise to the call?'

'You know. You will know.'

'Who? Me?'

'I mean that whoever aspires will know if and when he or she is ready. The call and he or she will become one. But come. Let us try and get some proper rest.' Vinayak got up and then said: 'Madan, I think we have a spy in our midst. I'd like you to be observant and tell me what you see and think.'

'I will, *Tatya*,' Madan replied. 'You can trust me.'

'I know. And I do.'

At the same time that Madan and Vinayak were talking in the early hours of the morning in Highgate, in India, Chaman Lal Dhingra, barrister-at-law and one of Madan and Bhajan's elder brothers, having bathed and breakfasted, came by to see their father on the way to his chambers in Amritsar.

'They have printed my letter, father,' he said with a smile as he carefully unfolded his copy of *The Civil and Military Gazette* to the letters page and handed the paper to his father. He had written to the paper to express his deepest sympathies on the outrage at the Muzzafarpur bomb and the tragedy of the death of two innocent women. In the letter he went on to say:

'We could never have been so happy under any Oriental Government; no other government would have extended so much to raise us by conferring upon us the blessings of modern civilisation and culture. We have advanced in every way – materially, mentally and morally – and bare justice demands that we should be grateful for what they have done in our interest.

Enjoying peace and security in the British regime, we are in a splendid position to develop our resources and to improve ourselves in intellectual, social and religious matters. Association with England is helpful to us in various ways.

I firmly believe in the blessings of British rule and because I see that some of our men are grievously misguided and are retarding the progress of our country. I know that such ideas are likely to be pooh-poohed by some people.'

Dr Ditta Mal nodded his head in agreement. 'Quite right. It needs to be said. I am glad that you have said it.' He handed back the paper to his son with a smile and returned to his thoughts.

'Is something wrong, father?' asked Chaman Lal.

'No, no, I am all right. There is a letter today from Bhajan,' he said, pointing to the sideboard with his chin.

'But nothing from Madan?'

And Dr Ditta Mal shook his head. 'You remember, I never felt sure about sending him abroad. But all of you went on that he needed the chance, that he needed to find himself.' There was irritation in his voice. 'I didn't need to go abroad to find myself. You find yourself where you are, where you belong, in the circumstances into which you are born, maintaining the traditions of your forebears. You find yourself in yourself. Bhajan writes regularly. Why doesn't Madan? Does he need to lose us to find himself?'

Chaman did not reply. There was nothing he could say and he, too, was annoyed by Madan's silence and the distress it was causing.

23.
1989: DIANE

*"Teach your subordinates, that we are all British gentlemen
engaged in the magnificent work of governing an inferior race."*
(Lord Mayo to the Lt Governor of the Punjab)

'Hello. Diane here. Are you busy this evening?'

'Nothing planned. Why?'

'Why don't you come over? I'll cook something and we can celebrate your commission. And you're off to India soon, aren't you? I'll make something simple, and we can have a quiet catch-up.'

'OK. Sounds good. I'll bring the wine.'

'Do that. What are you doing during the day?'

'My green fluorescent sticker says "Greenwich Maritime Museum". And on my way back I've got to pick up some material from the SOAS library.'

'Well, enjoy. Tell me about it in the evening. Byeee.'

The idea of meeting up with Diane at the end of the day gave a spring to my step. On the journey, I thought about it. I remembered how pleased my mother had been when she had come to live in the adjoining street and how irritated I'd felt when she'd told her that I needed a friend.

In the years following Diane becoming my neighbour, the relationship developed: neighbour, friend, fellow writer, mentor, sister. She was also a human rights activist, trades unionist, always inspiring, always there and the fact that she didn't suffer fools gladly meant her friendship give me a confidence.

There were other shared connections and intersections: India, as she had one point been married to an Indian; mixed-race daughters around the same age; single parenthood. There was also the Commonwealth/colonial connection in that she came from New Zealand – possibly through the mists of another history, that of the Irish potato famine. But she was white and could blend into landscape.

And interestingly, there was also Madan Lal, because we had first met during the Indian Emergency protests when I had started my initial research into Uncle Madan.

My mind had wandered into such a distance that I all but missed my stop and stumbled out of the train in Greenwich just in time.

I had long thought of visiting the Maritime Museum, to see what I could find out about the SS *Macedonia* on which Madan sailed from Bombay to Tilbury.

At Greenwich, the library was tucked away behind the museum, which, when I arrived, was full of enthusiastic and boisterous schoolchildren. So the quiet was a surprise. I looked around the place, all very library-like, with open shelves and large tables with a few enthusiasts. I explained that I wanted to get a sense of the time and space. Of what life was like onboard ship. The librarians were helpful and kind. I looked at the pictures, skimmed the descriptions, activities on board, menus and magazine articles for potted bits of culture, history and advice for new arrivals.

Then, with a chuckle, I found myself remembering: John Irwin, keeper of the Indian section at the V&A and a family friend had invited me for lunch and a talk he was giving, during which he recounted an anecdote of when, as a young man fresh from University in the 1930s he was on board a ship about to dock in Bombay, when all the young new arrivals were invited to a serious talk about the dos and don'ts when in India ending with, 'above all, never, ever let a native see you naked'.

I asked the librarian whether she knew if there was any segregation on the ships between the English and Indians.

She looked astonished at my question, indignant, affronted even.

'Oh no. I shouldn't think so. Not then.'

'Why, not then?'

'Well, there weren't so many of them then, you see.'

'What on earth's that got to do with it? There was segregation in India at the time. Plenty of places where Indians and dogs were not allowed. Oh, but of course that's because there were so many of them there you see.' My tone had become quite high-pitched.

The librarian looked bewildered. Her face flashed a moment of doubt, vaguely aware that she might inadvertently have said something … But what? Then it settled and reassumed its librarian's calm. She gave me a reassuring smile.

But I was flying in a bloated balloon, inflated with rage and rejection, and I couldn't stop myself: 'Surely you must know that race and racial superiority was a cornerstone of Empire. It's part of *your* history, your conditioning, not some strange aberration I've dreamed up or … plucked … from thin air.' I had involuntarily raised my left arm in the air and as I brought it down the balloon deflated, shrunk and caught me, naked.

'I mean … Oh, I don't know what I mean … I'm sorry. I'm really sorry.'

I could almost feel sparks emanating from me as I gathered my things as quickly as I could and left the library feeling indignant, irritated, upset, ashamed – and just awful. I wished I could rewind to a 'before' and do and say things differently. I even turned and retraced my steps as a physical expression, a statement of that intent. I just wanted to get home and abandoned my carefully laid out plans for the rest of the day.

As I walked to Diane's house I thought of the librarian. Poor Sylvia, as that was her name. She was probably a lovely lady who watered her geraniums, looked out for her neighbours and loved her cat. And it wasn't entirely her fault she hadn't been taught her history! I resolved to leave her in the street as I rang Diane's bell.

'Mm. Nice wine,' said Diane, 'Good choice.'

'Well, I left the choice to the man at the Oddbins shop.'

'You mean Ian. Ah yes. He knows his stuff.' Diane raised her glass, 'So, sister, chin-chin. Here's to your project, to you, to Madan Lal, and may your film be a real success. I'm proud of you. Why are you making a face?'

'What if I fail?'

'Come on. You haven't even started yet. When are you going to India?'

'Well, I'm doing a reading and a workshop at the Commonwealth Institute at the end of October and then I fly – into the sky.'

'So you're here for a few more months.'

I nodded. 'I was remembering earlier that I met you the very summer I first started my search for the story of Madan Lal.'

'We met at a protest meeting about the Indian Emergency in the '70s.'

'That's right. It was organised by the IWA and it was as a result of meeting them that I started to look for his photograph and unearth his story.'

'And then what happened?'

'Life happened. Other priorities. It sort of went on to the back burner.'

'I think it's just great you got the commission from Channel 4. Good on them.'

'But it's confusing, also. I feel a bit out of my depth and don't know what to ask to enlighten me.'

'Well, I'm sure it will become clearer in time.'

'Hope so. Like I went to see the House in Highgate where all the revolutionaries used to meet. According to my research there were many of them. But there's a single blue plaque saying "Savarkar" – and I don't know that story. So I was going to go to the library today to get a book but I sort of messed up.'

'Well, you can go another day.'

I nodded and sipped more wine.

'Remember I told you what my aunt in India said.'

'Which aunt, the nice one or the other one?'

I laughed. 'Oh dear. Neither of them. No, my historian aunt.'

'Ahh.'

'She said, that when you start to find out about family history you start to find out about yourself. Well, as I try to flesh out and get a picture of the past I seem to keep encountering my own ghosts and fears and insecurities and buried hurts.'

'Well, that needn't be a bad thing.'

'But it's unsettling. I never know what will present itself. Then there are other times when I can see the – 'then': see my Uncle Madan swing off a tram, see him climb the steps of India House, see him go to Gamages to look at pistols. Does that sound strange?'

'Not at all. Writers do visualise and the characters take on a life of their own.'

'My plan is to visit the places that were at the forefront of the Independence movement: Bengal, Punjab, and Maharashtra, where there are freedom fighter memorials. I'll start in the Punjab, to follow the route taken by the cortège when Madan Lal's coffin was returned to India. My mother was there and my aunt Danti.'

'Is that the nice one?'

'Yes. She's the one who worked for the refugees and the "rescue" of women abducted at Partition. And I'll see the Punjab. My ancestral province.'

'Will you go to Lahore?'

'Lahore? No, no. Why would I do that? It's in Pakistan.'

'Well. In relation to loss maybe?'

'It doesn't fit into this project about the exhumation of Madan Lal and the return of his remains.' I said firmly and then added, 'I hadn't even thought about Lahore.'

On my way home, I started to think about it. 'Lahore!' I breathed out. It was my parents' lost world. Their exile, which I lived vicariously.

Back home I grounded myself and looked at the itinerary of the return of Madan Lal. Below the title 'Pay your last respects to the great Hero on his final journey,' were listed the towns in the Punjab the cortège had passed through. But for Partition, Lahore would have been there, too. But then again, but for Partition, I might not have been in England needing to find the story. I sighed and looked out of the window at the familiar skyline.

24.
1908: AMRITSAR

In early June Dr Behari Lal Dhingra was making his way up to the hills in Simla in the Maharaja's white train. He was going to stop in Amritsar on the way. He was using the journey to catch up on his correspondence and reading. Looking through the bundle of papers and journals that had just arrived, he caught sight of *The Times*' report on 'India House'. 'India House,' he wondered. The name meant something to him, but what? He read the article.

THE TIMES, London 23 May 1908
SEDITIOUS INDIAN PROPAGANDA IN LONDON

Three years ago this summer Mr Shyamji Krishna Varma, M.A. of Oxford inaugurated the 'India House' at Highgate as a hostel for Indian students in London, the inmates being lodged and boarded at very moderate fees. There can be no question that the real object of the enterprise has been to promote the bitter anti-British feeling and the revolutionary views set forth in *The Indian Sociologist* ... may be judged by the terms of a red ink circular distributed to many Indian students in this country inviting them to attend a meeting held at the hostel on the 51st anniversary of the commencement of the Mutiny by the revolt of the Sepoy regiments at Meerut. The gathering was secret, Europeans being carefully excluded, and Indians present are reticent as to what took place. The circular invitations, headed '*Bande Mataram*', are in the following terms:

To Commemorate

The Anniversary of the

INDIAN NATIONAL RISING

Of 1857

A MEETING OF INDIANS

Will be held at

INDIA HOUSE

65, Cromwell Avenue, Highgate, N,

On Sunday the 10th of May 1908,

At 4 p.m. precisely.

You and all your Indian friends are cordially invited

To be present

The 'programme' printed on the opposite page shows that a purpose of the meeting was to hold up to admiration as 'martyrs' the principal leaders of the rebellion, including the infamous Nana Saheb who was responsible for the breach of faith with the Cawnpore garrison and the wholesale massacre of women and children. The programme commences and ends with 'National songs', and the other items are: 'National prayer, Tributes to the sacred memory of Bahadur Shah, Shrimant Nana Saheb, Rani Laxmibai, Maulvi Ahmed Shah, Raja Kuvar Singh, and other martyrs. Declarations of self-denial. President's speech. Distribution of Prasad.'

It is evidence of the activity of the anti-British propaganda among Indian sojourners here that close upon 100 Indian students attended, some of them having travelled from Oxford, Cambridge, and even Edinburgh to be present. The meeting lasted four hours, and much stress was laid upon the poverty alleged to be inflicted on India by alien rule.

❀

Behari felt a chill as he put down the paper and grappled with thoughts racing through his head: a hostel for Indian students? Didn't Bhajan mention something about a hostel for Indian students in London? Was it called India House? And wasn't Madan living there? He couldn't remember the details and was impatient to reach Amritsar. The journey started to feel very long.

Once in the house he headed straight for the *baithak* to find his father, and after the briefest of greetings got straight to the point: 'Father, do you remember the name of the hostel for Indian students that Bhajan wrote about?'

'Oh, the one with the good Indian food? India Building, I think. Madan's living there now.'

'Could it be 'India House'?'

'Yes. That's it. India House.'

'Father, please find the letter that Bhajan wrote. This is very serious. I just read about the place in the newspaper. It is a centre for sedition.'

'He said they serve Indian food there and celebrate Indian festivals.' Dr Ditta rummaged in the box for the letter. 'Ah, here it is. Yes, you're right, it's called India House.'

Behari Lal showed him the newspaper. 'It's a most dangerous place father! Krishna Varma and the extremists.'

'The extremists! Oh my God! It can't be! Oh no! I always knew I should have kept him with me. Why did I listen to your arguments? I never questioned my father's judgements and neither did anyone else. He was the head of the house. One didn't even think of arguing a different case.' Dr Ditta was shaken and agitated. 'Very dangerous. Write to him at once and tell him to leave. Call your mother. Write to Bhajan as well. Tell him – It's an order!'

When his wife walked into the room, he turned to his son and said, 'Behari, tell your mother what her son has gone and done.'

'Well!' said Ammaji when she'd heard the story. 'You were always the one for this English education, new ideas and independent thinking. Now you are complaining when Madan is doing too much of this independent thinking?'

'Ammaji. You don't understand.'

'I understand more than you think. I understand also that my son is in danger.'

'Write the letter, Behari. I will dictate it. No, send a telegram at once. Also the letter.'

'Tell him his father's wishes are mine as well,' said Ammaji quietly.

25.

1908: MADAN LEAVES INDIA HOUSE

As summer progressed, India was much in the news. There was continuing unrest. Tilak's trial was in full swing and followed with interest. Tilak, known as the father of Indian unrest, had taken his opposition to British rule into the streets, reviving Hindu festivals and transforming them into mass protest movements. In addition, he had used his editorship of his two journals to disseminate his views and was being tried for sedition. Questions were being asked in Parliament about the repressive legislation in India that was being rushed through.

India House was also in the news, in newspaper articles with headings such as 'House of Mystery', and 'Devil and his Dirty Dozen'. Vinayak Savarkar was even mentioned by name. Inside there was a heightened sense of urgency. The Sunday meetings were well attended; there was always a talk, often extolling martyrdom, and Savarkar usually opened and closed every meeting with a reading from his book *The First Indian War of Independence*.

On the last Sunday in June, Dr Desai, a student of chemistry at London University, gave a talk on the making of bombs.

'What about giving us the exact ingredients to make a bomb?' came a voice from the audience.

Dr Desai looked around him and then said quietly, 'Whenever any one of you is ready to throw a bomb, and to take the consequences, let him come to me and I will provide the correct proportions.'

Savarkar got up to read a chapter from his book. He concluded with:

'God is the essence of freedom; slavery is the absence of freedom. Hence where there is God, there cannot be slavery, and where there is slavery there cannot be God or godliness. Slavery is the road straight to hell. We need to fully understand this and ask ourselves – Can our *swadharma*: the path of our true selves and our duty, can it be anything other than the struggle for *swaraj*, self-rule?'

At the end of the meetings there was always tea and *pakodas*, and animated discussions in at least four or five different languages: English, Hindi, Marathi, Bengali and Tamil. Madan and Bhajan had strolled out into the garden. Madan pulled out a newspaper cutting from his wallet and handed it to Bhajan.

'If the whole nation is inspired to throw off its yoke and become independent, then in the eye of God and the eye of justice, whose claim is more reasonable, the Indian's or the Englishman's? The Indian has come to see Independence as the panacea for all his evils. He will therefore swim even in a sea of blood to reach his goal. The British dominion over India is a gross myth. It is because Indians hold this myth to their bosoms that their sufferings are so great today. Long ago the Indian rishis preached the destruction of falsehood and the triumph of truth. And this foreign rule based on injustice is a gross falsehood. It must be subverted and true *Swadeshi* rule established. May truth be victorious.'

'What do you think?'

Bhajan nodded his head thoughtfully.

The following morning a telegram for Madan arrived from Amritsar. Bhajan had stayed over at India House and was just about to leave after breakfast. Madan had never given his parents the address of India House. The message told him to leave India House at once and get in touch with the family solicitor. Madan let out a howl, but by the time people came or called to see if he was all right, he had regained his composure and was making his way back to his room. His body felt heavy. He felt betrayed. His heart seemed to thud in his throat.

'Look what you've done!' Madan threw the telegram at Bhajan on entering the room. 'Why did you tell them I was here?'

Bhajan read the telegram. 'I only said that there was a hostel for Indian students and that we liked the food.'

Madan looked at him darkly. Bhajan recognised the look.

'I'm very sorry Madan *bhai*. It was long before it got in the news.'

'And what am I going to do?' Madan felt his head starting to whirl. 'He'll cut my allowance, won't he?' He sank into a chair and then got up again. 'I need to go for a walk; I can't breathe. I need to think.'

As he walked out of the room Bhajan said, 'I can always share my allowance with you, Madan *bhai*.' But Madan was already down the stairs.

Later that evening he talked to Vinayak who said, 'The important thing is to do your duty. You have a duty to your father and your mother, and we all have a duty to our Motherland, the mother of all our fathers, mothers and our whole race. At different times we might have different duties. But only you can know where your duty lies.'

'I don't know. My father will cut my allowance and I ... I don't want to disappoint my father again.'

'Then you must leave India House.'

'But what about my duty to the cause?' asked Madan.

'As I said, at different times we have different duties. The Cause can still be served. As yet there is much to learn.'

Madan found lodgings elsewhere. He stayed away from India House, avoided meeting his brother and spent a great deal of time on his own, walking, in Hyde Park or by the river, where he'd look into the water and try to imagine it was the sea. He needed to think; he needed to listen to himself; he needed to get through all the noises in his head. Sometimes he'd find himself talking. Once he asked a tree, 'Where does my duty lie?' and then, 'Father, I wish I could make you understand, make you trust me. But you have never understood me. I wish – you could be proud of me.' He tried to untangle his feelings, his thoughts and his reasons for leaving India House. He thought of his family amongst whom he'd always felt an outsider. A misfit. And then he thought of his mother and he wondered what they had told her.

'*You know my son, when Ram was told he was to be exiled into the forest for fourteen years, he asked, "Did the order come from my mother or my father?" When he was told it came from his mother, albeit his stepmother, he said, "Then I'll have to go because a father's order can still be questioned, but a mother's order – never!"*'

'Oh Mother! What have they told you?' he asked the Thames.

At the end of July, Madan learned that Tilak was to be transported to Mandalay jail in Burma for six years. He threw the newspaper down and started walking towards India House. Anger welled up inside him and Vinayak filled his thoughts. Vinayak had come with a personal recommendation from Tilak and regularly contributed to his newspaper, *Kesari*. Now when he returned, Tilak would no longer be there. Mandalay! It was a terrible blow for the Motherland. It made him mad, and as he walked up Cromwell Avenue he had to stop and remove his spectacles to wipe away the tears.

At India House two comrades, Nitisen Dwarkadas and Gyanchand Verma, had just returned from a visit to India. They both strongly urged that the time had come to act quickly to help the comrades at home. They were standing in front of the fireplace in the dining room and Madan noticed that above them was a new banner with '*Remember the Martyrs of 1908*'.

'Well, I am pleased to see you, Madan,' said Nitisen. 'Where are you staying now? I was told you left because you were worried about your allowance, but I didn't think that sounded like you.'

'I read about Tilak's deportation. I came to see Vinayak.'

'He's upstairs, but come and see me before you leave. We need to set something up now.'

Vinayak was at his desk, just starting a letter. Across the top he had written 'May the Goddess of Independence be pleased', and was underlining it when Madan knocked on the door.

'*Tatya*,' said Madan. 'I had to come. I felt so angry.'

'I'm pleased you came. Anger is a powerful energy, when you learn to harness it.'

'How do you do that?'

'By becoming clear. But you know that, don't you?'

26.
1908: ESCAPE TO LONDON

In India, as the new laws took effect to gag the press and enable further arrests, floggings and deportations, those who could started to flee, via French Pondicherry and Portuguese Diu, to Europe and London.

In Parliament, Sir Henry Cotton asked the Secretary of State, 'whether his attention had been drawn to a case in which a person was sentenced to seven years transportation for sending a telegram of a seditious nature and whether there were any reasons to justify such a severe sentence.'

Lord Morley's reply was that he could appeal.

The India Office also tried to get to grips with the situation and stepped up its vigilance. Indian students were shadowed wherever they went. When they did meet, they exchanged tips on the best way to shake off their pursuers.

'I had hoped,' said Curzon Wyllie, 'that when Krishna Varma left, matters would quieten down.'

'Well, they haven't. They've got worse. Meetings are being held everywhere and Indians are found on the platforms of all the motley crew of dissenters. It's like dealing with a Hydra-headed monster – cut one off and two appear.'

'Like Mahisha. Just one of their mythologies.'

'But this is reality.'

'They are using their myths potently to serve their ends. Here,' Wyllie pulled out a paper to show to Sir William Lee Warner and explained, 'they are using the Ramayana story, which is familiar to millions, in which Sita is depicted as Mother India, ensnared by Ravana (British imperialism), and being rescued by Lord Rama, the righteous king with his army of nationalists.'

Warner nodded and shook his head at the same time.

On a late September afternoon, a group of Indian students gathered at Victoria station to receive Bepin Chandra Pal and Khaparde, two of the leaders who were arriving from Paris. More were expected to arrive the following month. Khaparde had come to appeal against Tilak's deportation and Pal had come on an India House touring 'lectureship for political missionaries'. He was supposed to have arrived the previous year, but because of a speech he had made he had been arrested and had had to spend the year in jail.

Madan met Harish on the way, so they both arrived together to join the reception party.

'Their spies are going to get quite confused,' said Harish as they joined the group. 'They can't really see the difference between us, you know; all they see is colour.' He then told an amusing story of

179

how three of them, who actually looked quite different but who on this occasion had dressed in identical suits, had managed to lose their shadows. Everyone laughed.

'Don't underestimate them or be too confident,' retorted Vinayak soberly.

The party made their way to Highgate. Once there, Pal called for an urgent, impromptu meeting at which, to everyone's surprise, he condemned the use of violence.

'You have all been out of India too long and you do not know the situation there. I have just come out of jail and I can see what has happened since the time I was incarcerated. This kind of action is leading us nowhere,' insisted Pal. 'It is all very well for Shyamji, sitting in the luxury of his Paris apartment, to preach violence for which he will not have to suffer the consequences. I seem to remember he had a different tune when he lived in London and could be accused of sedition.'

The young revolutionaries were taken aback and admonished Pal for being a coward, and for having become frightened and intimidated. 'We have to show them that we are fearless.'

Pal contradicted this statement. 'Look, you are all here safely in London. I have just spent a year in jail. By behaving as we are now behaving, we are defeating our purpose.'

'And what is our purpose if it is not freedom? Bayonets hold us down. They have disarmed us – and it is they who have forced bomb-throwing on us.'

'You have to assess the time and this is not the right time,' Pal retorted.

Madan and Harish looked at each other with an expression of resignation. They had heard this line of argument before in this same room, the Hyndman library.

'The national ideals and aspirations of India, at this stage, can exist within the multinational British imperial system. Britain and India should jointly contribute as partners for the highest ideals of humanity. We need to show how this can be done.'

'What are you saying? What did they do to you in prison?'

Pal decided not to stay at India House. Instead, he found lodgings in Sinclair Road, Shepherd's Bush. Soon this became another Indian centre and Pal's prestige as a leader, together with his recent incarceration, meant that he gathered a following around him. The rival groups both supported and competed with each other, vying for members and their loyalty.

Savarkar was unperturbed. He had already started to activate his plan and was simply too busy to care – sending propaganda to India, personnel for military training, gathering know-how on the use of explosives and the acquisition of arms.

A number of private and public meetings were planned. As *The Indian Sociologist, Free Hindustan* and other papers were banned in India, holding meetings, inviting journalists and then using their reports proved a useful way to let people know that the struggle continued.

'A revolutionary war knows no end, save liberty or death,' said Savarkar.

27.
1989: LONDON – INDIA OFFICE LIBRARY

I filled out some requisition slips and ordered files chosen somewhat at random and then sat down at my desk to wait for half an hour. In the meantime I opened my notebook to continue planning my impending trip .

In India I would follow the route of the coffin through the Punjab, as I might have done if I'd accompanied its return in 1976. This, I imagined, might form the journey of the film. I was quite engrossed with my lists of 'To Do', when a bound volume of files for 1908 was placed on my desk with a heavy thump. It was enormous; to open it I had to stand up. I opened the file of L/P&J/6/903 and skimmed along its pages. The first two had cuttings pasted on them:

Daily Chronicle 4.11.08
'DISLOYAL STUDENTS
INDIANS' HOSTILE DEMONSTRATION AT LONDON MEETING
A demonstration of disloyalty on the part of Indian students was witnessed yesterday afternoon at a meeting at the Caxton Hall...'

The Times, 4 November 1908

INDIAN STUDENTS IN ENGLAND

'At Caxton Hall, Westminster, yesterday afternoon, under the auspices of the East India Association, Dr John Pollen CIE, read a paper on "The Indian Student in England". Lord Lamington presided and there was a large attendance of Indians. There were also present the Dowager Lady Lamington, Sir W. H. Curzon Wyllie, Lt. Colonel Sir Donald Robertson, and Sir M. Bhownagaree.

Dr Pollen said the most important thing was to help young Indian students on their arrival in this country to find comfortable and respectable homes. It was not good ... that they should fall into the hands of designing persons.

An animated discussion followed in which a number of Indians took part. Some of the speakers maintained that it was the colour question that was at the root of this disaffection ... One said that the policy towards India should be changed so as to inspire mutual confidence. A speaker said the cause of mischief both here and in India was that the Indian students claimed equality with English students and this was not conceded. Mr Bepin C. Pal who received quite an ovation from the students present said that he had received his inspiration for freedom from western civilisation.'

There were further cuttings: a copy of *The Indian Student in England* by John Pollen, C.I.E., LL.D., and on another sheet, entitled 'Reference Paper Political A.D.C.', in clear, rounded handwriting, was a report for the J & P department on *Meeting of Indian Students at Caxton Hall, November 3rd, 1908. Dated 5/11/08.*

Sir Charles Lyall

'I was present at the Caxton hall the day before yesterday ...

'An unusually large number of Indian students attended the meeting and the hall was filled to overflowing ...

'In my opinion Dr Pollen's paper was ill-timed and in questionable taste, and calculated to provoke the heated discussion that followed. ...

'One point was clearly brought out at the meeting, viz, that Indian students wish to have nothing whatever to do with the India Office, and that they thoroughly distrust any measures which may be taken for their betterment. They claim to be on the same footing with Englishmen, entitled to equal liberty of action and equal freedom of speech, and they strongly object to any exceptional treatment.

'The demonstration of disloyalty was most marked, and reference to the King's recent "message" and mention of the King's name provoked loud hissing in various quarters ... Anglo Indian officers who were present are also desirous that the behaviour of the Indian students should be brought to the notice of the Secretary of State. There can be no doubt that the feeling of disloyalty among the Indian students is growing day by day and the majority of the students in London are neither afraid nor ashamed to openly manifest their disloyalty.

'Among the many Indians in the Caxton Hall, not a single protest was raised against the hissing at the mention of his Majesty's name ... I have no hesitation in saying that the disaffection in India is to be found among the Indian students in this country.' Sig: W. H. C. Wyllie. 5/11/08

28.

1908: LONDON – CAXTON HALL

Madan and Bhajan came together to the meeting at Caxton Hall. There had been notices about it at all the colleges, and Indian nationalists, now quite plentiful in London because they were on the run from India, had decided to use the meeting as a platform to suit their purposes. All Indian students were urged to attend and the organisers were astonished at how many came, so many that they spilled outside the hall.

The Highgate revolutionaries were there in full force, scattered in small groups. The atmosphere was electric. Madan's spirits lifted as he came into the room and saw his comrades here, and then there, and then again there ... He smiled, and could almost hear Savarkar's instructions about spreading themselves around the hall.

On the podium Dr Pollen was talking about the bad climate between Indians and the English:

'I, for my part, think the time has come for the mending of manners on both sides. Indians are readily responsive to sympathy but they are chilled by an icy manner and depressed by a lofty, condescending attitude ... On the other hand Englishmen find it difficult to tolerate anything that resembles aggressiveness, self-assertiveness or bounce and they have little patience with undue loquacity and what they regard as unctuous ambiguities ...'

'What about their aggressiveness?!' Madan whispered.

'But,' the speaker continued, 'for Indians to give themselves independent airs or to talk of separation from Great Britain is simply suicidal ... British Domination must, in the interests of India herself, continue for many generations to come.'

'Boo! Boo!' came a voice, and this cry was soon picked up here, there and all over.

Curzon Wyllie and the others in the front turned their heads to identify the booing. Madan just managed to slip out of view, pulling Bhajan with him.

'That's Wyllie of the India Office. Kundan *bhai* knows him. He spies on us. Vinayak has an Irish contact at Scotland Yard. He told us.'

Dr Pollen was still reading his speech.

'India was never conquered by the English – India was won ... by the winning ways of the English. We may or may not be the absolutely superior people ... but we are – where we are – the rulers of Ind – by the grace of God and by the qualities we undoubtedly possessed; and thoughtful men, both in India and England, recognise that while in some ways we are superior to the Indians, they are in other ways superior to us, and it is in the cordial recognition and frank acknowledgement of this simple truth that the higher interests of both really rest ...'

Later, as Madan, Bhajan, Harish and Nitisen waited on the pavement at the exit, Sir William Curzon Wyllie suddenly appeared. He looked straight at Madan and gave a nod of his head.

Madan acknowledged him with a bow, instinctively. And elegantly. Sir William, tense from the exchanges in the hall, felt slightly relieved and smiled. Suddenly Madan started to feel awkward and Harish and Nitisen were looking at him questioningly. He felt awkward with himself, that he'd bowed, so instinctively, and he felt uncomfortable that Harish and Nitisen had been there with him.

Coolies! he thought. That's what we are to them.

29.
December 1908:
Madan Returns to
India House

Madan returned from the Caxton Hall meeting feeling exposed, angry, hurt and confused. He told his landlady that he did not wish to receive visitors. Often, he did not put his light on if he stayed in.

There was still the odd person who couldn't be avoided, of course, so Madan was in touch with what was going on – meetings taking place, and such like – but he didn't make any attempt to attend them. Space was thus created for gossip and rumours, and people surmised why he remained absent – that he was, after all, rich and privileged, that he wasn't serious or even that he was under suspicion, maybe even a spy. But Savarkar would have none of it

It was now nearly six months since he had left India House. Six months in which he had felt very torn. In a way, though, he'd always felt torn. Torn between two worlds, or maybe it was two parts of himself. He'd always wanted his father to feel proud of him, but this was never easy to achieve. All his other brothers seemed to find it easier. In his father's house he'd always felt an outsider, the one who didn't quite fit. He didn't want to disappoint his father, and yet in trying to fit he'd felt stifled and squeezed. As he had when he'd acknowledged Sir William at Caxton Hall and bowed. It was as though he'd triggered a nerve that went through his body like a current. It was a strange sensation; even as he remembered it, he could feel it. But what was the feeling trying to tell him?

When he'd come back from the village to the grand house in the city and had had to put on the stiff, city clothes, the knee-length trousers and the socks and shoes that had restricted his movement and crunched up his toes, they'd all said how well he looked, so smart, a natural. He didn't tell them he felt uncomfortable. Ratan Kaka had said it was all part of growing up. So he learned to fit and did it quite well.

Coolies! He remembered, and angrily thumped his fist into the arm of the chair and got up. He stoked the fire, closed the curtains and started to pace the room. 'Duty, duty, duty. Duty to family, to parents, duty to Motherland, what about duty to myself? What is my duty to myself, my *swadharma*?'

He went over to the cupboard, took out his blue turban and put it on. 'You are an Indian,' he said to his reflection. 'An Indian in English clothes. The very finest suiting and tailoring. But who are you in them? And what are you?' He started to feel anxious. It was an uncomfortable feeling and he longed to be free of it. He returned to his chair and watched the flames of the fire devouring the wood, tongues of red and orange and tinges of blue, crackling and calling out to the wind. Fire the purifier, he thought. He wished he could feel purified.

He'd always wanted to be himself, even if he didn't always know what that was, but he wanted to find his own way, become his own person. That night, before he went to sleep, he opened the window and asked the night, the moon and the stars, 'What is my *swadharma*?'

The following day Madan decided to go and see Madame Cama. He'd heard she'd come from Paris to organise a conference at the Caxton Hall. So many Indian leaders had escaped from India to either London or Europe that it had been decided to hold a conference of all the Indian nationalists to coincide with the meeting of the Indian Congress in Madras. The Madras meeting was the first since the split between the 'moderates' and the 'extremists' a year earlier. Now with so many eminent extremist leaders in London – Lajpat Rai, Bepin Chandra Pal and Khaparde as Tilak's representative – the conference would serve as a protest.

Madame Cama, or Bhiku as she was known, was not staying in Highgate. Madan was pleased about that. At India House there were many dissensions and tensions. Rivalries had set in and Madan did not wish to get sucked into factional fighting. He didn't find it helpful. Often Vinayak wasn't there, and there were frequent mutterings about his leadership style and ideas. Madan felt he still needed to think, and mostly kept away from India House.

Madame Cama had avoided staying at India House for much the same reasons. She saw her role as remaining independent and keeping on good terms with all the various factions so that she could keep the dialogues going and meet everyone.

'Madan! How good to see you. You've lost weight. Have you been eating properly?' she said on seeing him. Madan smiled, remembering that his mother had said much the same when he'd returned from sea. She hadn't reprimanded him or questioned him, just given him food.

Bhiku opened up tin boxes of delicacies and rang for tea. To his surprise Madan found he had quite an appetite.

'You must take some copies of my leaflet. It's called '*Bande Mataram*. A Message to the People of India'. We're posting the leaflets from different parts of London. Would you be willing to post some as well? These are difficult times.'

Madan nodded and picked up a bundle. 'I have been thinking about duty and about where my duties lie.'

'We all have to ask ourselves these questions. I, too, have had to carve out an independent journey, beyond the expectations of a dutiful daughter or dutiful wife. A dangerous journey in strange lands far from home. And yet …' She walked over to the window. 'Sometimes it feels as if there isn't a choice. Or the way, just presents itself. And you find yourself on it.'

'I feel just at such a crossroads; so torn.'

'I know what you mean. That's quite natural.'

'When I think about the direction my life has taken, I feel that I have chosen both nothing and everything. It doesn't make sense, does it?'

'It isn't such a paradox.'

'I've been asking myself the extent of my commitment. What would I be able to sacrifice for my Motherland?'

'Well, you know my motto.'

'Yes. I do,' replied Madan, and then together they said: 'Resistance to tyranny is obedience to God.'

Madame Cama continued; 'And for God, you can say truth, or freedom, or justice. Obedience to our divine nature. To that which transcends us.'

Madan nodded.

Madame Cama continued: 'Sometimes, situations or encounters with people make one realise one's destiny. I remember having a long talk with Sergei Pavlovich in Paris about ends and means, about choices, about a life of exile. It is not easy being in one place with your heart in another. We need to help each other. After I spoke to Sergei I realised we all shared the same reality, that it transcended nationality. It is the reality of our time. We are at the vanguard of humanity's march forward. We have a historical reality and a personal duty.'

'I would like to return to India House. But I wouldn't like to endanger my family. I can ask myself how much I would be willing to sacrifice for our Motherland. But I cannot force that sacrifice on others. Vinayak is fortunate; his brother and family are as committed as he is.'

'Have you spoken to Vinayak?'

'No. I wanted to see you first. But please don't tell him about our meeting.' Madan rose and started to pace around the room.

'Sit down, Madan. You're making me agitated. Sit down and talk.'

'At India House I feel so much more myself, I feel – almost free,' said Madan as he sat down again. 'But I don't know how far I can go. Or which route to take.'

'You are thinking too much, Madan. You are beginning to worry, and that is never healthy. Some things can only become clear when the mind is quiet. We serve the Motherland in whatever way we can.'

Madan furrowed his brows and then explained: 'Well, I am a member of the Free India Society. I am determined and committed to the Abhinav Bharat (Young India). But I have not taken the oath.'

'Look,' she said and got up to get something from her desk. 'When Aurobindo Ghose was freed from prison, he gave a speech in Bombay that someone sent me. I've copied out a section. Let me read it to you:

"Have you got real faith? Or is it merely a political aspiration? Is it merely a larger kind of selfishness? When you believe in God, when you believe God is guiding you ... what is there to fear? What can all these tribunals, all the powers of the world do to that which is within you, that immortal, that unborn and undying one ...?"

'Here. Take it.' Madame Cama smiled and held out the paper. 'When I copied it I didn't quite know why. But maybe, without knowing it, I copied it for you.'

Madan took it and read it again before folding it away in his pocket

'But I need to know. Could I sacrifice my life?'

'Death is the only certainty in life. We need to trust. To listen and be guided.'

When Madan got home he put the leaflets on the table and read:

Bande Mataram
A message to the Indian People
'Countrymen, lend me your ears...

'Hindustanis! Our revolution is holy. Let us send our congratulations to our countrymen and women who are struggling against British despotism and for new liberty. May their numbers be daily increased. May their organisations become ever so formidable ... I beg of you young men to march on. March forward, friends and lead our helpless, dying, downtrodden children of the Motherland to the goal of *swaraj* ... India for Indians.'

'India for Indians,' Madan said under his breath. He could still taste the Indian delicacies Madame Cama had given him. His mother had done the same; she'd pull out of a box something good to eat whenever he came to visit. He could imagine his mother standing up in Hyde Park for some noble cause.

When India is free everyone will have the opportunity to become who they truly are and what they want to be – free.

A few weeks later, Kundan Lal, Madan's eldest brother, arrived in London on buisness.

He was relieved to see that Madan was not living in India House and tried to persuade him, with the full authority of an elder brother, to stay away and concentrate on his studies, prepare himself for his return where he would have good prospects. And to impress upon him that this was the wish of all his elders.

Madan for his part tried to impress upon his brother that he was learning more than just what could be read in textbooks. By being in England he was also experiencing what life in a free country felt like. He had been sent to England to broaden his education and his experience and he was doing just that in the widest way possible. He was meeting people from all parts of the world. It was a time of change. People with no voice were finding theirs.

He told him that he had attended meetings in the House of Commons where the India budget was discussed late at night in the mostly empty House … and knew all about the drain of wealth and resources that kept India poor.

Kundan Lal tried to reason, make him understand … cajoled, pleaded, dictated, even threatened, but to little avail. Madan remained calm and defiant – and surprised even himself.

Soon after, Madan moved back to India House. He was warmly welcomed when he arrived but there was also much excitement.

'Madan, Listen, listen, Vasudev, have you met Vasudev? Never mind he's staying here and he went to the India Office …'

'Yes,' interjected another voice 'He met with Lee Warner and said, I have come as a representative of the Indian students to tell you how we feel about the present situation in India …'

'I think it was a stupid, counterproductive thing to so …' said a third voice.

The voices were talking to him, to each other …

'Listen Madan. He had this rolled-up scroll in his hand, which Lee Warner thought was a petition, put out his hand to receive it …'

'And Vasudev, guess what he did. He bowed, like this and then went forward …'

'Stupid useless gesture. In India you could be transported in leg irons for less.'

'He went forward and struck him across the face with it!'

There followed laughter and an animated discussion of those who condoned and those who didn't. And Madan Lal looked on, happy to be back.

30.

April 1909: The Shooting Range

On the days Madan had lectures, he would spend the day in the city and regularly go for target practice to the shooting gallery in Tottenham Court Road. The owner shared the same surname as the Secretary of State for India: Morley. It generated a chuckle among the students. This particular day he was unsettled, thinking his friends, Harnam Singh and Savarkar whom the benchers of Gray's Inn were refusing to call to the Bar. So he went to the shooting gallery early. He asked for a round of six shots. Usually he took twelve.

As he looked at the target he could almost hear his mother's voice telling them the story of the Pandava brothers undergoing target practice.

'Can you see the fish?' asked the teacher, and they all said yes. All except Arjuna, who said: 'All I can see is the eye. Nothing else.'

Vinayak has just that clarity, Madan thought, focused and guided. Madan looked at the target in front of him. What did he want to shoot at? What oppressed him? What did he want to dispel? The voices that made so much noise. The Empire, with all its huff, bluff and oppression. He could feel the anger in his body as though it was on fire.

'*Anger is just energy. You can harness it to guide you to clarity.*'

Madan looked at the target and saw British imperialism – the arrogance of Empire, pomp and protocol, bluff and sham. The sounds in the shooting gallery seemed to pull away into the distance. He felt quiet. He aimed. He could only see the target. He pulled the trigger – a clear hit.

'In the next target are all the myths that prop it up; mystique of omnipotence, invincibility, superior race,' he muttered to himself. 'All bluff!' He pulled the trigger.

'The myth that Indians are cowardly.' Again he hit the target.

'This is for the veils of ignorance, the shackled minds, Western education, in which we collude.' He pulled the trigger. Then he thought of his family, the English drawing- room with its heavy Victorian furniture and it angered him.

In the fifth target a face emerged. Lord Curzon. Again he felt the heat of anger rising. 'Heathen dog!' he said. 'This is for partitioning Bengal so as to divide us from our Muslim brothers' He pulled the trigger. 'Divide and rule, Britannia; for this you will never be forgiven.'

At the sixth shot, the sombre grey-wigged benchers of Gray's Inn came to his mind and he thought again of his friends whom the benchers were refusing to call to the Bar. The emotion disturbed his mind. But as the target went fuzzy another clarity emerged – of all the martyrs, the detainees, all the sacrifice.

Madan didn't fire the last shot. Mr Morley called after him, 'There's still one more shot, Sir,' but Madan was already in the street, walking.

On returning to India House, Madan found a letter from the India Office addressed to him. It was from Sir Curzon Wyllie, who wrote:

Your brother Mr Kundan Lal Dhingra, whose acquaintance I had the pleasure of making in England, has written to tell me that you are in London, and asking me to be of any assistance I can to you.

I shall be pleased to see you at the India Office if you can conveniently call between 11 and 1 or 2.30–3.30.

I remain,

Yours faithfully,

W. C. H. Wyllie, Lt. Col.

He crushed the letter in his hand tightly as he could and then threw forcefully against the wall. Well, that's that, he thought. Once more he would have to leave India House, and have to do this soon, before the required visit to the India Office. Somehow all this served to strengthen his resolve.

The house was still quiet, as most had not yet returned from the city. Outside an April shower was beginning to splutter.

When he heard people returning, he sought out Savarkar.

'*Tatya*,' he said, 'I'm now quite clear. I am ready to take the oath of the Abhinav Bharat. Quite ready.'

Savarkar nodded slowly, 'I am very happy for you. My brother. My comrade.' They embraced.

Later they were in a darkened room at the top of the house, a small ceremonial fire in the grate illuminated the image of the ten-armed goddess Durga riding her tiger. In front of her a candle flickered.

Beside the image there was a book wrapped in red silk and a dish of sweets for the *parsaad*.

In front of the goddess, facing each other, stood Madan and Savarkar. On the other side were Harish, Aiyer, Chatto, Das and Madhava Rao.

Savarkar chanted a *sloka* to Durga, whom the gods had invested with all their weapons to rid the world of the demon Mahisha. Then he unwrapped the red silk and handed Madan the book of the *Bhagavat Gita*. Madan held it and raised his hand.

'Now repeat after me,' said Savarkar 'In the name of my sacred religion, for the sake of my beloved country, invoking my forefathers, I swear ...'

Madan repeated after him,

'I dedicate my health, wealth and talents for the freedom of my country and for her total uplift.

'I will work hard to my utmost capacity 'till my last breath.

'I will not spare myself or slacken in this mission.

'I will follow all the rules and regulations of the Young India Society.

I will never disclose anything about the organisation.'

They all turned to the deity and stood in silence with folded palms, and then Madan bent down to touch Vinayak's feet. '*Tatya!*' he said.

Vinayak raised him up and embraced him. Someone then put on a gramophone record of *Bande Mataram*.

Bande Mataram
Mother I bow to thee!
Rich with thy hurrying streams,
Bright with thy orchard gleams,
Cool with thy winds of delight,

Dark fields waving, Mother of Might,
Mother free.

Thou art wisdom, thou art law,
Thou our heart, our soul, our breath,
Thou the love divine, the awe
In our hearts that conquers death.
Aurobindo Ghosh

31.

1989: India – Return from Exile

'Better to be half an hour early than one minute late.'

With a smile I remembered this phrase of my father's, an attitude that doubtless derived from his colonial upbringing, as I sank into one of the comfortable chairs in the departure lounge at Heathrow.

I had arrived early, checked in and now had time to relax and collect myself. Airports were good for that. However impersonal, glassy, brassy, for me they were reassuring, comforting, familiar, peaceful little havens of constancy and promise. We were all always on the move. Always there were airports.

As I alighted from the plane, it occurred to me that I was stepping on this soil, and for the first time since Partition I would … be staying in my mother's flat, and not as a guest. I was also an independent woman in my own right. A return from exile. I smiled. I was still smiling standing in the queue, when a uniformed official approached me instructing me to follow him and picking up my hand luggage.

'What are you doing? Why?' I asked.

'Yes, madam. You come. Please to follow me.'

He cleared the way and guided me to a counter marked 'Unaccompanied Ladies'.

I frowned. Then, seeing that there was no queue there, I accepted the convenience and thanked him. Unaccompanied lady!

My mother's flat was on the second floor. It was the same height as the branches of the trees – the domain of the birds. In my half-awake state I could hear them fluttering in and out through the window, busily building a nest on top of the wardrobe. I opened my eyes and smiled; the birds twittered, dust particles danced in a shaft of sunlight and at that moment everything felt right. For the first time since the Partition in 1947, my mother had her own home in India, a place where she could at last retrieve her precious possessions and gather together the fragments of her shattered life. I had a commission that had brought me back to India where I, too, could locate the fragments of my lost connections.

Yes, at that moment everything did feel right, but it was to be a very short-lived moment. The spectre of Partition. My mother was distressed. Not everyone was forthcoming in returning her 'precious things', as she called them. Some considered it an affront that after so many years she should even consider claiming them. The most precious of all my mother's previous belongings, the Roerich painting, was not returned.

The painting was undoubtedly my mother's most meaningful possession. It was a gift from the artist himself in return for my mother having sat for him, and in every house she had ever designed a special place had been allocated to it. In the stories of my childhood it featured as 'the one and only thing that had been saved from Lahore' – and which would save us all. Her distress was unfathomable and evoked the mean monster of my childhood nightmares ... the litany of injustices inflicted on my mother and the burden of feeling responsible and helpless.

'But you go on your travels,' she insisted. 'You must.'

I felt I was letting her down but at the same time I was grateful that I had a focus of my own. I looked through my planning folder and thought of my journey to the Punjab. As there was no phone in my mother's apartment, I strolled over to my aunt 'Painji's' house, trying to centre myself as best I could.

Walking through the gates into my aunt's garden, I could see the front room crowded with family and visitors, all talking. On seeing me my aunt raised her voice and said authoritatively: 'You can forget about travelling to the Punjab; it's out of the question. The Punjab is in turmoil. It's very dangerous. If you're a Hindu they'll kill you.'

'Quite right, quite right,' my cousin agreed. 'You'd better wear a *kada*, take off your *bindi*, wear a *salwar kameez*, fold away your sari ...' said another.

'You'd better stay here.'

'It's under President's Rule. There are curfews.'

'They want it to be *Khalistan*, you see, Aunty,' interjected one of my nieces.

'That's right, Khalistan, land of the pure.' Retorted my aunt, 'First it was Pakistan, land of the pure. Every time it's us Hindus they want to throw out.'

'It's very dangerous. We're not Sikhs, you see.'

'We are partly Sikh, aren't we?' I responded.

'Yes, but not enough for some.'

And everyone spoke at the same time. Everyone had an opinion that felt like pellets being fired at my head.

'Are you telling me that I can't go to Amritsar?' I asked.

'Amritsar!? Noo! Nev-ver!' they all said together.

'But, but … I have to. For my research. I have a job.' I was bewildered.

I felt jet-lagged and muddled. I loved being in India, but it also scrambled my mind. I decided to make my calls from the telephone booth in the nearby market and made my way there.

'Don't take any notice,' my aunt Romila reassured me. 'Here in Delhi they all get a bit hysterical. We've got Sikh family in Chandigarh; they will advise you best. If they're travelling back and forth from Amritsar, then so can you.'

The next day I flew to Chandigarh, the Le Corbusier capital, and recalled seeing it when it was being built on one of my 'home leave' trips from Paris. We came to India every two years. Home. As guests. Staying in other people's houses. Refugees.

In Chandigarh I stayed with Sikh relations. In my aunt's comfortable house I felt welcome but also a 'something', which made me feel awkward. I put it down to the business of families, family obligations and the million little Indian rules I didn't know.

In the evening my cousin's wife suddenly blurted out: 'There's something I must ask you.' There was a sharp frostiness. 'Why did you come from Delhi to Chandigarh by plane? It's almost next door.'

I felt trapped and fearful. Clearly I had transgressed some invisible rule and had been the subject of some discussion. I could see that in my cousin's half-smile, my uncle's intense concentration on his food, my aunt's look of embarrassment and the flashing eyes of my cousin's wife. I stammered a reply

'Oh well, I have this ticket, you see; fly-as-you-like-for-three-weeks.' I explained, unsure of what was at issue.

Suddenly everyone at the table was smiling and a tangible sense of relief could be felt in the room. The frostiness dissolved.

My aunt laughed. 'I knew it was something simple. Chanda thought you'd come by plane because Delhi people might have discouraged you about coming to the Punjab. You know, saying it was dangerous for a Hindu.'

'No, no. Nothing like that, Just a cheap ticket.' I blushed slightly.

At the government offices I was introduced as the descendant of the great martyr and treated as an honoured guest: 'a visitor from foreign'. A schedule had been arranged for me, as well as an escort to guide me through the labyrinth of offices and bring me back for lunch.

The newsreel film of the return of the remains of Madan Lal was ready for viewing. To soulful music and a sombre commentary, it showed a plane landing.

'You understand Punjabi?' asked the director.

'More or less.'

In the picture six or seven men were carrying a coffin.

'They're mostly dead, now,' the director pointed with his chin to the film. 'All assassinated.'

'Sorry?'

'The coffin-bearers, I mean. Dead. Mostly shot.'

In the newsreel, Madan Lal's coffin draped in the Indian tricolour – orange, white and green – was being garlanded by Prime Minister Mrs Gandhi and her son Sanjay Gandhi.

'You know what happened to them?' he said, again indicating with a sharp movement of his chin.

'Yes,' I replied, feeling somewhat awkward.

'Both dead. Mrs Gandhi shot by her bodyguard!'

'Yes. I remember.' I replied

'We have been approached by the Philately Department in New Delhi,' said my escort, guiding me through the labyrinth, 'for the bringing out of the commemorative stamp of Shaheed Madan Lal Dhingra. Our publicity officer would like to consult you, so I will please take you to him. We are needing a photograph.'

'A photograph! Ah yes, I have a photograph,' I replied.

After lunch, a videotape of the film was handed to me. I had finished all I had set out to do and my escort dropped me at one of the shopping precincts. As I walked around I considered the fact that I was the right colour, wore the right clothes but somehow everyone knew that I wasn't homegrown. '*A visitor from foreign*'!

The next day I was on the bus as it thundered through the villages and towns of the Punjab, flanked by two soldiers with machine guns who would jump out at every stop and scour the neighbourhood as passengers stretched their legs, drank their sweet tea and cracked their monkey nuts. I surveyed the landscape to which I might have belonged and tried to imagine myself blending into it.

'If you catch the early bus to Amritsar,' I had been advised 'you can stop off at Jalandhar and visit the Martyrs' Memorial Museum, and then you can catch the next bus on to Amritsar. There is a curfew in Amritsar so you need to get there before 4 o'clock …'

I got off at Jalandhar. It featured on the itinerary of the cortège, so I was on the trail. The Martyrs' Museum was a dusty old building comprising a large, columned hall with framed portraits or photos of young men and women adorning the walls, garlanded like deities. I walked around, making a point of looking at every face and name, and stopped in front of the portrait of Madan Lal. I was then taken to see Babaji, an ascetic, 'retired' revolutionary. Dressed in white with a loose turban, he squatted on the floor of his first-floor office surrounded by books and papers and an old Gestetner machine.

'In the Gadhar Party we had many songs. About Madan Lal, Madame Cama, Krishna Varma, Savarkar, and all the revolutionaries of India House. People could be flogged, imprisoned, transported for singing Gadhar songs, but they still sang them. The authorities created a climate of fear. Madan Lal and others showed what fearlessness was. How love of Motherland and love of people could transcend fear.'

'It is good you are doing this. It needs to be done. I have tried my best to know about all these old revolutionaries and India House, because India House was the main place from where this whole movement sprang, but the government has not done anything much about the revolutionaries. So it is very good that you are doing this. That you are paying respect to the Martyrs of India and to your ancestor,' said Babaji. Then he broke into a song that he translated as he went along:

'Dying for the country is the highest joy of life
Sacrifices will pave the way to India's freedom
The martyrs are the elect of fortune ...

'A martyr in heaven is glorified in the world below,
It is a bargain to retrieve the jewel of Hind
At the price of one's life.
Gadharites would not speak to men who want to live.'

In Amritsar, I had arranged to stay at the university campus. It was on the outskirts of the city and named after the great Guru Nanak, founder of Sikhism. Riding in the rickshaw, I recited a Sikh prayer to myself – the first prayer I can remember learning. I didn't even know what it meant. My long-forgotten mother tongue.

The guest room was large, airy and comfortable. I had assigned only three days for visiting Amritsar, and the first was nearly over. I went downstairs to the dining hall. It was a chilly night. I became intensely aware that outside there was a curfew, that there were 'terrorists' around, and that only a few miles away was the severed end of India.

'I suppose Pakistan must be quite near,' I said.

'Oh yes. Very near. But also quite far, if you know what I mean,' said the academic at my table.

'My family lost everything, because of Partition, you know.' I was thinking aloud. 'Now I come back and there's this whole business about Khalistan, which is basically about another partition. It's as though we are repeating ourselves because we cannot heal. Do you see what I mean?' I said with intensity. The partition seemed to resonate with my own life through every phase: childhood, profession, marriage, motherhood – each had been patterned with partitions.

That night my mind wandered between thoughts and dreams.

'*We didn't live together in tolerance, we lived together with love.*'

I went to sleep with my mother's words and dreamed of her melting into one of her rich ochre paisley Jamevars, blue French exercise books with the little squares in her hand, in which she was designing her house with a special illuminated niche for her Roerich painting.

The next day I went out early; curfews made the days short. I went first to the Golden Temple, walked into the inner court, all marble, water and gold, and found myself once again reciting my first prayer: *Ek Onkar* (one god*) Sat naam* (name is truth) *Kartha Purak* (creator). An aunt had taught it to me in Simla, when, eight years old, speaking mostly French and German, I'd had been returned to India.

I'd attended a convent, Tara Hall, and learned the Lord's Prayer and Hail Mary and been praised: 'Well done! Good girl!' And back home my aunt taught me the Sikh prayer and also praised me 'Shabash! Good girl.' And I liked that.

But when I came home to Paris everyone was busy, so I'd thought maybe I should ask to be taught a prayer and I'd get some attention and maybe even praise. So I asked.

'You pray that your heart be filled with so much love that it just overflows from you to all.' My mother smiled. 'That is the only prayer.'

I smiled at the memory and how disappointed I'd been.

The Jallianwalla Bagh, the scene of the Amritsar Massacre, had been made into a memorial shrine to the martyrs of the nation. All around there were plaques that told the story: the single, narrow entrance that was blocked by guns and through which General Dyer would have brought his tanks if it had been possible. But the entrance was too small; they'd fired into an unarmed family crowd … I looked down the well into which people had jumped to escape from the bullets and drowned.

In the centre was the Martyrs' Memorial Hall. Inside there was a tapestry depicting the massacre, as well as portraits – Madan Lal, Uddam Singh, Bhagat Singh, Kitchlow, and other heroes of the Punjab. The stories of Madan Lal and Uddam Singh often became intertwined. People mixed them up – they were the only two who had been executed at London's Pentonville Prison, and both came from the Punjab.

I had arranged to meet a journalist. He was the oldest resident of the city, had lived in the Dhingra buildings, and had known members of my family. He recounted some anecdotes of the family, mostly about their wealth and privilege. Then he gave me a file of papers, saying that he couldn't quite remember how he came by them. 'There is Dr Ditta Mal Dhingra's will and other things besides ...'

He had also managed to get in touch with some members of my family who had insisted on coming to pick me up and take me to their house.

'A sister must stay in her brother's home,' said my unknown cousin. 'Those are our traditions.' And so I awoke the next morning in the Dhingra buildings near the Hall Gate.

'We didn't show the building in the film,' the director of the newsreel had told me in Chandigarh. 'It didn't look good to show a decaying building in a film about a great hero.'

I thought the building looked sad, beaten about, scarred, like the city. And that night the curfew had also felt real, a cold, dark silence broken only by the sounds of army patrols and protesting dogs.

It was clear that this had been a beautiful house, built with great attention to detail. Walls of filigree stonework that cast luminous patterned shadows enclosed the terraces. A network of roofs on different levels connected the courtyards to the terraces. I tried to imagine the place inhabited by my forebears, but it was a world

I didn't know. Although if I closed my eyes I thought the sounds might be similar.

'There used to be twenty-one houses stretching all the way there,' my cousin pointed in the distance, 'but they were sold long ago. Some were broken down to make that cinema.' This time she pointed down the rooftops.

In the afternoon we went to the Ram Bagh Gardens of Ranjit Singh to find the memorial to Sahib Ditta Mal that had been erected by his sons. It was a pavilion of red stone and white marble.

'*It is said that Sahib Ditta Mal died of grief after Madan's death.*'

I looked at the date on the memorial. 1916. Just seven years after the execution. On our return they showed me the room where Madan Lal was supposed to have been born.

I had decided to take the train from Amritsar and retrace Madan Lal's journey from the Punjab. The same station, the same railway tracks, the same route, the same landscape.

My cousin had brought me there on his scooter. When I tried to sit astride it, I was informed with some embarrassment, that 'In Amritsar, ladies don't sit like that.'

'Oh', I replied and perched myself side saddle – decorous and dangerous.

The station was a squat, square, redbrick building, probably the same as in Madan's time.

My cousin's wife had given me a tiffin box with some food and a thermos of tea. The guard brought me a bedding roll and told me to lock my door.

'But do not to worry about anything, sister. I am just nearby.'

❧

The train pulled into Delhi station and two porters squabbled over who would carry my small bag. The one who was successful balanced the bag on his head and I followed his red shirt like a dutiful wife as he threaded his way though the crowds clearing my passage, every so often turning to make sure I was following him and was all right. I felt grateful and gave him a good tip. He smiled appreciatively. The taxi driver also smiled, anticipating I would do the same for him.

Dawn was just breaking as the taxi drove through the waking city, past the shanties, the queues at the municipal water taps, along the old Red Fort, through the colonnades of Connaught Place, Lutyens' Imperial Secretariat, past Moghul mausoleums. As the changing views drifting by, my mind also drifted … to another time, and another drive through Delhi.

My India moments often felt like sealed capsules and I was never sure what might burst or surge. The drive through Delhi I was remembering was in the summer of 1968. The monsoon had just ended and the air was muggy. I had arrived in India with my Belgian fiancé and two friends having driven overland through Germany, Austria, Yugoslavia, Bulgaria, Turkey, Iran, Afghanistan. In Kabul I'd had to take a plane to India as I could not cross Pakistan with my Indian passport.

We had left Europe at a heady time; a few months earlier the events of May had ignited an international awakening and all along the route we encountered the infectious spirit of the time and the solidarity of idealistic, rebellious youth wanting to make a better world. I had also remembered Madan Lal then.

It was in Paris. I had come to see my father before the journey. He was anxious that we were going overland. Some years earlier he had organised an international conference on Tolstoy and Gandhi in Venice and wanted to give some names and addresses of Tolstoyans and Gandhians along the way – just in case we might need some help.

Madan Lal appeared when I was with my friend Alix, my only friend in Paris, who was telling me about her involvement with the events of May' 68.

'Everything needs to be re-examined if we are to create a better and more humane world.

'Look!' she said, pointing to some words painted on a poster we were passing. It said *L'imagination prend le pouvoir*. 'Isn't it wonderful!'

She talked of the Paris commune and expressed her pride in the tradition of revolution of which she was a part.

'You know I have an ancestor who was a revolutionary,' I said.

'Oh?'

'Yes. He was part of a revolutionary group and executed In England.'

'And to be executed by the English certainly gives him a cachet and places him in good company.'

As I must have looked perplexed, she added, 'Surely you haven't forgotten our Joan of Arc?'

'Ah, yes, of course. Our Joan of Arc. How could I forget?'

'Tell me about your ancestor?'

'I don't know much, really.'

'Well, find out when you're in India.'

But when I'd arrived in India, I didn't quite know how, who to ask, or why. Driving around Delhi, I noted that more English road names had been replaced by those of the freedom fighters. Madan Lal did not feature because he had been classified as a 'revolutionary'. And our freedom struggle had been waged with dignity through non-cooperation and nonviolence, and we had been taught to be proud of this, for it befitted our most cherished traditions, traditions that we were rediscovering and reaffirming. The nascent republic had taken as its emblem the three-headed lion and wheel at the top of the Ashokan pillar – Ashoka, the great humanitarian monarch of the third century BC who had embraced Buddhism, renounced aggressive warfare, espoused the cause of nonviolence and erected rock edicts stating this, throughout the length and breadth of India. We were the proud inheritors of that tradition and India now belonged to its people. I had also come to understand, though I had not been directly told, that in India, there were the 'people' and the 'masses'. The people inherited India and the masses were part of that inheritance.

Apparently, I, through birth and 'connections', was part of the people. Nonviolence was our creed, the Congress our champions, and it was the champions' names that replaced those of Curzon, Irwin, Minto and Morley. These were 'freedom fighters'; the others were 'revolutionaries' – also known as 'terrorists' or 'misguided youths'. They didn't feature as road names; neither did their descendants obtain 'freedom fighter' pensions and privileges.

India was my homeland, the place to which I belonged. I had an Indian passport and long hair, and anything that made me too conspicuous, or different, or which didn't quite fit in, or was a bit of a jumble was best ignored or drowned in the well. It was only if I conformed, fitted in and disappeared that I could stop being a refugee. So I censored myself and I censored Madan Lal.

The taxi turned, lurching me into my present – and into another past. The turning was opposite 'that land', which my mother had found and where she had paid for a plot to build a house for our homecoming and which had become – another partition. The memory smarted.

As I climbed the steps to my mother's flat I felt weighted down by more than my bag. My mother was still grieving. 'Home' remained elusive. 'Partition' had slunk under the door and into the flat where it enveloped us like a malevolent shroud.

As I bathed and prepared myself for the day, I reflected on how misfortune gets traduced as shame. 'It's all *karma*' fudges the edges for injustice to prevail. I also acknowledged my timidity and fear of defending my mother in case I would get lashed like her.

'I'm meeting Kiki for lunch at the India International Centre, would you like to come?'

'*Accha*, you're meeting Kiki?'

'Yes, for my research.'

'No, darling. You do your work. I'm so glad you are doing this. I'll be okay. But thank you.'

My cousin Kiki was also a great niece of Madan Lal, and was happy I was bringing his story to light.

'Call me when you get back from the Punjab,' she'd said, and then added: 'You know I met Savarkar. Madan Lal's friend.'

'Did you?' I remembered the plaque with his name and said, 'Yes, I'd like to know who he was.'

'He talked of uncle Madan. He admired him a great deal. I'll tell you about it when you come back. I think you will find it interesting.'

Kiki had booked a table by the window overlooking the lawns. She handed me the menu, saying that she knew what she wanted. As I looked at it, she got busy – shifting the items on the table:

salt, pepper and the vase with the single flower. It made me a bit nervous, so I said:

'I'll have the same as you.'

She called the waiter and placed the order: 'Two masala dosas.' And as soon as he was gone, she started: 'I remember Veer Savarkar very well. In fact,' she continued, 'I remember it very well indeed, because it was quite an occasion. It was before Independence, and I was aged fourteen. Veer Savarkar was very important. He was president of the Hindu Mahasabha, and he came to preside over some meeting that we attended from school. Somehow he got to know, I don't know how but someone must have told him, that Madan Lal Dhingra's great niece was in the audience and they came and told me that he wanted to meet me and to join him on the podium. He specially asked to see me.' She closed her eyes. 'But there was more than that. He had a chair placed for me on the podium with him and then, in front of everyone, he paid this obeisance to me. There in front of everyone.' She shook her head. 'Imagine!' I was only a fourteen-year-old schoolgirl. And he was the head of the Hindu Mahasabha.' She elevated her right hand and looked at it.

'That happened to me once, too.'

'What? You met Veer Savarkar?'

'No, no. Just someone, you know, sort of wanted to honour me because I was from the family of Madan Lal.'

'Ah. *Accha.*'

'What did he say about Madan Lal?'

'Ooh! Madan Lal! He was full of admiration. He told me they had been in London together. They'd been friends. And he said how much he admired him and what a great and courageous man he was, that people like him were rare, that he'd never forgotten him and how intensely he remembered him. Of course, I didn't know very much then, but I found out later and read his statement. Have you read it?'

I nodded.

'It was very moving. It's good you're doing this,' she said, rearranging the salt and pepper once again. 'For years they didn't bother about the revolutionaries at all. And now they're remembering for their own purposes.'

'And what are they?'

'Well, It's the Nehru centenary this year so they are trying to remember all the freedom fighters. So it's a good time for you to be doing this.' Then she said: 'And this year also the BJP at their conference have officially adopted Savarkar's philosophy of Hindutva.'

'What does that mean?' I ask

'Well …' Kiki half-shrugged her shoulders 'They're against the Congress and Nehru and secularism and they are very against Gandhiji.'

'Why?' I asked.

'They blame him for Partition.'

I knew that my father was a great admirer of Gandhi and my mother was more critical and as I grappled to find a question that might enlighten me, Kiki looked at her watch and I could tell she was ready to leave.

'You know that Godse, who shot Gandhiji was a member of the Hindu Mahasabha and that Savarkar was briefly arrested.'

'In London, there's this house where the young revolutionaries used to meet and live. A roll call of freedom fighters lived in that house and there's a commemorative plaque which has only Savarkar's name on it. Why do you think that is?'

'Well Savarkar has a big following. He is the father of Hindu nationalism. His followers must be in London, too. And they would have arranged the plaque, no doubt. Go to the London authorities and find out from them.

'You know that Madan Lal's younger brother was also in London at the time? He registered at Gray's Inn as Bhajan Lal Dhingra and was called to the bar as Bhajan Lall. Only our grandfather kept the name Dhingra, all the others dropped it. Did you know that?'

'Yes. My mother told me. Actually I wanted to ask you about Bjhajan Lal. Did you know him? Or do you know where I could find out about him?' I asked.

'I saw him when I was quite young and then I heard he'd become a recluse. But Litto knew him. Ask her.' Kiki smiled. 'Litto herself was quite notorious. Ask her about that, too. She's in America at the moment but is due back soon. Next week I think.'

'Well, I'm travelling for the next ten days and then I'm back in Delhi for while'

'*Accha*. Where are you going to?'

'Calcutta and Bombay.'

'That's good. They were at the forefront of the freedom struggle at that time – It was the partition of Bengal that set the whole thing off with *Swadeshi* and things, around the time of Uncle Madan Lal. You can ask Litto about that. She married a Bengali. A Bengali communist, too.' Kiki smiled conspiratorially. 'So when you get back get in touch with her.'

After walking Kiki to the gate, I noticed a solitary garden chair and walked over to it. I smiled as I sat down and a voice came through:

'Baldoon deserved a much bigger platform that he got. But for that you have to return to your homeland. And he got lost in Paris. Also, he was a very modest man.'

The voice was that of Mulk Raj Anand, a writer and friend of my father's from Lahore whose name featured in my father's list of people to contact.

Just a year earlier, our paths had crossed – with an initial clash. He was among a group of Indian writers, stopping over in London, on their way back to India from the Frankfurt Book Fair and meeting had been arranged at the Commonwealth Institute.

I'd introduced myself, he'd looked at me and frowned 'You are the daughter of Baldoon Dhingra. What have you done about reissuing his work? Don't you know that there are people who loved and admired him and to whom you owe that?'

I was dismayed. Being scolded. In public. I stammered. 'He was in Paris. you see, I was in London … and there was Partition, you know …'

'Tell you what. You gather together whatever writings you can, bring them to me and we'll edit them together. Visit me when are you next in India. And call me Uncle Mulk. Okay.'

I rose from the chair and made my way to the gate and hailed an auto-rikshaw to take me back to my mother's flat.

How was the lunch with Kiki?' said my mother on my return

'Good. I thought of Papa whilst at the IIC.'

'Now you see running the IIC was a job he would have loved and would have suited him well. But he never put himself forward, never asked. I don't know why. He would have been so good at it.'

'When I come back, mama, I'll take you to Ahmedabad. Would you like that?'

'Yes, I would like that. Thank you. God bless you,' she replied.

32.

1989: LETTER FROM DELHI

Dearest Diane,

I am sitting in the Nehru Memorial Library. On the desk is my notebook and a large volume entitled *Indian Unrest* by Sir Valentine Chirol, published in 1910. Both are unopened. Instead, I have been just sitting here staring at the bullock peacefully pulling a lawn mower across the lawns. A sort of 'settling' sight, which makes me smile.

I have visited the Punjab in the north, Calcutta in the east, Bombay in the west, the centres of the early nationalist movement. In all those places Madan Lal is remembered and features in their memorial halls and also in their textbooks.

Apparently the central government produces one series of history books but the state governments can produce their own – and each state has its own narrative, its own heroes. In all these places, which erupted before Gandhi, Madan Lal is an icon of heroism, courage, selflessness, but with different meanings and for different agendas.

In Calcutta, where there is a 'Left coalition' Madam Lal is a great inspiring revolutionary. At the National Library a man, on hearing my connection, started to recite parts of his statement , which he knew by heart. I became very English and embarrassed.

He went on: 'There has been a falsification of Indian history. It is important to counter the image that India was made free by nonviolence, drinking goat's milk and weaving Khadi. There are thousands who did not choose the nonviolent path and who laid the ground for others and the official reason in the end for quitting India that Mountbatten gave was that of the Naval Mutiny and that was not a nonviolent thing. You can read that in his autobiography.'

In Bombay, Madan Lal is a 'great Hindu hero', worshipped as the god of patriotism. And with his close connection to Savarkar, 'father of Hindu nationalism', he is co-opted on to that agenda. My lodgings in Bombay were in Madame Cama Road. At the end of that road was the seafront. In the evening I strolled along, gazing at the water, and thought Madan Lal might have done the same, seen much the same view before he sailed away, never to return again.

Now back in Delhi, watching the bullock mow the lawn! My mother is still distressed so tomorrow I will fly with her to Ahmedabad to the Sarabhais, old friends who love her – as this is what she needs. She looks forlorn and feels much abandoned.

Much love,

Leena

33.

June 2019: *Doctor Who*, Savarkar and 'A Visitor from Foreign'

My time travel through my manuscript is jolted into the present with persistent calls on my landline: 'Leenaji, this is Acchar Singh from IWA, Coventry. I have sent you messenger, and email but have not heard so I am calling.'

I apologise profusely.

'17th August this year is the 110th anniversary of Shaheed Madan Lal's martyrdom and we would like to hold a meeting to commemorate. Will you be available to attend?

'Actually, I'm just in the process of writing about Madan Lal and that is why ...'

He continues, 'This year the anniversary on 17th of August falls on a Saturday. We usually have our meetings on a Saturday so I will try to book a hall on that day itself. Is that date suitable for you?

'Yes, yes,' I reply.

'It might be the last one that I will be able to organise. The next one will be the 125th anniversary.'

'You know, the 17th August is also the date the Radcliffe Line of the Partition was made known. WH Auden wrote a poem about it called "Partition".'

'Yes, yes, you can read that poem. Others will be reading poems about Madan Lal. So I will go ahead and book the hall?'

'Yes the date is fine. I will be there.'

'Radha will be attending so you can both come together from London like you did last time for the 100th anniversary.'

I am about to say that I will not be travelling from London and instead say: 'Yes. I'll do that. I'll come with Radha. Like last time.'

I put down the phone with a warm sense of validation. Out of my window my June garden is abloom with colours, beckoning me. I step into it with my notebook and accompanied by images of Doctor Who, landing with Yas in the clearing on that fateful day ...

'Tread softly,' the Doctor tells Yas as they walk along together,' you're treading on your own history.'

My character, Nani Umbreen, had given her granddaughter Yas a special gift: a watch with a cracked face, along with the stipulation 'that it must never be fixed'.

'Why not?' asks Yas.

'I don't want to talk about it anymore,' says Nani, 'you wouldn't understand.'

'Please,' implores Yas, 'Your life is our heritage.'

Nani is unmoved. The topic is closed. I smile, remembering how in my performance I'd copied my mother – who would gracefully raise her right hand and say in Punjabi '*Bas, hun mere kan na kha*' ('Enough, now don't eat my ears!')

Yas is troubled. She is also resolved to discover the mystery of her history. She takes the watch with the cracked face and pleadingly persuades the Doctor to travel back in time. 'Family history and time travel, very tricky,' says the Doctor. They arrive in a clearing in a forest surrounded by fields and learn that it is Sunday 17 August 1947, just a few hours before the Radcliffe Line (Partition) will irretrievably crack the face of India

I make my way across my garden towards the bench nestling under the tall purple rhododendron. Native of the Himalayas, like me, I think as I sit down, for I was born in the Himalayas, in Simla - where the Simla Conference on Partition was held. I wonder, with some irritation, that Mountbatten ('Master of Disaster') chose a Sunday for unveiling that Partition Line and reflect on the chronology: On Thursday 14 August Pakistan celebrated its Independence, Friday the 15th was Indian Independence Day and the next day, Saturday 16 August, Mountbatten sent the British troops home to be safe from any blame and far from the slaughter that he knew would be unleashed the following day when the Radcliffe Line demarcating the two countries was revealed.

'Never in my wildest dreams, did I ever imagine that I would ever leave Lahore,' my mother would often say with a look of utter bewilderment trying to make sense of Partition and dislocation. And she never really did – either leave Lahore or make sense of it all. (And neither did any of us.)

'We lived together with so much love. It was not possible to imagine.'

I thought of my Uncle Bashir, also from Lahore, whose family in London were the nearest thing I ever knew to family. Like my parents he, too, had come before Partition and travelled on a 'British Indian Passport of the Indian Empire'. Later we would become citizens of different countries. But it made no difference. We were in London and the friendship, the love, the loyalty was never partitioned. Like the story behind the watch with the cracked face.

'I want to take care of my Nani,' Yas tells the Doctor with feeling and I remembered as I'd watched her on the screen I, too, had shed a little tear – for her, for me and for that shared feeling. I, too, wanted to take care of my parents, make things better for them, dissolve Partition.

I pick up my notebook, at the back of which I have 'jottings' – among them a quote from Carl Jung: 'The greatest burden a child must bear is the unlived life of its parents.'

Yas discovers Nani's secret story: that her Muslim grandmother's first love was a Hindu neighbour and childhood sweetheart called Prem. The watch was a wedding gift. The marriage would be thwarted, the groom would be killed, the watch would crack and the Radcliffe Line would rip through their land as Partition cracked the face of India, leaving a wound that wouldn't heal. Just fester.

With the help of the Doctor, Yas learns that she can't change things, that she can only bear witness and accept and, in doing so, move into an expansive, healing understanding. And how extraordinary that Doctor Who, in helping Yas, should have helped me, too. As Yas on the screen realises, I, watching her, realise this, too.

'Love abides in the face of everything,' says Doctor Who, rescuing the situation she has landed into by conducting the wedding ceremony between Nani Umbreen and Prem. Though Prem will die, the love will live on, and in the years that follow it will nourish Yas. 'Prem' in Sanskrit means unconditional love.

I look up at the beech trees in my garden, birds flying in and out, leaves fluttering in the breeze. I smile. Well, never in *my* wildest dreams did I ever imagine I would be living in the English countryside and inherit a glorious cottage garden with its wall of scented roses, settled shrubs, lupins, peonies and tall foxgloves.

'We didn't change when that line was drawn' says Prem, walking with his brother towards the Demons and his death.

'But we did', replies his brother with a narrowing look of cold hate.

I feel a cold shiver and stand up as though to shake it off and, leaving my notebook on the bench, start to pace in the garden. I think of Savarkar, as he is emerging in my manuscript in the here and now where his idea of India was taking root and the emails about him waiting to be read which, until now, I have shelved.

As I pace the garden I reflect on the nature of hate and the nature of love. Are they opposites? I ask the tall foxglove. I pick up my notebook from the bench and make my way back to my desk.

The first email reads: *Subject: Savarkar'*
'Hi Leena,

Glad to hear that you are back to writing. You mentioned about Madan Lal and Savarkar being close friends. I'm sending you two links. I thought it might interest you to know where he fits into the landscape of our new India with Modi and the BJP winning a second term. They are "old" but relevant and paint the picture of "now".'

The first link is from *The Economist*, dated 17 December 2014. It shows a colour photograph of Modi paying obeisance to a garlanded and illuminated portrait of Savarkar. Savarkar, Modi's mentor.

The man who thought Gandhi a sissy
The controversial mentor of the Hindu right.
17 Dec 2014

'... In 1906, in a lodging house for Indian students in Highgate, a pleasant area of north London, a young lawyer called Mohandas Karamchand Gandhi dropped in on a law student called Vinayak Damodar Savarkar, who happened to be frying prawns at the time. Savarkar offered Gandhi some of his meal; Gandhi, a vegetarian, refused. Savarkar allegedly retorted that only a fool would attempt to resist the British without being fortified by animal protein.

The meeting is said to have begun hostilities between the two young Indian nationalists; whether or not the story is apocryphal, there were real reasons for antipathy. The two men had very different approaches to the struggle against Britain. Gandhi, who became leader of the Indian National Congress (INC), was a pacifist with an inclusive attitude towards Muslims and Christians. Savarkar, who would lead the Hindu Mahasabha, was a right-wing majoritarian who spawned the idea of *hindutva*, or Hindu-ness – the belief that the Hindu identity is inseparable from the Indian identity. Congress eclipsed the Mahasabha and, since history belongs to the victors, the story of India's Independence movement became one of nonviolence. But the strand of thought that Savarkar represented was more important than is generally recognised, and is enjoying a revival ...'

The second click reveals an article two years later in 2016, this time a black-and-white copy of a picture of Savarkar animated on a podium and titled: **Reading Savarkar: How a Hindutva icon justified the idea of rape as a political tool.**

I decide not to read that one and move on to the next mail. This is the recent one by Pankaj Mishra:

The New York Times, 23 May 2019

'How Narendra Modi Seduced India With Envy and Hate.

The prime minister has won re-election on a tide of violence, fake news and resentment.' I set my computer to print the article for reading later.

I sighed, closed my eyes, furrowed my brow and rubbed my forehead, as though that would clear the space for some insight to get through.

'*A visitor from foreign.*' It was kindly said, implying I be treated as an honoured guest – but, at that time, it got tarnished with the 'outsider', 'non-belonging' projection from my experience of 'Englishness'.

Opening my eyes I looked at the photograph of Madan Lal, then pulled out my notebook and started to write:

'Dear Uncle Madan,

You look so young, so handsome, so full – of idealism, patriotism and, dare I say, love? Love of India, of freedom, love for a better world. And maybe, some hatred, too: for empire, racism, exploitation, injustice, the unnatural state of affairs.

When I was your age, in my early twenties, the *zeitgeist* of my time was also of change. My background music was Bob Dylan's 'The Times They Are a-Changin.'" We marched and protested against racism, apartheid, the Vietnam War, the nuclear bomb, and the peddling of fear. We tried to practice solidarity, sharing, decency, and like John Lennon to 'Imagine' that the world could 'be as one'.

Our icons included Che Guevara, who declared that the true revolutionary is guided by a great feeling of love. And Nelson Mandela, who had been a 'terrorist' espousing guns and violence, but who much later, in 1990, came out of twenty-seven years of incarceration with a message of love and reconciliation.

But, your friend and comrade, Savarkar, left his revolutionary, inclusive self in the Cellular Jail in the Andaman Islands and emerged from his incarceration with a divisive message of stigmatisation which then sprouted hate and which made me feel unsure and like a 'visitor from foreign.'

Getting up from my desk, I looked absently at the garden, once again exploring the energies of Love and Hate, as though for a character I have to play – combining words and gestures: what do they feel like, look like, sound like?

Hate: hard, heat, omniscient, intoxicating, affirming, self-righteous, entitled, firing up, defining, separating, indignation, anger, divisive ...

And Love? – soft, nebulous, uniting, embracing, expanding, dissolving, even disappearing, so that Cleopatra can sigh: 'Oh! My oblivion is a very Anthony and I am all forgotten.'

I am interrupted by a call. My friend Diane tells me that she has just received her naturalisation for British citizenship. 'I seriously think you, too, should apply, especially now, with this Brexit business and who knows what laws they might bring in.'

I listen. But don't fully register as I grapple with this new bubble of feelings and voices swilling around: *'You don't lose your identity*

*by getting a more convenient set of travelling papers, darling.' You
need an Indian passport to enter politics and work for the uplift of
your Motherland.' 'What, stand in the queue marked British and
cope with the askance looks.'*

'I know until now,' continues Diane, 'as Commonwealth
citizens we've been secure, but then, the Windrush generation
also felt secure and had been here as long as us. And look what
happened to them!'

How funny, I think, that Diane should call me now, when I'm
writing to her in the manuscript ...

'Are you listening?' she asks.

'Yes, yes', I reply. 'I am listening.'

34.
1909: SHELLEY AND TOLSTOY

Madan was sorting through his things and his thoughts. It needed to be done. It was more than three weeks since he had left India House. It was his fifth change of address since he had come to London three years earlier. And it would be his last before he returned to India. Until then, he needed to prepare himself in every way. On all fronts. He had maintained his routine of attending classes, taking walks and doing revolver practice. He had not disclosed his address. He needed this spell of solitude. But messages had been left for him at the college, including one from Bhajan. He now intended to visit him and was looking for a volume of Shelley that he had purchased for him a while back from Watkins Books in Cecil Court. He located the book and placed it on his desk alongside his open engineering books and two others: Dadabhai Naoroji's *Poverty and Un-British Rule in India* and a slim volume on Thomas Paine, containing as a bookmark the letter from Curzon Wyllie. The letter that he had angrily crumpled in his fist and thrown across the room. Later he had tried to iron out the creases in case he needed to show it when he attended. But it hadn't proved necessary. He hadn't gone. He'd gone as far as Whitehall, then changed his mind.

As he slipped the letter back and picked up the book for Bhajan, he had another thought: that warm Austrian coat that his brother Behari had had altered for him in Amritsar, he would give to Bhajan. After all, he would not be spending another winter here as by the end of the summer his exams would be over and he would be back in India. And, as he and Bhajan were the same build there would be no need for alterations. Yes, he thought, it was a good coat and he liked the idea. He would deliver it for cleaning on his way over and tell Bhajan

Bhajan was sitting at his desk, looking over the pages he had just finished copying: Leo Tolstoy's 'Letter to a Indian'.

Some of the Indian revolutionaries had written to Tolstoy enclosing copies of their journal *Free Hindustan*. It was a twin journal to *The Indian Sociologist*; both shared the same masthead quote of Herbert Spencer: *'Resistance to aggression is not simply justifiable but imperative; non-resistance hurts both altruism and egoism.'*

Copies of Tolstoy's reply had been circulating among the Indian students; one of them had fallen into Bhajan's hands. He found himself resonating with the ideas, the sound, profound case for nonviolence. He wanted to share this with Madan. Bhajan had attended a meeting at India House, hoping to find Madan, but he wasn't there. Bhajan found himself disagreeing with Savarkar's views on violence. He was exploring his feelings about this when Tolstoy's letter had fallen into his hands. He had copied extracts of the letter to give to Madan. As he read it through once again, he marked a few passages with a pencil.

'I have received your letter and two numbers of your periodical, both of which interest me extremely. The oppression of a majority by a minority, and the demoralisation inevitably resulting from it, is a phenomenon that has always occupied me and has done so most particularly of late ...

'The reason for the astonishing fact that a majority of working people submit to a handful of idlers who control their labour and their very lives is always and everywhere the same ... the reason lies in the lack of a reasonable religious teaching which, by explaining the meaning of life, would supply a supreme law for the guidance of conduct and would replace the more than dubious precepts of pseudo-religion and pseudo-science with the immoral conclusions deduced from them and commonly called "civilisation".

'If the people of India are enslaved by violence it is only because they themselves live and have lived by violence and do not recognise the eternal law of love inherent in humanity.'

Bhajan was interrupted by the arrival of a visitor and was delighted to see it was his brother. 'Madan bhai!' he exclaimed, 'I have been attending the meetings, hoping to find you.'

'Well, that's good!' laughed Madan.

"Nobody knew your address. I'm so glad you are here. I was copying something for you. Have you come across Tolstoy's letter?'

'No. I've been busy. You know, exams coming up.' He said absently looking around the room. 'I dream of home sometimes, see the courtyard, the *champak* tree, mother sitting under it.'

'Preparing for some festival.'

'Yes. But although I dream of home, when I think of returning, of being there, I feel shackled, timebound. I imagine the best of what could be in store for me, and it feels like a prison.'

Bhajan listened, attentive, as it appeared Madan was half-talking to himself, clarifying his own thoughts.

'I don't want to go back to be a brown Sahib, aping the white man. I don't trust or believe in the integrity of this government. I know you'll say there are good Englishmen, and there are, like Dunlop Smith or Aitcheson and others, but you see I don't believe that our destiny lies in the connection with England. In fact, I believe that this connection has been very harmful for us, and that we've been badly infected by it. The sooner it's severed, the better, because only then will we be able to hear our own voices.' Madan sat down as though to listen to the voices. 'If I'd been an Indian at another time, when Ashoka reigned or Buddha taught, I would know who I was. But now, I don't. We've been educated to feel ashamed of ourselves, our religions, our race. We've been educated to see ourselves through their gaze, their definitions.' Madan got up as though as though he'd been tied down. Suddenly he laughed. 'I now understand what Hamlet felt like.'

'Hamlet?' said Bhajan, who was relieved to be able to laugh.

'Yes, Hamlet, with all the voices telling him what he should do, and he, trying to listen to his own voice amidst all that noise. It's not that he can't make up his mind, just that he wants to make up *his own* mind.' Madan was now pacing up and down the room thoughtfully.

'You know. I've been thinking the same things. Really,' ventured Bhajan.

'Yes?'

'Acting from our own way … our essential nature, acting from there. I'm not being clear, but you mentioned Buddha and Ashoka as expressing something ... intrinsic to Indian culture – and both had nonviolence as central.'

Madan shook his head. 'But we were attacked and subjugated through violence. The only thing the English understand is violence; it's the only thing that they respect.'

'But why do things *they* understand? Why not find our own way? It's not just freeing us from their rule in our land, but in our heads as well. You've said that yourself.'

'Yes. But things have to be looked at in the context of their time. As long as they're there, we can't be who we are. It isn't our way. It's not our *swadharma*. Neither internally nor externally. I've also thought a lot about *dharma*, about duty. The ideal son is like Shravan, devoted and totally self-sacrificing to his parents. But imagine if Siddhartha Gautama had devoted himself to his duties as son, prince, husband, father – then he would never have become a Buddha. Instead, he had to sneak out into the night like a thief, turning his back on duty and responsibility, because he had to become what he was truly meant to be. If he hadn't, if he'd been dutiful, he wouldn't have been able to fulfil himself, to become a Buddha and give us all that fine knowledge. Am I not right?'

'Well, yes. One can look at it that way.' Bhajan walked to his desk.

'Why, we were a great civilisation when they were running around in bearskins! Now they treat us like children needing to grow up. And what will we grow up to be? A brood of Indians who are as alien to their native Indian culture and to the spirit of India as the white man is?' Madan walked over to the window and looked out into the street below. 'I must go now. The days fly so fast. Life, too. Look, I also have something for you. Actually, I came to see you to give it to you.'

Madan handed Bhajan the book he had for him.

'Shelley! And so beautifully bound.'

'The One remains, the many change and pass,' Madan started to recite.

'Heaven's light forever shines, earth's shadows fly,' Bhajan joined in and they continued together:

'Life, like a dome of many-coloured glass,
Stains the white radiance of eternity.'

'That's just it, Madan bhai. It's all One. It's all life. Even the bits we don't like.'

Madan took the sheets from Bhajan's hand, folded them, put them into his inside pocket, whilst continuing with his recitation of Shelley:

'Until death tramples it to fragments - Die
If thou wouldst be with that which thou dost seek.'

Bhajan watched him from the window for as long as he could, clutching Shelley to his heart. When he could see him no more, he had a strange sinking feeling. At first he tried to brush it aside; later he acknowledged it.

Madan returned to his room with a feeling of peace. He had been able to express himself and felt tenderness towards his brother for enabling that. He declaimed the line from Shelley to his room: 'Die – If thou wouldst be with that which thou dost seek'.

Since he had taken the vow to devote his life to the cause a sense of spaciousness would pass through him in waves. The full impact, that he had surrendered his life started to impress itself on him. He sat down in the deep armchair, closed his eyes and observed his breathing. In and out. He felt himself expanding as if his body had no contours but was just an energy, pulsating with and part of the energy around, in the air, everywhere, ever-expanding. When he half-opened his eyes, his mind felt utterly quiet. His life now belonged to the cause, to the Motherland, to Shri Krishna. It really was so clear. So simple. An old memory surged, aged six going with his mother to the Golden Temple, and then to visit a very quiet man. He'd watched her bow down before him and touch her forehead to the ground and later when he'd asked why she had bowed to him.

'He has given his life to God. So now is free.' She'd said it simply and smiled.

He smiled as he remembered it and this brought his awareness back to the room, the armchair, his body sitting in it. He opened his eyes.

35.

1909: THE PHOTOGRAPH

*'Only he who could keep his hand on the candle for the longest
would do it ... And it was your Uncle Madan. A man in Paris told
me. He was there, too, in the same room.'*

Madan was concentrating on his exams and was either revising in
the library, sitting in the exam hall or taking a walk in one of the
many little parks that surround University College.

Once he had decided on a course of action, he was resolute,
disciplined and focused. And he *had* thought it through – and
decided. Doing well in his exams was now part of the overall plan,
which was to secure a post in one of the independent princely states
of India and from there work for the cause – to free the Motherland.
At one of the meetings, Savarkar had pointed out how in spite of
the Arms Act there was plenty of warlike material in India, 'What is
wanted is active propaganda work in the Indian states and among
the troops. We must teach our people to hate the foreign oppressor
and success is sure.' Madan took notes at meetings and sometimes

studied them. In his wardrobe he had a small case, which he kept locked. In it was his revolver, which he used for target practice, his journal, some letters, money and valuables and the badge 'Remember the Martyrs of 1857'. On the lid he had pasted pictures of some of the martyrs and to these he had recently added the picture of Khudiram Bose, the eighteen-year-old who had been sent to the gallows, and that of his accomplice Prafulla, for the Muzaffarpur bomb. These he had been brought from Calcutta recently by Vasudev Bhattacharya and he had been given them when he returned to India House.

Sometimes he would open the case and look at the portraits for inspiration and to strengthen his resolve to study. The exams would end in the first week of June and then would follow the Institute of Civil Engineers in October, after which he would be ready to go home.

A few days after his exams had ended, Madan was sitting on a bench in Russell Square, planning to visit India House, when he saw Harish coming towards him.

'There you are. I was looking for you. There is some bad news,' said Harish.

'What news?'

'Vinayak's two brothers, Ganesh and Baburao Savarkar, are to be transported for life to the Andamans.'

'What, for publishing poetry?'

Harish nodded.

'What? For life?'

'And all their property is to be forfeited and their families left with nothing. Vinayak is beside himself. I was there earlier. He says it's time to act.'

'Did he? I will go there now. Are you coming?'

'I'll be there later. There will be a meeting in the upstairs room. Now, I have to see my tutor.'

Madan Lal got up immediately and made his way out of the gardens while trying to recall one of the brothers' poems he had helped translate:

> 'Who obtained independence without a battle ...
> Was glorious Rama, sable as a cloud,
> a fool to have freed his mother the earth from servitude?
> Did he fight a battle for no purpose?
> Who obtained Independence without a battle?
> Ask the Greeks how they achieved their national
> emancipation.
> There are no paths leading to emancipation other than war.'

When he reached Euston station, he decided that he would walk to Highgate. He had done it before and knew it would take an hour and a half, and at this moment, with the turbulent emotions he was feeling, he did not want to sit in a tram. Walking helped him to think, to ground himself

He knew how close the Savarkar brothers were and that they were all dedicated to the cause. He admired them all immensely. Vinayak, he knew, would be distraught. He rehearsed what he might say: '*Tatya*, please remember that you have other brothers. I am here. Tell me what I can do.' Or, he thought, he might say simply: 'Tell me what I must do.'

He knew that some of the other students thought he was a 'rich man's son', dabbling in trivial pursuits, because he liked dancing. But then he liked ju-jitsu, too! In any case those were just externals. What did they really know? Madame Cama, Bhikaiji, she knew and Savarkar knew the nature of his resolve and depth of his determination.

Like the time long ago when he began work as a stoker and Babu Ram noticed his soft hands ... he'd worked extra hard, getting burns and calluses that he didn't even feel – until he was urged to stop by Gulzari.

Walking up Dartmouth Park Hill he decided to detour through Waterlow Park. Being close to nature always lifted his spirits.

As Madan Lal climbed the steps to the front door a wave of presentiment flooded through him. He stopped on the porch until it had ebbed away.

Inside the house, Savarkar was incandescent with rage and pain: pacing up and down, he was suffering ... Madan's prepared speech dissolved; he stood at the door and had no words. Sometimes, there are no words. You can only show, and be, and as Madan stood there and looked at his friend, he physically felt his suffering.

Savarkar stormed and raged, vowed Vengence, Retribution. Action. Here. Now. 'What we need are martyrs. My brothers are now martyrs. Their sacrifice will fuel fires of rage that will ignite our cause. But I will not see them again!'

He howled.

In the evening, those who had taken the oath of the Young India Society met for discussion and to make a decision.

Chatto found the poem by Bahadur Shah, the last Moghul Emperor exiled by the East India Company. He read it in Urdu, and then since not everyone was familiar with Urdu he read it again in translation:

'So long as there remains the least trace of love and faith
in the hearts of our heroes

So long as the sword of Hindustan remains sharp,
One day it shall flash – even at the gates of London.'

Sometime later, in the same room, they gathered again. The ceremonial fire was lit in the grate, the curtains were drawn to darken the room – because it was summer and the days were long.

The young men, all initiates, had arranged themselves in a semicircle around the fireplace. In the centre of the room a tall plant holder with a ceramic top had been cleared to hold a candle, its flame flickering.

Each initiate was a member of the Abhinav Bharat and had taken the vow of sacrifice. None looked at any of the others but each stared at the candle – and one by one came up and put his hand above the flame for as long as he could stand. Then the length of time was recorded.

Madan felt the same wave of premonition he'd experienced earlier. He sensed now, that Savarkar was willing him as he closed his eyes and put his left hand over the flame … he didn't know for how long, until a hand gently pushed his away from the heat. He looked at it and said: 'Get a raw potato from the kitchen and a knife and slice it as thinly as it can be.'

The thin slivers were then placed on the burn to draw out the heat and replaced by new, cool ones until the heat was drawn out and the hand felt more comfortable.

Later Savarkar said to Madan: 'You will be remembered forever. You will never be forgotten. Your sacrifice will fire hearts for further heroism and sacrifice until the Motherland is free from servitude and cleansed.' Then he added: 'I knew it would be you.'

Madan nodded.

But time was at a premium. There was much to be done. Foremost was the photograph. It had to be taken and printed before it could be suppressed. The target was to be Lord Curzon; hatred for him was effortless. After shooting him, Madan would then shoot himself; he would carry two pistols and a knife. In his pocket he would have the statement they were preparing, explaining the logic and justice of his action.

For the photograph, Madan Lal decided he would wear the fine suit made for him when he had first come, just three years earlier. Then he would give it away – and he tried to think who he might give it to. He opened his wardrobe and surveyed what else he would give away, what he would destroy and what he would leave to be found. His notebooks he might throw in the river. He found the postcard of Curzon on which he scrawled 'Heathen dog'. This he would leave in his room.

He caught sight of himself in the mirror and walked across to it. He looked at his reflection, at his expression, then closed his eyes and considered the qualities he needed to project. He opened his eyes again to see if his expression had changed.

Then he sat down in the armchair. He felt utterly calm, utterly at peace. He didn't know how long it lasted but when it finally dissolved, he felt reassured that it was there, somewhere, a space and a feeling within.

Taking the photograph was a clandestine affair. Only four people in India House knew about the vow and impending assassination. Guy Aldred, an anarchist and supporter, had arranged the logistics of the photography, though he didn't know its purpose. On the assigned day they chose a quiet corner at the back of the garden and a time when most of the inmates of the house were out or occupied. Chatto stayed indoors to be sure that no one ventured into the garden.

Madan Lal sat in the chair and looked straight and resolutely into the camera.

Back in Ledbury Road, Madan continued with his routine of revolver practice, clearing his things, and coming to Highgate for the regular Sunday meetings. His statement of martyrdom was being prepared, a collaborative effort in which he participated.

On Sunday 27 June he felt absent, thinking that it was his last meeting and that in four days he would no longer be alive – and trying to grapple with what that meant. He thought he heard his name called in the distance, and then he heard it again, closer. He turned to look at the room, where they were all looking at him.

'We have elected you to run the proceedings for today,' came Madhava's voice.

He felt unprepared, awkward, shy, then he felt flattered and relieved to be the focus of their attention. He spoke softly and the meeting started. When it was over Nanu sang a patriotic Bengali song and then everyone went into the garden for tea. Madan stayed behind trying to get to the bottom of what he was feeling.

'I feel a pang, a yearning, difficult to describe. But I long for a song in a language I know, in Punjabi or Urdu.' Asaf Ali was nearing the garden doors when Madan almost sprang upon him and made his request. Asaf looked surprised, then obliged – and Madan felt the song go through him, through all the soft organs in his body and right into his bones.

Weekly report to the Director of Criminal Intelligence

'At the usual Sunday meeting at India House on 20 June, Savarkar very violent and advocated the wholesale murder of Englishmen in India. He asked everyone present to serve the country by sacrificing his life at the earliest possible moment. For the next moment would be denied him.'

M Asaf Ali: Memoirs

'Dhingra was the most rare bird – a wistful, uncommunicative person who gave you the impression of being cross with life. He attended every meeting, never spoke, and was seldom noticed by anybody. That day he was in a strange mood, I looked hungry for something. I thought that he was feeling terribly nostalgic. As Nanu's Bengali song did not satisfy Dhingra's longing for an Urdu song, he turned to me with his request. I went to the organ and sang and played an Urdu *Ghazal* and a *Thumri*. He went into a transport of joy, which seemed to me rather extravagant. I left him looking out of the drawing room window in what appeared a far-away state of mind. All this got fixed in my memory by carefully reconnecting every detail, when what was to follow called for these recollections.'

56.
23 July 1909: Pentonville Prison

Madan, asleep in his prison cell, dreamed of the sea. He was floating weightless in the ocean, held and stroked by the soothing water and listening to the wisdom of the waves, the messages of the fish being busily relayed in glide and flutters for his safe transportation to the other shore.

He saw himself, six years old, standing by the river with his mother and younger brother, Bhajan, throwing little fistfuls of rice into the rushing water and praying for the safe voyage of one of his older brothers travelling to England.

'Ammaji,' he looked up at his mother, 'if the sea is so very far away, how will the fish get from our river to there?'

'They'll get there, my little Raja,' his mother had said, smiling. 'The water will carry the message. For the water connects everything, from the highest mountains up in the sky to the deepest depths of the sea. For the ice in the mountains melts into the waters of the rivers, which are then washed down to the great ocean. The water is charged with all that ancient knowledge.'

'And the air, too, Ammaji?' Bhajan had chipped in. 'Like when Madan bhai calls me from the top veranda and I'm in the kitchen courtyard, the air carries the message and then the air knows it?'

He was sinking now, deeper into the sea, swimming with the fish, with his comrades, fish with faces. Harish, Nitisen, Basu and Vinayak, Madhava with whom he almost collided as he'd nearly done that time before.

'Your *Tatya* is proud of you. Very proud.' Sometimes he was swimming, sometimes floating, sometimes man, sometimes fish.

37.
1 July 1990/1909: London – The Assassination

Early one sunny July morning in 1990 as I was waking, I found my attention drawn to the bookshelf in my bedroom, and the long, protruding roll from the Public Record Office. It had arrived by post in a thick cardboard tube, and I had wedged it, unopened, on to the top shelf by the wall and forgotten about it.

Now, as I reached for it, I noticed my calendar said July 1st – the same day as the assassination, eighty one years ago. I pulled it down carefully dusted it and prised out the papers coiled tightly inside. The fading blue ink, now photocopied, made the long, looping handwriting easier to read than the original:

'I do not want to say anything in defence of myself, but simply to prove the justice of my deed …'

There was a lot of noise around me, but I was still surrounded by that silence. It was like a cocoon and I was in it.

DOUGLAS WILLIAM THORBURN, journalist, saith
'I saw the prisoner apparently speaking to Sir Curzon Wyllie.
Prisoner raised his arm and rapidly fired four shots in Sir Curzon's
face – into his eyes ... Prisoner had his right hand free and he placed
the revolver to his own temple. But there was merely a click."

*When I first saw that it was to be him, I was slightly shaken.
Harish was looking at me. I felt my resolve as I thought of the
Motherland, the cause, my sacred duty. I felt alert.*

*We were talking and when he turned to me again to hear what I
had to say. I looked straight at him and pulled out my pistol. I said:
"It is my duty. To my Motherland."'*

SIR LESLEY PROBYN , saith
'At about 11 o'clock ... I heard the sound of three or four shots.
On going forward I saw the prisoner, who fired another shot ...
he then turned the pistol round to his own temple. I immediately
went at him, held his arms and got the pistol from him. There was
a struggle ... I handed the prisoner over to the police constable ...'

*The handcuffs were heavy and cold and I was still in a daze –
wondering why I was there and how it was that I had lost that last
shot, the bullet which was meant for me.*

*What is everlasting in this world? The sun sets, the sea ebbs, all
things rise and fall.*

The papers sprang back and voices went. I picked up the roll
and went downstairs to spread them out over the dining table.
There was a drawing and a plan of the Jehangir Hall at the
Imperial Institute. I placed it in the centre of the table. It showed
the entrance hall, the lobby, the steps, the two landings and the
vestibule, leading to the hall itself. Today, there would probably
be a set of photographs, but these were fine ink drawings. It was

a grand place, full of pomp. Uncle Madan would have walked up those steps; five steps to a landing, seventeen steps to another landing, then five more to the vestibule and into the hall ...

I was in a waking dream, but I was alert. So alert I could feel my heart pumping, and I could feel the blood in my veins, and I could feel my breath in-going, out-going, and my limbs as I walked, up the steps and then into the hall. I looked around at the people I knew.

EMMA JOSEPHINE BECK affirming saith
'I am single and live at 160 Kingston Park Road. I was at the 'At Home' on 1st July ...

'I had a conversation with him (Dhingra) about half an hour before the tragedy. I noticed nothing peculiar about his condition. He remained quite normal ... He seemed quite calm.'

I hadn't expected it to be him, and for a moment I was taken aback. Harish was behind me to remind me of my resolve. When I looked at Harish, however, it dawned on me that his own resolve was questionable; he was weak. I felt my own resolve growing stronger. To teach courage, you have to show it.

He had been asking me about my studies. We had just finished conversing and he was about to leave. There was no time, no time. I said: 'It is my duty ... you see.' He looked astonished. I pulled the trigger. He didn't have time to understand ...

But I knew we would meet in another place. That was what we believed.

MADAN MOHAN SINHA affirming saith:
'I live at 36 Maida Hill, West London. I am a student of the Middle Temple ... I saw a loaded revolver taken out of his inside pocket, also a hunting knife. The only thing he said was that he wanted

his glasses. His manner was very calm. He was the only person not agitated or excited.'

I sat there wondering how it was that I was still alive; how was it that the bullet had clicked and not fired. Was I still alive? I had flashes when I wasn't sure about that, either. I was there, but it was also like a scene I was watching.

I said: 'My specs,' and they were given to me and I said: 'Thank you.'

FREDERICK NICHOLLS sworn saith:

'I am police constable 476.B. At 11:10 p.m. on Thursday night I was on duty in Institute Road. I heard several people blowing whistles and shouting "Police ..."'

'I took charge of Dhingra and took him to the station with a detective sergeant. Dhingra never spoke. He was charged and made no reply. He was very quiet.'

They took me to Walton Street Police Station. I was surrounded by silence, although the silence had a specific sound.

CHARLES GLASS, sworn saith

'I am signal inspector, B Division ... I was present at Walton Street Police station ... I read the charge over to the prisoner and he nodded his head and said "Yes". I said "Do you wish any of your friends to be communicated with?" He said "I don't think it will be necessary tonight; they will know later on." He was then placed in the cell.'

In the cell and I lay down, but couldn't sleep. I thought about that last shot. That last shot that was meant for me. That I was alive when I should have been dead. Dead on the floor with him, with my statement in my pocket. Now they've taken away my statement.

I'd completely forgotten that I had to arm the gun. When I put it to my head and it didn't fire, for a moment I didn't know where I was, and then it was too late. I couldn't get to my dagger – there were so many of them trying to hold me down. Now I'm here and not dead. Why?

At Westminster Police Court for the formal charge, I was asked if I had anything to say.

I nodded and said: 'The only thing I want to say is that there was no wilful murder in the case of Dr Lalcaca. I did not know him. When he advanced to get hold of me, I simply fired in self-defence.' In my head I said to him that I didn't mean to kill him and wished that he could be alive and that I could be dead in his place.

Back in my cell I remembered that at the shooting gallery I'd left without firing that last shot. It was when I decided I would return to India House. Why had I not fired that sixth shot?

I dreamed I was in the dock. Everyone was watching. In the gallery there were comrades from India House. In the centre was Tatya. As I looked around the courtroom I felt as though I was growing larger and taller and I was reading – my statement: 'I admit the other day I attempted to shed English blood as a humble revenge for the inhuman hangings and deportations of patriotic Indian youth. In this I have consulted none but my own conscience and conspired with none but my own duty ...'

When I awoke it was all quite clear. My sixth shot – to stand trial, to stand defiant, to proclaim the love of Motherland and the justice of our cause. To demonstrate the courage of our race and to inspire the spirit of patriotism and love of freedom. And so I prepared myself:

'The only lesson required in India today is to learn how to die, and the only way of teaching is to die ourselves. So I die and glory in my martyrdom. Bande Mataram.'

I folded the documents from the Public Record Office. I scanned through some photocopied newspapers and documents; it felt as though the voices of the past came alive in the present.

The Times, London, 3 July 1909
'It was ascertained that the assailant is Madha Lao Dhingra, a Hindu from the Punjab who has been studying engineering at University College. He remained quite cool and collected after his arrest. He was taken to Walton Street Police Station and is said to have slept well during the night.'

Weekly Report of the Director of Criminal Intelligence
'The murders were carried out with an automatic magazine Colt pistol purchased on 26 January 1909; the assassin was also armed with a loaded Browning magazine automatic pistol ... He also carried a 6-inch steel blade hunting knife.

'At Dhingra's lodgings there were two picture postcards, one of which was a reproduction of a picture recently published in *Free Hindustan* depicting the blowing of Indian rebels from the mouth of the cannons and the other a portrait of Lord Curzon on which is pencilled "Heathen dog".'

W. S. Blunt – *My Diaries*
'3 July. A most important thing has happened in connection with India. Sir Curzon Wyllie has been assassinated by a young Indian at the Imperial Institute.

'The whole English press is united in its religious horror at the crime, forgetting how it applauded exactly such crimes in Italy fifty years ago, and in Russia the other day. Krishna Varma's position is precisely the same as Mazzini's then was, whom we all now justify since his plan of assassination led to the liberation of Italy, and if ever people had justification it is the people of India.

'... a document found on the prisoner shows that the murder was political in character. At the present stage the police are very reticent as to the contents of this paper, which consists of three foolscap sheets in crabbed handwriting.

'But it is understood that the paper sets forth the political conviction of Dhingra as a bitter enemy of British rule in India.

'It declares that rule to be unjust and iniquitous, and says that any and every means are legitimate on the part of Indians to gain Independence.'

Daily Chronicle 3 July 1909

Madan Lal Dhingra. Life Story of the Imperial Institute Fanatic.

'I know Madan Lal Dhingra. I know both him and his family and there will be sad hearts in the distant Punjab today when they hear the dreadful news.

'The Dhingra family is well known and highly respected at Amritsar. The father of the assassin is a prosperous physician. He is more, for he takes a leading part in municipal affairs, and he is a sort of father confessor to the people in the neighbourhood who come to him not only for medical help but for guidance and advice in the affairs of the world.

'Though I knew Dhingra in India I did not meet the boy Madan Lal until March last ... as I knew his people we naturally became rather intimate. But I noticed he liked to turn the conversation to political channels. He spoke of the Bengal extremists with only qualified approval, this was not because they went too far but because they didn't go far enough. The government does not care what hard words are used against them – the only thing that would move them is physical force.

'I took Dhingra to be an idealist who looked forward to the time when Indians would drive the British from India, but it never occurred to me that he was an anarchist who would develop into an assassin.

'Dhingra, wearing a jacket, was able to conceal the revolvers and the dagger with which he was armed. This would explain why he did not wear evening dress. He also wore a turban, which was unusual for him. I think it was a symbol and sign of his nationality. Sir Curzon was in conversation with Dhingra for at least ten minutes, to all appearances the talk was quite friendly and their voices were not even raised. The flash and report of the shot was the first intimation that anything was wrong ...'

38.

3 JULY 1909: BEHARI LAL, DEHRADUN

Dr Behari Lal stepped out onto the veranda, and as always, the view took his breath away: the morning mists were just lifting from the luminous, glistening green jungle and would soon reveal blue mountains in the deep distance, then the silver streak of the snow peaks stretching across the sky and melting into the horizon, disappearing, reappearing in the changing colours of the monsoon sky ... blue, pink, grey and gold.

Barsaat, the rainy season. He loved this season, season of renewal, joy, delight. Everyone and everything loved this season. He took a deep breath, lifting his arms to allow the clean, rain-washed air to enter his body as deep as it would go.

A blessed season, a blessed time – and he felt blessed. He was a father for the fourth time to a third son. A beautiful, perfect, healthy baby, just seventeen days old. As was the custom, his wife had come to her family home for her confinement and the customary forty days of seclusion for mother and child that followed the birth.

He had woken earlier than usual and put it down to the excitement of the previous day when the *Namkaran* naming ceremony had been held. His wife's family were Sikh and so it was performed accordingly. The priest had arrived in the morning, the family had all gathered in the specially designated prayer room on the first floor, placing the baby next to the *Guru Granth Sahib* holy book. After the prayers and recitations and moistening of the baby's lips with Amrit, nectar, then the *Hukum nama* was taken: the holy book was opened at random to reveal or decree the choice of syllables for the name – it was *Bal*, signifying strength, inner power and the baby had puckered his little mouth in agreement and all had smiled. To *Bal* was added *doon*, because the baby was born in the city of Dehradoon and so would be called Baldoon, a concocted name that only he would own. Following the ceremony there was the *langar* – more than a hundred people were fed and given gifts of shawls and blankets.

Before coming out on to the veranda he had tiptoed in to take a peek at his sleeping son who again puckered his perfect little mouth and Behari Lal's heart swelled. The black mark placed near the baby's ear to ward off the evil eye had streaked down his cheek, which Behari gently touched as he blessed his new-born and carried this glowing feeling with him onto the veranda.

It was time for his walk and he decided to take a longer one than usual, to take full advantage of his time in the cool hills, because he had a feeling, now that the naming ceremony was over, that his time there might be interrupted by a call to return to the plains to attend to his duties. Although he was the Chief Medical Officer, he was also close to the Maharaja, who liked to consult him on all sorts of matters, including the welfare of his hundred or so dogs who were treated like little princes.

Thinking that he might walk the forest path, he put on some suitable shoes and then pulled out an umbrella, which he surveyed briefly. It was a quality umbrella, 'Made in England' and he remembered purchasing it at the specialised umbrella shop a short walk for University College Hospital when he was studying. He'd liked it enough then to return and get two more, for his mother and father. Then he thought briefly of his younger brothers in London and that Madan would soon be on his way home, a qualified engineer.

He stepped out just as the household was stirring. The mists, lifting, had unveiled the blue mountains, but the clouds were still low and there was no knowing when the rains might start again.

Behari returned from his walk via the back of the house, past the cowshed and vegetable garden and into the kitchen courtyard (still not wholly cleared of the celebrations of the day before). The staff greeted him.

Gulaam Mohommed, Behari Lal's trusted manservant, followed his master into the house. He had prepared the breakfast table, ironed the newspapers, put out the day clothes and was ready for any further instructions.

When the telegram was delivered, Gulam Mahommed took possession of it with a flicker of a smile. He was not averse to returning to the plains primarily because he, too, had a baby son, Niaz, less than a year old ... and who was his delight. But on seeing that it was from Amritsar, his brow furrowed. Had something happened in the family?

'Dr Sahibji', he said on entering the study where Dr Behari was sifting through some papers.

'Yes. What is it?'

'Ji. Telegram.'

Behari nodded. He had been right to go for a long walk but still, if this was a summons, he had not expected it quite so soon.

Gulamm Mahommed, instead of leaving, stood there.

'What is it?'

'It's from Amritsar, Dr Sahib.'

Now Behari furrowed his brow as he quickly tore it open. There were three messages or three pieces of information: That he should proceed to Amritsar at once. That Sir Curzon Wyllie had been killed. That Madan was under arrest.

What was the connection? It took a while before he realised that it was one message and then a wave of feelings and thoughts rushed through him in quick succession – heat, cold, fear, anxiety, anger, hurt, pain, distress, incomprehension, fury, disbelief, terror.

'What needs to be done?' came Gulam's voice.

'Prepare the bags. Find out the times of the trains. We must leave for Amritsar.' His mouth was parched, and his voice was deep and rasped. Gulaam Mohommed quickly walked to the side table and poured a glass of water. The only sound in the room was the clink of the beads around the net covering the water jug and the sound of the water filling the glass.

'I'll take care of everything,' Gulam said, as he handed the glass to Behari Lal. He in turn nodded his assent as he gratefully drank the water.

Gulaam Mohommed did not know what had happened, but he guessed it was about Madan Lal. He didn't ask. In time he would find out. He was a man of empathy and had great love for his Dr Sahib, whom he had come to work for as an illiterate teenager; he could now read and write and even knew a smattering of English! He set about taking charge of the situation so as to alleviate his

Dr Sahib's distress. He was familiar with travel routines and knew what to do.

Before leaving, Behari Lal went again to see his beautiful baby son, but found himself keeping a distance so as not to contaminate him with his own toxic emotions. Then, remembering how Laxman had drawn a protective circle around Sita in the *Ramayana*, he started to do the same: with his right hand and his eyes he drew a protective circle around the baby, thus creating a protective cocoon; he made a wish – that nothing would enter to hurt the little one, that the innocent child would be protected from any repercussions of his young uncle's folly. Then he whispered his name: Baldoon.

Taking leave of his wife, he also found himself keeping a distance, but she leant forward and took his hand and said, '*Rab Rakha*' ('God keep you'). At that moment he could have broken down, but Gulaam at the door called to say the *tonga* was loaded and they must leave.

Behari had managed to remain outwardly composed, but once seated in the private compartment in the moving train, images rushed towards him and flashed by in dizzying succession, changing like the landscape from the moving train ... he saw his mother needing to be comforted, his father needing to be reassured, Madan needing to be rescued, Bhajan needing to be supported, moments of their life flashing by, disturbing images, turbulent emotions, regrets, misgivings, fears encircled, he felt responsible, burdened, helpless ...

Gulaam handed him a glass of water. Handing back the empty glass he thought of his wife, her touch, her blessing, *Rab Rakha*. And then he thought of his little baby boy, Baldoon, and then chanting in the prayer room of the Mool Mantra came gently through into his mind and grew louder: *Ik onkar, Satnam,*

Karta Purak, Nir Bhau, Nir Vair, Akal Moorak, Ajooni, Saibhang, Gurparsaad.

('There is only one God, Eternal truth is his name, He is the creator, without fear, without hate, Immortal beyond form, without birth or death, self-existent, by the Guru's grace.')

And then he wept. And so did his trusted Gulaam.

39.
4 July 1909: The Family in Amritsar

As all the family gathered in Amritsar, Dr Ditta Mal took charge. He hadn't properly registered what had happened; there hadn't been time. All he knew was that he had to take care of things, he had to act, to look out for the family. He had to take the helm and steer everyone through.

The English drawing room and *baithak* had been combined to create as much space as possible. Dr Ditta was dictating telegrams and letters, reading reports and papers, greeting advisers and family – all at the same time. Every so often he would bury his head in his hands and shake it, exclaiming: 'What has this mad son of mine done? Our good friend Sir William and, oh, the good, dear Lady Wyllie. It is all too unbearable. He has definitely gone mad. They can't hang a man who is mad. Can they? No, no, they can't.

'Come here, someone. Take down a telegram:

'**To Bhajan Lal Dhingra**
'REFER MENTAL UNSOUNDNESS FROM CHILDHOOD
'EXPRESS FAMILY ABHORRENCE THROUGH SOLICITOR'

'Send it at once and take down another one:

'**Col. J. R. Dunlop Smith, Private Secretary to H. E. the Viceroy**
'You can imagine the shock I have sustained at this age on reading the news that my son has been the murderer of our esteemed friend.

'The whole family expressed deep abhorrence of the horrible deed of this mad son of mine. He has no doubt shown signs of unsoundness of mind for the past ten years, but I never expected that the cursed India House would prove so much an exciting cause ... I am not quite myself at present and cannot write more.'

Ditta Mal worried about all his sons, and he felt the absence of the two in London acutely. He convinced himself that Madan was of unbalanced mind and that it might save him from the gallows. He also worried about any repercussions of Madan's act for the rest of the family in India. He knew that sometimes family property was forfeited. Behari Lal assured him that the English would act justly, that they had done nothing wrong, that in fact they had a record of loyalty. 'They know us father, Colonel Dunlop Smith has known us for years.'

'That's it. Send another telegram. You and Mohan get ready to go to Simla. I will ask him to see you. Tell him everything, how Madan ran away from home and worked as a lascar. Imagine working as a stoker on a ship! You have to be mad. Tell him about the time that he tried to cut off the whiskers of his landlady's cat. Isn't that it, Kundan?' he turned to his eldest son. 'That is after he arrived in London. Is that a normal way to behave? Tell him all that.'

Col. J. R. Dunlop Smith, Private Secretary to H. E. the Viceroy
'Myself too distressed, but deputing two sons to express abhorrence and give fuller particulars. Could you grant interview Wednesday afternoon?'

Dr Ditta Mal then opened a tin box containing letters, separated into different bundles. He picked out one bundle of five or six letters, tied together with a string, and handed them to Behari Lal. 'These are letters from Sir Curzon Wyllie. Take them with you to Simla.' As Behari took the packet, his father broke into a sob: 'This is too terrible. My son, my mad son, what have you done?'

Ditta Mal regretted having sent him abroad, his wife regretted having left him as a toddler. She placed an oil lamp, a *diva,* in the English drawing room together with a statue of elephant-headed Ganesh, remover of obstacles.

Dunlop Smith replied by return to Dr Ditta's telegram and prepared himself to meet the doctors Mohan Lal and Behari Lal. They had met many times over the years – very pleasant meetings. But he was not looking forward to this one. It was all too terrible, and it involved people he knew on both sides. All decent people. He felt himself to be intimately involved. He quickly wrote to the Criminal Investigation Department saying that he would shortly be sending them a note, as he knew 'all the Dhingra family'. Times like these had to be handled carefully. Here was an instance to demonstrate the even-handedness of British justice.

Mohan Lal and Behari Lal travelled to Simla, hardly able to talk to one another, only just able to hold themselves together. During the interview with Dunlop Smith they broke down, and

Dunlop Smith himself was moved. When they left it was he who felt unable to move and speak.

Colonel Dunlop Smith's rooms in the Viceregal Lodge looked out on to the Himalayas. The sun shining on their snow-covered peaks reflected into the crystal paper-holder and caught the eye of the colonel, inviting his gaze on to the mountain range. He walked up to the window. The mighty mountains. India. He loved India and had devoted his life to its welfare. Just like Wyllie. How had it come to this? He recalled discussions in which people had argued that giving Indians a Western education was as a grave miscalculation ... and this unrest was the outcome. And yet, he thought, the education and intellectual emancipation of India was one of the justifications for British rule. He once again thought of the Dhingras and the note about them that he had to write. He returned to his desk, collected the letters and telegrams from Ditta Mal and wrote...

Demi-official from Col. J. R. Dunlop Smith to Sir H. A. Stuart 8 July 1909

'As promised I send you two copies of my note on the Dhingras ...

'I've known the family for several years. The father, Rai Sahib Ditta Mal, was civil surgeon for a time in Hissar in 1896 when I was Deputy Commissioner of that district.

'He has six sons. I know Dr Mohan Lal, M.D. Medical Health Officer, Amritsar, and Dr Behari Lal, M.D. Chief Medical Officer, Jind State, both very well. They are the joint authors of the *Minto* Health pamphlets, called by permission after the Viceroy.

...

'They came to see me and gave me the accompanying letter. Both were very much moved and broke down more than once during the interview ...

'They are convinced that the outrage was the result of a conspiracy and that other heads planned it all. He was chosen, they maintain, as a tool because of his curious character.

'The interview was a painful one and I could only ask them to tell their father that I would deliver his message to the Viceroy, who fully sympathised with the family in their terrible position.'

Appendix, Simla, 7 July 1909

From Mohan Lal Dhingra M.D. and Behari Lal Dhingra M.D. To Private Secretary to the Viceroy

'We are the brothers of the ill-fated Madan Lal ... it is a deep irony of fate that in a family like ours, so deeply loyal to the government and so gratefully attached to the British people, a young man should degenerate into a murderer ...

'We are inclined to believe that as he was eccentric and subject to fits of rashness ... he was discovered as an excellent tool for the evil purposes of Krishna Varma and his lieutenants ...

'Madan left for England in May 1906. Our eldest brother Kundan Lal was there and Madan made an exhibition of his eccentricity in London during the first week by attempting to cut the whiskers off the pet cat of the landlady of his lodgings; when remonstrated about it by his brother, he quietly left the house.

'We believe that the real culprits have cleverly kept themselves in the background.

'We shall not consider Madan Lal as a martyr as the extremists would desire; we look upon him as a lunatic (who could not be influenced by the tradition and instincts of the family) and his act as a detestable act.'

40.

1991: The Preserved Body

Somewhere in my mind-store is lodged an image from my Paris childhood, picked up from a film or a play I no longer recall.

The image is of a mime artist simulating walking, bent and burdened with worries and thoughts. Alongside him is a moving backdrop, which denotes time passing, landscapes changing, events surfacing, people pleading attention. But, head bent, he doesn't notice as he trudges along Then, suddenly, a chink of sunlight shoots through and as he looks up to its source, his back straightens, he stands erect and a smile starts to flicker. Above him the clouds start to disperse and reveal a clear blue sky.

I returned from India feeling bent and burdened, with a case full of notes, taped interviews and photos. All weight. No idea what to do with them.

I surveyed my desk, with its three months of dust and the old Post-it stickers becoming unstuck. And then, like steam, the anxieties rose around me. The development money was finite, how long would it last? To go further, I would need to present a proposal, but of what, when I could see no shape or structure or focus or flow? And when that money was gone what would I do? I had some residencies as a writer, but they would only interrupt the work.

And there was my daughter's eighteenth birthday party, for which I'd returned. 'An eighteenth birthday is a milestone, Mummy,' she'd impressed upon me before I left and now she would be back for the half-term with friends to stay. Could I manage upbeat when I felt so blue? Maybe it's just jet lag, I thought, and it will all go away. But it didn't – until my chink of sunlight dispelled it.

My chink of sunlight came, when, five days after my return, Nelson Mandela, holding Winnie's hand, finally walked Free.

I was electrified. I watched it on every news channel, replayed it in my mind to fix it in my store of 'magic moments'. I screamed and danced and sang and wept and celebrated: on my own, down the phone, with friends, on the Heath.

The clouds parted, malevolence melted and the piles on my desk appeared as possibilities. 'The eye altering alters all ...'

Anti-apartheid and CND formed my first forays into teenage activism. And the seeds were sown in Rishi Valley, my school in South India, where every evening after prep our English teacher, Sardar Mohammad would read us chapters from a book, which rounded off our day in a comforting way. One of the books was *Cry, the Beloved Country* by Alan Paton. One time whilst reading, he stopped and lowered his head for a long pause. When he resumed, his eyes were red and he wiped away a tear; I felt the pain and injustice and wiped away my own tears and later in London supported and leafleted for the boycott of South African goods.

❀

One evening I returned to two messages on my answerphone:

'Martin here. Just to say, I have managed to find some information on Bhajan Lal, your Sufi uncle. So give me a ring when you are back.'

A second, from Ann, said: 'I have found some very interesting information for you from Pentonville. Give me a ring.

I had met Ann following a reading and talk I had given at the Commonwealth Institute some months earlier.

After the talk, I was sitting at a table signing books and noticed a woman from the corner of my eye standing there holding my book and waiting. I attracted her attention and invited her over, but she gestured she'd to like to wait. When the other people had gone she came to the table.

'I was waiting so I could get to talk to you. You won't know me, but we were at the same school, St Chris, in Letchworth. Of course, I was in my last year in seniors and only saw you around. But I knew your sister, Gita, and when I saw the book and the name, and then I saw Paris and Partition, I realized it must be you. So I bought it and read it in one go and so loved it that I called the publishers and they told me about this event. And here I am.'

We went out for a coffee and talked of our respective lives since school and shared news and she told me that she worked at Pentonville Prison.

'Oh my God, that is just so amazing!' I said. I then told her about my research, about Madan Lal, the execution at Pentonville, the exhumation and the 'D' notice. I asked if she could find out about it for me.

❁

We would now be meeting for lunch, after several months. I had arrived early.

'Right,' said Ann, sitting down. 'Lovely to see you and I hope your trip to India was successful.'

'Thank you,' I replied.

'Okay, now. First the bad news. Which is that I couldn't find out anything about 'D' notices. I don't think they come in the jurisdiction of the prison. But the good news is that I can tell you about the exhumation, and the information I have is from an absolutely reliable source.'

She pulled out a large manila envelope. 'I've also brought some information about Pentonville Prison for you to have a look at. Just to give you a sense of the place and its history. So that's for you to keep and look at your leisure.'

We ordered our food and wine and with a glint in her eye she started ...

'My source worked at Pentonville Prison in the 1970s and remembered the Indian exhumations very clearly. He said there were two of them, a couple of years apart. Is that right?'

I nodded.

'He said that exhumations always take place at night.' Ann sipped her wine. 'The prison community is volatile and highly charged, and they want to create as little disturbance as possible. At least that's the reasoning. What used to be the burial yard is now covered with grass and there are no marked graves.'

'Then how do they know where to look?'

'Oh, they were all very clearly logged and recorded as to the exact placement.'

'It seems that when they opened the coffin, they found that the body had remained preserved.'

'Preserved? How?'

'They sprinkled lime so as to hasten the decomposition, but in fact the lime created a cocoon around the body that preserved it.'

'Good heavens.'

'Yes. He said it was rather extraordinary. He was there, but that he can't talk about it on film because of the Official Secrets Act. He no longer works at the prison. But he still can't talk about it.'

'Would he meet me?'

'No. But he was happy for me to tell you. Oh yes. He also said that the Indians got the idea of the "exhumation" from the Irish.' Ann smiled. 'Being three-quarters Irish myself, I liked that.'

'What do you mean? Explain.'

'Well Sir Roger Casement, one of the leaders of the Easter Uprising of 1916 was executed at Pentonville and the Irish wanted his body repatriated. Every year on the anniversary of his death, a lone piper would circle around the walls of the prison at night playing the pipe ... until sometime in the 1960s, his remains were exhumed and returned to Ireland.'

'Sir Roger Casement, the lone piper, the preserved body.' I said grappling with the images. 'You know they used to call themselves the Indian Sinn Féinists.'

'Really? I like that, too. Well, they were both colonies fighting the British Empire.'

'Yes, and it was mostly the Irish MPs who would raise questions about India in Parliament. India had no representation.'

'Have you been to Pentonville?

'No. Not yet,' I replied, realizing that the prison didn't even feature on my list of places to visit. Why hadn't I given it a sticker, I wondered. 'I'll go tomorrow.'

'And how's your work going?'

'Slowly. India was confusing, with ever-widening horizons. I need more time. I have submitted an application to the British Academy and if I get funding, then that will buy time for me.'

'When will you know?'

'Soon. And I'm doing some short residencies for an Arts Council project called, "Artists in Education for a Multicultural Society".'

We decided to keep in touch and went our separate ways.

The next day, in the morning, I took the Overground to the Caledonian Road and walked up it to visit the prison – and very nearly missed it. There was no sign saying 'prison', just a well-maintained, nondescript building behind a raised forecourt – and a plaque with HMP Pentonville. It could have been an institution of any kind, although the enormous Gothic gate might be a give-away. Beside the gate was a door with policemen going in and out jangling keys. They smiled at me as they passed.

I wondered which gate they had brought Great Uncle Madan through. Then I wondered if he'd come in horse-drawn carriage or one of the early motor cars. Was he shackled? What was he feeling, thinking?

The insult of Empire. With imperial disregard they denied you a cremation, suppressed your statement, buried your story and tried to silence your name. You challenged and defied them – in life, in death and even after death.

Dear Uncle Madan, the great uncle I never knew, younger brother to the grandfather I never knew, who was the father of my own beloved father who got left behind on the platform at the

Gare du Nord when I came to London, the city where you died and where I now live.

I was crying as I walked into a café. They smiled at me kindly. Maybe thinking I'd come from visiting someone in the jail.

The book Martin had located for me was a slim volume in Indian English called *First Indian Martyr to be Executed at Pentonville*. By B. S. Maighovalia. I read in it:

'Introduction
The celebrated Dhingra family enjoyed a unique social status in the erstwhile United Punjab. The following pedigree-table will lend support to my contention for the convenience of the reader.'

It went on to list each of the eight children of Rai Sahib Dr Ditta Mal, all Doctors, Lawyers:

'(8) The youngest son of Dr Sahib Ditta Mal was Mr Bhajan Lal Dhingra, Bar-at-Law. He was in London during the trial of Madan Lal Dhingra. After his return to India, he practised for some time in the Amritsar Bar. Later on he shifted to Lahore, discarded his lucrative practice for all times to come, having become a disciple of a famous Muslim divine, Pir Lasuri Shah, and was installed at the Gaddi on the demise of this pious saint at Lyallpur (West Pakistan). He is alleged to have renounced the world, got himself enshrined in a small tomb with a small opening where he used to take morning tea, and become isolated from kith and kin. Ultimately he was buried in the same tomb which he had selected in his lifetime, for the purposes of "counting the beads of rosary" in the meditation of "Allah".'

I read the entry a couple of times as I remembered my meeting with Litto Ghosh in her little first floor flat in Bengali Market and that I had a cassette recording which then listened to my return home:

'I remember Bhajan Lal very well, even though I only met him that one time. He made a huge impact. My meeting him set the direction of my life: my going to Gandhiji's ashram at seventeen, setting up the women's wing of the student movement, the work in the Bengal famine, the Communist Party, all started because of my chance meeting with Bhajan Lal.

'My older sister, Kamala, had married into the Dhingra family. I had lost my mother, and had come to live with my sister and brother-in-law whilst I finished my schooling. Bhajan Lal was my brother-in-law's uncle. One day, he just appeared at our house and stayed for about three or four months ... in those days we had big houses and servants so it was not unusual for a family member to just arrive. He was a special guest, already a recluse, known as a wise man ...

I was aged fourteen at the time. He saw me and asked that I should be the one to serve him. This was quite something ... So, before going to school I would take him his small breakfast and in the evening I'd take him his tiffin and I often would eat with him. He would talk, tell me things, listen to me, ask me things. He talked in a way that a fourteen-year-old could understand ... He lived very simply, eating only one main meal a day. He always wore a white pyjama kurta. He never handled money, a young disciple who travelled with him took care of all those things but otherwise he was very normal. One day I came back from school and he had gone. Sometime later his disciple came and collected his things.

But things completely changed for me. I became a vegetarian, started to think deeply about things and decided I'd go to Gandhiji's ashram. I had to train myself. I was used to comfort so I stopped turning on the fan at night. I started washing my own clothes, cleaning my own room, then when I finished my schooling, I left my comfortable home to go and live frugally and work in the ashram. It was a very unusual thing to do.'

'I was told you were quite notorious'

Litto laughs: 'Yes I suppose I was once. When I was in the women's defence league. Women were expected to be compliant. But we wanted to change things. We wanted women to have a voice. I never meant to be notorious. I just wanted to be sincere, to be myself, be independent. I married out of class, caste, community. I married a Bengali communist! And everything unfolded from meeting Bhajan Lal – because he helped me to find my own way, my self - my purpose … When I think of Bhajan Lal it is always with great gratitude.'

Lyallpur, I learned, and was in the development known as the Canal Colonies, land reclaimed for cultivation through the extension of irrigation canals from the rivers. It was named after its founder, Sir James Lyall, Lt. Governor of the Punjab, who used the Union Jack as the model for the bazaar, a central clock tower with radiating avenues around it, each for a different trade. Lyallpur had been renamed Faisalabad and was the industrial centre of Pakistan. How would I get to there?

Soon my mother returned, a bit battered from her India ordeal. But even though she travelled on the cheapest airlines, with changes and waits, she never seemed to have any jet lag and just fell into her regular routine: waking early for her walk to commune with nature, returning for her bath, then her prayers and finally I would hear a gentle clatter in my kitchen and know it was eight o'clock. Although she had her own kitchenette on the floor below, she preferred using mine, which was stocked and maintained.

While delving into libraries to learn about a colonial period I hadn't experienced, it occurred to me to ask my mother how she had found out that India was colonised.

'Oh, I remember it very well,' she started, 'It was at the end of the First World War. I was seven years old and had gone with my aunt and an uncle for a walk in the Lawrence Gardens. We often did that. That evening the gardens were all lit up, people were dressed in nice clothes, there were fireworks and it was a celebration.

'"What's happening?" I said to my aunt. "It isn't Divali yet, so why are there all these lights and fireworks?"

'And she said that it was because the war was over.

'So I said: "Who won the war?"

'And she said: "The English did."

'So I asked: "But if the English won the war, why are we celebrating?"

'My aunt squeezed my hand and told me to be quiet.

'Now I was confused. I'd overheard grown-ups discussing how it might be better for India if the English didn't win the war and how we could never know the truth because the news came to us from Reuters, which was their version, so we could not be sure. So I insisted and said: "It might not be true that the English won, it might be just Reuters telling us that. We don't want the English to win, do we?"

'"Quiet," she said. "Don't say these things. Someone might hear you and we'll get into trouble."

'So I said: "Why?"

'Then she whispered to me: "Because the English are our rulers and if you say things they don't like, they can put you into prison."

'I was shocked. I didn't enjoy the fireworks and said I wanted to go home. And then the next year there was the massacre Jallianwallah bagh in Amritsar.'

We were walking together on Hampstead Heath. My mother was launched on her memories. 'Then, when I was in college they hanged Bhagat Singh and he was a great hero. We all cried and he was inspired by Madan Lal.'

'How do you know?'

'Asaf Ali told me. He was one of Bhagat Singh's defence lawyers. Later he became Indian ambassador in Berne and I stayed with him for a few days and that's when he told me. He also told me that he'd met Madan Lal in London.'

'Oh, I forgot,' I said. 'I haven't told you. I met someone who works at Pentonville Prison where Madan Lal was hanged and she said that when they exhumed the body, they found that it had remained preserved.'

'*Accha*? What does that mean?'

I explained about the lime creating a cocoon and doing the opposite of what it was meant to do.

'So, when we did the cremation in Amritsar, the whole body was there.'

'That's what I was told. You could say it was waiting.'

'That's very good. All Hindus want to be cremated and have their bones put in the Ganga.' We walked along and she said in Punjabi: 'They say you are reborn where you die.'

'Who is this "they"?' I asked.

My mother chuckled. '"They" usually means no-one.'

'So if "they" are right, Madan Lal would be reborn as an Englishman.'

'And your father reborn as a Frenchman.'

We both laughed. My mother had often said she would like to die in India, so after walking for a while I asked: ' How would you feel if you were reborn in England?'

'All right,' replied my mother. 'English people are very kind. In India we used to be in awe of them, but when I came here I found them to be very kind, very helpful and trusting.' She added: 'When I left Paris to bring you to London, your father said to me: "When you get to England you'll find that English people are very reserved and very difficult to get to know. But once you have an English friend, you have a friend for life!"'

'Well Papa had his friends for life didn't he?'

'And you, too. You've got Ginny and Soo and Marcus, too, and others, haven't you?'

'Why didn't you make a home in England?' I asked.

My mother turned on me. 'How could I make a home in England if my husband was in Paris?' she replied with a frown and sharp glance. It felt like a reprimand. And I felt like a child asking too many questions. And not knowing what questions to ask.

We walked on together, in our separate worlds, and then my mother said: 'I lived in Paris more than twenty years. Your father loved entertaining. But since the flat was so small, we'd have picnics in the Bois de Boulogne and go boating in the moonlight. And every Sunday I'd go to the Marché.'

'And the man who knew Madan Lal, did you see him again? Did he tell you more?'

'*Only he who could keep his hand on the candle for the longest would do it.*' He told us that. I went with your father once to his house in the rue de Voh-jee-rah.'

I laughed at her pronunciation. She smiled.

41.

JULY 1909: BRIXTON PRISON

When Madan Lal was taken to Brixton Prison, he found he was often able to access that blessed calmness he had felt when preparing to do the deed and this reinforced the sense that he was fulfilling his purpose, his *dharma*, his assigned path and duty.

He received letters from Koregaonkar and other comrades, wanting to visit, informing him of offers to defend him, of funds being raised and the fallout from his actions.

The letters told him about meetings of condemnation that were being held. The first had been on the day after he'd been brought to Brixton and the second the day after, on 4 July, a large meeting at Caxton Hall, where in a packed hall speech after speech voiced condemnation. He read that Bhajan had been dragged onto the platform in tears, unsteady on his feet, and instructed to condemn Madan – but had been unable to utter a sound, as his voice was gone and he was totally overwhelmed with emotion. Mr Thorburn, who had dragged him up, then raised Bhajan's arm and spoke for him and requested his assent, but Bhajan's tears blinded him and he did not know what he was being called upon to do. He then stumbled and had to be helped off the platform.

He also heard that when the motion of condemnation was going to be passed unanimously, Savarkar had stood up and shouted 'No', that a scuffle had followed whereupon Savarkar was punched and thrown out of the hall.

Madan appreciated the gesture but also felt troubled, shook his head and said softly: 'Oh *Tatya*, I hope you have not been foolhardy.'

When Savarkar came to see him and brought him some fresh collars, Madan saw the scratches and bruises on his face and reprimanded him, to which Savarkar said that he could not let a unanimous condemnation pass. Never. He also told him about the offers made for his defence, money raised, and that a trial with a defence might be further publicity for the cause.

Madan shook his head. He felt himself guided by a greater force.

'No. I know what is required of me and what I have to do. Twice I didn't take the last shot. In the shooting gallery and again in the hall. I put the pistol to my ear, but it was not armed and then it was too late. My sixth shot is to stand trial, on my own, get my statement read in the court and then reported in the press. I will defend myself.'

They looked at each other, digesting together the full import of the moment. Savarkar then stood up, still not taking his eyes off Madan. Madan also rose and when he did, Savarkar, with the guards looking on, bent down and touched Madan's feet. Madan raised him up and gave him a look that said: 'You will see. I will not flinch.'

Savarkar said softly: 'You are my teacher now. I will never, ever forget you. Nor will our Motherland. Never.'

The following day there came a note from Mr Pollen, requesting an audience and offering to defend him for free. Madan remembered the address he had given in Caxton Hall with irritation and resentment, and then those feelings dissipated. He agreed to see him and prepared what he might say: 'Your Queen's Great Proclamation of 1858, Indians saw as their Magna Carta. All the promises were broken. How they were led to believe that after the rapacious East India Company, there would be consultation and cooperation but all that had happened was continuing plunder, leaving Indians ever impoverished. Use your efforts to rectify that and see that promise is fulfilled. I do not want anyone to defend me. I will not be a mendicant or supplicant pleading for your justice from a court which has no legitimacy and I do not recognise.'

But when Mr Pollen came, Madan Lal just said: 'Thank you for your offer. But I have decided I will conduct my own defence.'

Mr Pollen protested that it might not be wise, that if he changed his mind …

'I will not change my mind,' Madan interrupted – and stood up, to indicate the interview was over. Mr Pollen looked at him, with an expression that validated for Madan that what Englishmen respected was violence. Mr Pollen then held out his hand.

The night before the trial, Madan saw himself in the court and his statement being read and willed himself to sleep. And he slept.

H.M. PRISON, BRIXTON, 22 July 1909
MEMORANDUM. REG. 9493 MADAR LAL DHINGRA

'This man has been in Hospital under my close supervision and observation since his reception here on 2 July 1909. I have seen him every day, and have had several prolonged interviews with him, the last this morning. (Thursday 22 July.)

'His general health is very fair, and he tells me that, with the exception of occasional but slight attacks of Malaria when in India, he has always had good health.

'He is well educated, and of an intellectual type, somewhat reticent in conversation, and retiring in manner.

'He eats and sleeps well, converses quite rationally and sensibly on all topics, has behaved generally in quite a sane and normal manner, and during the time he has been under my care he has shown no signs or symptoms of insanity.'

S. R. Dyer, M.D. Medical Officer

42.

1909/1991: The Old Bailey

23 July 1909. I looked down the index of the trials for July 1909 sessions. There had been eleven trials on 23 July covering: 'fraud', 'carnal knowing', 'robbery with violence', 'housebreaking', 'larceny', 'seditious libel' and 'murder'.

The last two, which were heard by the Lord Chief Justice, were also loosely connected: the trial for 'seditious libel that preceded that of Madan was that of Arthur Horsley, printer of *The Indian Sociologist*, who was being prosecuted for printing an article written by Shyamji Krishna Varma. It earned him four months imprisonment. (The next issue of *The Indian Sociologist*, printed in Paris, hailed him as the first Briton to go to jail for the cause of India.)

Madan Lal, misspelt as Madar Lal, was also a first.

'On being called upon to plead to the indictment for the "wilful murder" of Sir W. H. Curzon Wyllie, the prisoner said, "First of all I would say that these words cannot be used with regard to me at all. Whatever I did was an act of patriotism and justice which was justified. The only thing I have to say is in the statement, which I believe you have got."

They brought me into the courtroom and sat me in the dock. I was glad to sit down as they had taken away my shoelaces and my boots did not feel right. Vinayak had brought me some clean collars and I was grateful for that. I looked around the courtroom. There was not a single brown face there other than mine. Indians had not been allowed to attend.

The Clerk of Arraigns: 'The question is whether you plead "Guilty" or "Not Guilty"...'

Prisoner: 'According to my view I will plead "Not Guilty".'

'Asked if he had any counsel to defend him, the prisoner replied that he had not.'

I remembered my dream, remembered Vinayak's visit the day before, and conjured up in my mind and in my feelings the meaning, the purpose, the cause, the Motherland.

Mary Harris. 'I reside at 108 Ledbury Road, Bayswater, and the accused lodged with me since Easter last. He was very regular in his habits. He generally came home at 7 o'clock and had dinner. He was very steady ...'

Henry Stanton Morley. 'I am the proprietor of a shooting range at 92 Tottenham Court Road. About three months ago the prisoner commenced to frequent the range for revolver practice; he attended two or three times a week ... He took a lot of care in his shooting and acquired considerable proficiency. On 1 July about 5.30 p.m. he was at the range and I saw him fire twelve shots at a target of 18 feet.' (The target was shown to the Jury; there were eleven hits.)

One by one their witnesses came up, the policemen, the witnesses from the Jehangir Hall, the doctor. It was all the same things being said again as had been said before, at the other court. Every so often they asked if I had any questions. As far as I was concerned the whole thing was a question! It was all a big act of theirs, masquerading as justice. Whose justice?

'This concludes the case for the prosecution.'

The Lord Chief Justice *(addressing the prisoner): 'Do you wish to give evidence in the box or say what you have to say there?'*

Suddenly it was all over, and I was being addressed.

Prisoner: *'I have nothing to say. I admit that I did it. This evidence is all true. I should like my statement read.*

'I do not want to say anything in defence of myself, but simply to prove the justice of my deed. As for myself, no English court has got any authority to arrest and detain me in prison or pass sentence of death on me.'

That was not the statement! That was what I said in the police court when they confiscated my original statement. They were reading the wrong statement! It was strange to hear my words in someone else's voice.

'That is the reason why I do not have any counsel to defend me. And I maintain that if it is patriotic in an Englishman to fight against the Germans if they were to occupy his country, it is much more justifiable and patriotic in my case to fight against the English. I hold the English people responsible for the murder of eighty millions of my countrymen in the last fifty years ... for taking away £100,000,000 every year from India to this country ... for the hanging and deportations of my countrymen ...

'Just as the Germans have no right to occupy this country, so the English have no right to occupy India. I am surprised at the terrible hypocrisy, force and mockery of the English people, when they pose

as champions of oppressed humanity – as the people of Congo and the people of Russia, when there is terrible oppression and horrible atrocities committed in India, for example, the killing of two million people every year and the outraging of our women.

'I am a patriot working for the emancipation of my Motherland. Whatever else I have to say is in my statement, which is in the court.

'I wish the English people should sentence me to death for, in that case, the vengeance of my countrymen will be all the more keen. I put forward this statement to show the justice of my cause to the outside world, especially to our sympathisers in America and Germany.'

The Lord Chief Justice: *'Do you wish to say anything more?'*

Prisoner: *'There is another statement of foolscap paper.'*

The Lord Chief Justice: *'If there is anything you wish to say to the jury, say it now.'*

Prisoner: *'It was taken from my pocket among other papers.'*

The judge straightened himself up and raised his head so as to be able to look at me as imperiously as he could, to intimidate me. All a big act.

The Lord Chief Justice: *'I don't care what was in your pocket; the question of what you have written before has got nothing to do with this case. If you wish to say anything to the jury in defence of yourself, say it now. Do you wish to say anything more?'*

Prisoner: *'No.'*

The Clerk of Arraigns: *'Prisoner at the bar. You stand convicted ... have you anything to say why the Court should not give you judgment of death according to Law?'*

I realised that they were not going to allow my statement to be read. So I straightened myself and raised my head and addressed the court.

Prisoner: *'I have told you ... I do not acknowledge the authority of the court. You can pass sentence of death on me. You white* *people are all powerful now, but we shall have our turn in time to come ...'*

When he put on his black hood and told me I should hang by neck till I was dead, it all felt completely unreal. What was death? It felt like a charade, but I still had to fulfil my destiny. The prison guards moved to take me away, but I hadn't finished. I turned to the judge and said: 'Thank you, My Lord. I am proud to have the honour of laying down my life for the cause of my Motherland.' As they took me away, I looked around at the courtroom and tried to walk as best I could without my shoelaces.

Mr Tindal Atkinson, K.C.: 'My Lord, I have been instructed to watch this case on behalf of the family of the man who has just been convicted ... I am instructed to say on behalf of the father of this man and the rest of the family that there are no more loyal subjects of the Empire than they are.'

W. S. Blunt *My Diaries*

'23 July – Dhingra, the slayer of Sir Curzon Wyllie, has been condemned to death, having made no defence beyond a dignified justification of his act as one of political warfare. When the judge, the Lord Chief Justice, had passed sentence on him that he should be hang by the neck until he was dead, "Thank you, My Lord," Dhingra said, "I am proud to have the honour to lay down my humble life for my country."

'No Christian martyr ever faced his judges more fearlessly or with greater dignity. I discussed his case with Khaparde, who is here for the weekend, his first country visit in England. He is full of admiration, as I am, for Dhingra's courage. We agreed that if India could produce five hundred men as absolutely without fear she would achieve her freedom. It was recorded in the medical evidence at the trial that, when arrested, Dhingra's pulse beat no quicker than normal, nor from first to last has he shown any sign of weakening.'

45.

23 July 1909: Pentonville 3 – Pentonville Prison

From the Old Bailey I was taken to Pentonville. In the carriage, I could feel the turbulence building up inside me, a constriction in my stomach and in my chest. The trial had hardly started before it was over. And my statement! I wanted to scream, to bang my fists against something. I was upset. Upset about my statement and upset that they had managed to undermine me so that I couldn't remember it. They were just trying to blot me out. If I had accepted the offer of a counsel – Dr Pollen had offered to defend me – maybe my statement would have been read?

But I was not going to scream. I would not give them any more satisfaction. The carriage was rocking and I put my mind on that. I listened to the horse's hooves and closed my eyes.

'What is everlasting in this world? All things rise and fall.' I put my mind on my breathing and observed my belly rise and fall.

At the prison they took away all my clothes and gave me a number. As I changed into the prison clothes provided I calculated that I had spent twenty-three days in Brixton Prison and wondered how many days I would spend in Pentonville. To prepare myself for a final voyage, where they couldn't touch me anymore.

In the cell, once they had bolted me in, I felt the turbulence rising once again, waiting to burst forth. Then I cried, the tears streaming down my face. I sobbed and I remembered.

I remembered the silence in the hall when I put the revolver to my head and clicked and it didn't fire. Then came the sobbing. I wasn't prepared for that, the widow's grief, the sobbing. You were never the intended victim. But we are all victims of an unhealthy, unwholesome, unacceptable relationship that has damaged us all.

'Poor in wealth and intellect, a poor son like myself has nothing to offer the mother but his blood and so I have sacrificed the same on her altar.'

I remembered when we were composing the statement that I had felt so at peace. 'Oh mother! I vowed you unflinching devotion. Help me to fulfil myself.' So many images flooded my mind before I could even grasp them.

'Madan Baba, this time you are going properly, like the son of a noble house.'

I saw Ratan Kaka. The courtyard. The boxes, 'Wanted on Voyage', 'Not Wanted on Voyage.'

What about this voyage? What did I want and not want on this voyage?

Criminal Intelligence Office

Note. A. B. Barnard 29/7 – 'According to a London telegram to *The Pioneer*, the 17 August has been fixed for the execution of Madan Lal Dhingra ... The body will most probably be cremated and we do not want the ashes of this "martyr" sent to India by parcel post.'

44.
1909: BHAJAN LAL

From Director of Criminal Intelligence,
Simla, 13 July 1909

'The Scotland Yard report received last mail stated that Bhajan Lal Dhingra attended a meeting of the London Indian Society at which the action of the Benchers towards Vinayak Savarkar was discussed. My weekly reports contain many references to this society. It has been entirely captured by the Extremists and is now a dangerous organisation. If the Dhingra family don't take any action, Bhajan Lal may follow in Madan Lal's footsteps. I have asked Colonel Dunlop Smith who has an intimate acquaintance with some of the family to warn them of the undesirable connection which Bhajan Lal seems to be forming in London.'

23 July 1909

There was a glorious sunset, a bloodshot sky of crimson and gold, as Bhajan walked up the Caledonian Road, his pace steady and his eyes looking down. When he raised them to look up, however, it was not the glowing skies that caught his gaze but the grim prison walls of Pentonville. He stared at them in disbelief. Was this really happening? Or was it a nightmare? He had asked himself that many times over the last twenty-three days. Twenty-three days in which he had been living in an unreal space, a daze. He felt angry, frustrated, sad, lost and incredibly tired. He had been unable to sleep or eat properly, and just the day before he had received a telegram from his father asking him to get the trial postponed. Have the trial postponed?! How could his father imagine what it was like in London? That here he was not the son of a wealthy and influential man, but just a brown boy, an Indian? To be viewed with suspicion. By landladies, colleges and even in the street.

In any case what could he do? Madan had refused to see him. He had refused all offers of representation. Harish told him that Madan wanted the trial so that his statement could be read out. Then it would be reported in the press and everyone would know.

Bhajan looked at the grey walls and wondered if the air could carry his thoughts over or through them. There was so much he needed to say and to understand. All day he had been flooded with images from their childhood that had replayed in his mind again and again: Amritsar, Simla, Sahiwal, Bombay, London. He had been on his feet all day, first outside the Old Bailey; and then he'd walked through places they'd walked together. But this road was not one that they had shared. Bhajan looked round at its unprepossessing greyness, not enhanced by the glorious glows of the setting sun.

A tram slowed to its stop near the prison gates. Bhajan, who had previously been standing perfectly still, suddenly sprang forward and leaped into the carriage just as it was leaving. There would not be time to follow him; even though he knew that they would eventually catch up. For the present at least he was free of them.

In his lodgings Bhajan shut the door, drew the curtains and sat down. He looked across at the chair opposite, in which Madan used to sit. Then the window where he would pull back the curtains to peer into the street below, to see if he had been followed. The room seemed to fill again with his presence. On his desk was the book of Shelley's poetry.

He remembered Madan had been standing by the window, looking out. The light had caught his face as he turned and said, 'You know, Bhajan, If I truly believed that my death, the sacrifice of my life, could help to deliver our Motherland from this intolerable servitude, I'd pray that I would have the courage to do it – to give my life.'

'The ego needs to be surrendered.'

'But of course. I know that.'

As Bhajan remembered and saw his brother's face and the look in his eyes he felt the knot of a howl in his belly wanting to be let out. But how? And where could it go? And where could he go? Maybe even now he was being watched. Where did they think he could go? He suddenly felt cold. It was July, why should he feel cold? He went to his wardrobe and took out the Austrian coat and put it on and then, wrapping it around his face and head, he curled up on the bed and wept and wept and wept and then, finally, slept.

45.

17 AUGUST 2019: *DOCTOR WHO*, PARTITION, 110TH ANNIVERSARY OF MADAN LAL

The time had come to step out of my time travel and attend the event for the 110th anniversary of Madan Lal organised by the Indian Workers Association in Coventry. I arranged to spend a week in London so as to fit in a visit to the National Archives and travel up with Radha, whom I had first met ten years earlier for the centenary celebration of Madan Lal. It was three and half weeks after my mother's death and everything had felt unreal. But we had met up since and I was looking forward to travelling with her.

'I watched that *Doctor Who* programme about the Partition. I thought it very powerful and effective,' said Radha when we were settled in the train.

'Well, doing it was certainly very powerful and effective for me. But since then I've been told that this is a technique they use in neuro linguistic programming – you project onto an imaginary screen a trauma or behaviour pattern, watch yourself in it and this distancing enables you to change the narrative.'

'Well, if only we could change the narrative of Partition.' Radha sighed. 'When did you come to London?'

'I came two days ago on the 15th. Independence Day. And today, the 17th, is 'Partition' day – the day the actual boundaries were revealed.'

'Well,' Radha said, 'if you had taken the bus and gone the other way you would have run into the demonstration outside the Indian High Commission protesting about the revocation of Article 370 in Kashmir. The BJP government did that ten days ago – another continuing legacy of the unresolved issues of Partition. A recurring narrative – Pakistan, Bangladesh, Khalistan, Kashmir. And the Indian government is as high-handed as the imperial one was.'

'I know. And none of the repressive legislation of Empire has been revoked.'

'As a nation, we have never addressed Partition,' says Radha.

'So we repeat it?'

'It festers. There has never been a national conversation about it and there should have been. We needed to talk about it as human beings. South Africa had truth and reconciliation. What did we ever do? A few months after Partition there was a war with Kashmir.'

'My mother's favourite cousin died in that war.'

'Our national motto is *Satyamev Jayate:* Truth alone prevails. But the truth has never been addressed. When things don't get addressed they become subterranean, creating a sort of malaise. A nether zone into which divisive forces like the RSS/BJP can muscle in and take root – as they have done.'

I think about it and say: 'It seems to me that from the start there were lots of competing narratives and an incompetent imperial power past caring.'

'*What do you say in a country with 33 million Gods?*' I close my eyes to catch that memory from thirty-five years earlier: the words are those of J. Krishnamurti, the philosopher whose school, Rishi Valley, I attended at thirteen and where I heard of Madan Lal, and now, with a view to sending my daughter there, I am in Madras, attending a talk of Krishnaji. People are going up to him, touching his feet, he is objecting: 'Please sir, please, no need for that,' he keeps saying, but they all just smile and take no notice. The question, too, is received with nods of agreement and all are smiling to be in the presence of the 'reluctant' sage. Krishnaji looks over the gathering and sighs, 'Well, with so many gods they can at least play together and have fun.' The audience all smile and roll their heads in agreement. Krishnaji speaks with an English accent, having been adopted as a child by the Theosophists and brought up in England. Memory captured, I smile and open my eyes.

'You tired?' asks Radha.

'No, no. just catching memories. I have these voices in my head, that sort of descend upon me.'

Radha smiles and asks: 'Have you prepared something for the meeting?'

'I thought I'd like to express my debt of gratitude to the IWA in that it was meeting them that spurred my quest to find out about Madan Lal. That I feel moved and affected by their commitment to his memory. That he was a hero of the Indian people, not the Indian elite. Although he came from a privileged background, he had a wider experience of life and struggle. He'd worked at a stoker, been out to sea, knew ordinary working people, used to visit the sailors' home in the East End and finally sacrificed his all for the cause and what he saw as the greater good: Indian Independence! That it feels right that they should be the ones who honour him and I am deeply touched that they include me. Something like that.

'And if I stumble or get timid I will read from the manuscript – I have a short scene of his confinement in Pentonville and another when I address his photograph.'

'You won't get timid. How's the book coming along?'

'It's coming steadily. Sometimes a bit slow. I'm exhuming old "selves", reliving what was, at times, a painful journey for me, my family, my ancestors, my country, trying to break through layers of voices, silences, censoring and self-censoring.'

'Censoring?'

'Yes. I've been trying to understand why I let the manuscript lie for so long and the knot of fear tangled there.' Sensing the knot, I stop. And then continue: 'You know in *Doctor Who* I struck a rich and resonant vein, which keeps unfolding. Not only did it liberate me from an inherited trauma, which I find extraordinary, but the whole image of time travel, Time Lord, in my case Time Lady, trying to set things to right, to restore, rescue, offered a powerful, enabling, creative device. It's difficult to explain, it manifests as I go along and I hope it works.'

Kali is the goddess of time and the fifty-two skulls around her neck are the fifty-two letters of the Sanskrit alphabet and when they are all said together they make the primal sound of OM.

'At the end of May, two and a half months ago I had reached a difficult point in my manuscript: it is 1989, I meet a cousin who tells me she met Savarkar before Independence who told her of his admiration for Madan Lal. That he was president of the Hindu Mahasbha and had written a book called *Hindutva*, which the previous month had been adopted by the BJP. At the time I do not understand what any of this means, later I learn a bit more – but in the present I have some emails waiting to be read entitled "Savarkar", so I step out of my time travel into the now and read the mails, which tell me that Savarkar is the mentor of Modi, who has just won second term as PM on a dubious platform of resentment, hate and lies and I feel uncomfortable that they appropriated Madan Lal.'

'Not only Madan Lal,' Radha interrupted, 'they've appropriated Bhagat Singh, the great hero, who was a socialist and they don't like socialists. They've appropriated Ambedkar, who wrote the Indian Constitution and would never have supported them at all and at the same time they don't like him because he was a Buddhist. They've even appropriated Gandhi, whom they hate because he was a pacifist. And Sardar Patel, who was a Congress Freedom fighter and they don't like Congress.

'The RSS, to which Modi belongs, never fought for Independence, they were stooges of the colonialists. And they have the gall to appropriate all the folk heroes as they haven't got any of their own at all.'

'I once heard the RSS described as the Hindu Nazis!'

'Well, they've always been open in their admiration for Hitler and they sing from the same song sheet. It's a mindset imported from European nationalism, nothing indigenous about it.'

'Aren't we all just still caught up in the colonial and postcolonial narratives? I find it confusing and complex. Even the little bit that I am trying to make sense of.

'When I shut my computer two days ago before coming down here, I had reached a scene in which, once again, Savarkar was looming. The scene was December 1991: I was in Delhi, with my aunt, telling her that the young Savarkar in London who was Madan Lal's friend, had an inclusive view of India, a place enriched by its assimilation of diversity. I explained that in London he had Muslim friends and it seemed odd that he evolved into a virulent anti-Muslim fanatic. And that I wondered, had something happened when he was incarcerated in the Andamans? Could he have made a deal with the British to let him out in return for his sowing divisions in support of the Empire? There was a fellow revolutionary called Harish Koregaonkar who had given the evidence that convicted Savarkar and that I had a feeling about it. And my aunt had said she didn't know, but these sort of things did things did happen.'

'But it did happen,' interrupted Radha. 'Your "feeling" was right. He did make a deal. He sold out, became their man. The RSS worked for the British. During the "Quit India" movement, Savarkar was telling people to join the Army and fight for them. It's all out now. All his pleading mercy letters were all made available in 2015 or something. You can find them online even. He might have been a freedom fighter in London, but he wasn't back in India. He wrote about being a "prodigal son" wanting to return to the parental embrace of the British government or some such thing. It's all there in the open now. Okay, you can understand wanting to get out of that awful jail, but not ...' Radha shook her head.

We arrived in Coventry into a dull, dank drizzle of a day. Walking down the platform I said: 'You know Radha, I mentioned about censoring. It's a deep conditioning I have, this censoring. And I feel I censored the project, let it lie and nearly die – because of my confusion and ambivalence about the older and rather sinister Savarkar looming behind Madan Lal.'

'I can understand that. And he was Madan Lal's friend. But that was the young Savarkar, before he became ...' Radha shook her head and sighed.

The discussion on the train had left my mind buzzing and I felt bad that I wasn't wholly engaged in the meeting I had travelled up for. But everyone was welcoming, and I was relieved when I was told that the time allocated to me was in the second half after tea. Since the meeting was mostly in Punjabi, which I didn't fully understand, I was able to sit and smile and let my mind wander free. 'Visitor from Foreign', I thought, as I listened to the poetry and songs inspired by Madan Lal. When my slot came, I managed my appreciation of IWA in Hindi and then read from my manuscript in English. Everyone smiled and applauded and in the summing-up expressed their wish that the book be published.

'You know this censoring business can be challenging,' I said to Radha back on the train.

'What are you thinking in particular?' she asked

'Well, when I was writing the scene of Madan's trial, I decided to use the actual trial deposition. They make short shrift of his request for his statement. He's asked if he has anything else to say ...'

'He replies: "I have told you ... I do not acknowledge the authority of the court. You can pass sentence of death on me. You white people are all powerful now, but we shall have our turn in time to come ..."

'And I censored the bit about "you white people", then I felt uncomfortable both about it being there and about editing it out.'

'So you put it back?'

'Yes. I put it back in because I had decided to use the trial deposition itself – to be "truthful". I didn't feel I had the right to censor. But when I was travelling through it and saw it again, I remembered, and I felt that that knot of emotion was still there.'

'Was it not wanting your white friends to feel uncomfortable?'

'I don't know. I haven't really interrogated it. But what I felt was the vulnerability of his situation, being in that court, the only non-white person there because no Indians were allowed to attend, the summary trial, that he's going to be snuffed out and I felt his vulnerability and felt my own. Was I censoring him or censoring myself? I don't know for sure. I feel that it will manifest in time.'

'I'm sure it will. And you are interrogating it now.'

'By the way, thank you for listening and allowing me to spell out my thoughts, as it's really helpful.'

'It's helpful to both of us, Leena. You want to know about contemporary India, which of course I can help with. I was there, it's my experience and so easy to fill you in.'

'Thanks.'

'But for me, I'm a new immigrant and I'm really interested to know your experience and the changes in this landscape.'

I think: I've never really embraced the idea of being an "immigrant", but rather seen myself as a "dislocated" person.

'Also,' continues Radha, 'I'm really glad you are doing this. I think it's important and timely.'

On our return to London I said: 'Are you hungry?'

'Maybe a little.'

Would you fancy going for a masala dosa in Drummond Street? And another story on the way?'

'Yes. Let's go.'

As we walk, I tell her that during my research I had given my contact details to a number of people I met in India, who had then, at various times, contacted me with requests to take them around. Some wanted to visit Highgate Cemetery, others the house in Highgate. And I would take photos of them standing below Marx's head or the Savarkar plaque.'

'There's a Savarkar plaque?' Radha asked.

'Yes. And that's another story. In any case, they all appreciated my help, were very kind and warmed by my connection to Madan Lal. I made some enquiries about how the plaque came into being and at one point was invited on a "London Tour for Indians" which started in Gower Street.'

We stop in front of building in North Gower Street, with a plaque which reads: '*Guisseppe Mazzini. 1805–1872. Italian Patriot lived here.*'

'What's this?'

'This, my dear, is the first stop of the tour of Savarkar's time in London. Here we were informed about how he was inspired by Mazzini and his cult of targeted assassinations and secret societies. That Mazzini set up the Young Italy, while Savarkar set up Young India or Abhinav Bharat. That from Mazzini he also understood that the struggle to gain Independence involved sacrifice and suffering. And that he wrote a book about him. Then the tour went on to University College, where Madan Lal studied and different places connected with Savarkar and other Indian revolutionaries – ending in Pentonville, where we were told the great Hindu hero Madan Lal Dhingra, disciple of Savarkar, was hanged. The guide then recited his "statement".'

As we walked to the restaurant and ordered our dosas, I continued: 'Around those years, it must have been the mid-1990s, after emails started, because I received an email, from I don't know who, telling me to boycott anything Muslim, not use a Muslim shop, a Muslim tradesman, or a Muslim anything – or else the curse of Hanuman would fall on me. I was taken aback, mystified, annoyed, upset and carried these feelings to work the following day, where I was recording a play for the BBC. In the cast was Saeed Jaffrey, a Muslim actor and friend and I unburdened myself to him about this email, whereupon he laughed heartily, gave me a "Muslim hug" and said: "Don't worry, darling. Hanuman wouldn't curse you. He was wonderful and he never cursed anybody. He couldn't. He was just love. Remember how, when he opened his heart all that was in it was love, nothing but love for Ram and Sita." Then he added, "But I think, if I remember rightly someone cursed him."

'"How do you know all that?" I asked

'"Darling. I'm an Indian. I grew up there. And everyone loves Hanuman."'

'That's a nice story,' said Radha, as our dosas arrived.

'I have a headful of stories and disembodied voices, loose ends that dangle around and sometimes drift down. But I suppose we all have that, don't we? In any case around that time, I put my project away in a boxfile. It wasn't a definite decision, just that it felt confusing, acting jobs came and my head filled with other people's lines.'

After a while Radha said: 'Tell me, when you think of Hanuman, how do you see him? What image comes to your mind?'

'Hanuman ... I see the fine Chola bronze at the V&A of Hanuman with his hands outstretched and palms upturned in a gesture of giving or receiving. The statue was the gift to the museum from William Morris, no less. Otherwise, I see him flying in the sky carrying the mountain. My granddaughter composed a song to him when she was five: "*Hanuman, he will fly, in the sky, like the wind and save you. Praise him! Praise him!*"'

'Well nowadays in India he's mostly depicted like a body builder: All muscle and macho. And Modi, too, professes to have a chest of 56 inches.'

'And that's a good thing?'

'Shows he's a he-man.'

'Oh dear,' I reply. 'You know, a few years ago I went to Simla, where the highest point was the spire of Christ Church set against a vista of trees, melting into the sky. And now there's a gigantic statue of Hanuman 100 feet tall, so … you've got this orange head of a monkey sticking out incongruously from the treetops! They probably think it's marvellous, I thought it was bizarre. Hanuman the body builder!' I laugh again.

'People have changed. Society has changed. It's no longer as it was … It's tragic.'

As we walk along to catch our respective public transport, I ask Radha where Gandhi and nonviolence sit in the new India.

'That's a whole new discussion. Get in touch when you come to London again. I would say that there are nonviolent traditions in Jainism and Buddhism, Ashoka's edicts and all that. But India has always been violent. Brahmanism itself is violent. There's physical violence, emotional violence, violence against women, violence of the caste system. Definitely another masala dosa.'

Riding in the bus home I remember another bus ride with my mother when I'd asked her: 'You're not a great admirer of Gandhiji are you, Mama?'

'What rubbish you talk. Of course I am. He was a very great man.'

'Yes, but you don't wholeheartedly admire him like Papa did, do you?'

She smiled and said: 'Your father was a poet.'

'What's that supposed to mean?'

'Well, he was a poet, wasn't he? You're a bit like him.'

I had pursed my lips and looked out of the window.

'Gandhiji felt that there were good Britishers and appealed to them and tried to make them understand, so he took too long, much too long and so Partition happened.'

The bus reached the intersection at Camden and I noticed one going to Highgate and remembered that I'd forgotten to tell Radha the story of the plaque.

46.
1992: THE *URS*

'We don't believe that you just come, we believe
that you are called ...
Your life will now change.'

In the spring of 1992, I received a letter from the Department of
Posts, India, informing me that the commemorative stamp of Shri
Madan Lal Dhingra was ready to be launched. 'We would prefer to
release the stamp either on the date of birth or on the date of death
of the personality.'

I put the letter on my desk and looked out of the window. 'Death
of the personality', I grappled with the words, their meaning, their
mystery:

You are born and then you die and life goes on – it is only the
personality that dies. Death is the opposite of birth. Not of life.

I let the voice pass. So many voices, so many languages, so
many places ...

In the early days of the project, I had envisaged incorporating
the making of the stamp as a sequence in the film. But the script

had been lying in a drawer for the last four months. As I pulled out the file I felt its weight, and the weight of the project.

The previous winter, everything had looked promising. There was the possibility of a co-production; Channel Four was still on board and the Ministry of Information and Broadcasting in Delhi were interested. But on the eve of my departure for Delhi, I learned that Mr Ghose, my contact in the Ministry, had been transferred. As far as India was concerned I was back at square one.

It was a case of one door closing and another unexpectedly opening.

On the plane to Delhi I found myself thinking of Bhajan Lal, wondering how he became a Sufi mystic and how Madan might have affected him. I recalled what Romila had said: 'The Revolutionary and the Mystic – the search for utopia.' But even though I knew the name of the city where the tomb was, I didn't know his Sufi name or how I would ever get to Pakistan.

On my arrival in Delhi, my mother announced excitedly that there was an International Sufi Conference taking place, that she had got me a ticket and I might find out something about Bhajan Lal. Two days later, still jet-lagged, I was sitting in a lecture hall, listening to a Mr Afzal Iqbal from Pakistan delivering the plenary talk on Rumi. Later I sought him out and told him about my quest; when he found out that I was the daughter of his beloved professor from Government College, Lahore, he gave me an enormous hug and said that he would arrange everything I needed to go to Pakistan, including my visa.

'Don't thank me. Have you any idea of the store of goodwill your father has left behind in Pakistan? You can now claim it as your inheritance.'

Ten days later I flew to Lahore with my mother. Our gracious hosts, the Aalams, were also refugees from India – from Lucknow, the aristocratic Moghul city. They received us with great warmth. My mother, delighted to be in the city of her birth, was like a young girl and keen to show me the house she had designed and built and where I had spent the first three years of my life. Its new owner, Mr Batalvi, was a prominent lawyer. He wouldn't, however, return our calls.

Our hosts felt for her, and through their intervention Mr. Batalvi was shamed into making contact. He took us to see the house. On the way he explained that he was no longer living there as the house needed repairs.

My mother whizzed around the house looking happy and explaining her design dilemmas and their resolution. As we left, I noticed on the window ledge a prominently placed pamphlet: 'The Case for Pakistan'.

On the drive back my mother reminded Mr. Batalvi, 'You promised you'd let me have something of mine, either my dancing Shiva or my green Buddha head, I'd be very happy to have anything. You see, I have nothing from my house anymore.'

I was embarrassed and wished I could hide. Then I felt a bit bad and said to my mother: 'It's such a shame that no one thought of picking up any of your things when they left Lahore.'

'Let alone things,' retorted my mother. 'They forgot to pick up my cousin Jamuna biibi from the mental hospital. Imagine! They all went and left her behind.'

Meanwhile contacts in Faisalabad were established. My host, Maqbool Ilahi, had also been a student of my father. With his help we located the *mazaar*, the tomb of Bhajan Lal, known as *Sufi Lal Shah*, found out that the *Urs,* the annual pilgrimage, was on 14 December, and met the family who looked after the tomb. We even found an old woman who remembered him, and as Uncle Maqbool served her tea and sweets she recounted her story: 'Bhajan Lal was a successful barrister who came from a rich Hindu family and the British Raj offered to make him a civil judge, which in those days was a great thing. But he, whom we call Lal Shah, had some difficulty of accepting because of something in his past, so he came to see the Divine Pir Lasuri. As soon as he arrived, the Pir said: "Ah! So you've come at last. I have been waiting for you." And he became a disciple of the Pir. He didn't become a judge and gradually he even left his practice and went to live in the jungle. But I remember him from when I came to live here when I was thirteen; I was married to the grandson of the Pir. We used to all go to the *Urs* in Ajmer. We'd go in four or five carriages. Fakirs and people like us were not allowed to travel first-class. So Lal Shah would book the carriages in advance from his barrister's office and then come to the station in his suit and solar topee. All the doors would be opened and then, fifteen minutes before the train's departure, we would all rush on and fill the first-class compartments. Then we would sing and play music all the way to Ajmer.'

The evening before my departure, the family who took care of the tomb invited us for dinner to their house.

Our host opened a tin trunk and lovingly showed us its treasured contents. There wasn't much – my great uncle's solar topee, a jacket, a handwritten recipe book with items such as 'cinnamon toast', letters, letterheads, notebooks and a little volume of poems by Shelley. While we looked at them he started his story: 'My father was a disciple and looked after the tomb. He asked me to do this when he died. I did it as a son's loving duty. I had been married ten years without issue. People said why not ask at the *mazaar*. But I was not sure that I believed.'

His wife took over the story of how she did believe and went to the tomb and asked for a child and the next year she had a son.

'Now it is no more a loving duty to my father but the joy of our lives.'

'I will be here next year for 14 December.'

'Inshallah,' said Uncle Maqbool.

I looked again at the letter from the Department of Posts. I would write and tell them to arrange a date in late December.

My Pakistani writer friend Rukhsana gave me an introduction in the Pakistan High Commission. The embassy official scrutinised my visa application form.

'You have been here such a long time, why have you not got a British passport? If you had a British passport, you would not need a visa for Pakistan.'

'No, but I would need a visa for India.'

He smiled. 'In Pakistan we allow dual nationality. Will you be travelling alone?'

'No. My daughter is accompanying me. She's British and she needs a visa for India – but not for Pakistan.'

Passports and visas, visas and passports – all my life. As the official went about his business, I thought of the many times I'd almost applied for a British passport, my father encouraging me, my mother ambivalent, all making a noise in my head.

With my Pakistani visa safe in my bag, I started to make my way to collect my daughter's Indian visa from the Indian High Commission. The building was called India House, and as I walked down to the Aldwych towards it, I thought it ironical that it should have the same name.

'For "India House" – see S for Sedition.'

I collected my daughter's visa and returned home, thinking again of passports and visas. I'd never needed a visa for England. Once the man at Heathrow had said 'Welcome home!', even though I was in the queue marked 'Others' rather than 'EU'. I remembered another period when it was 'British' and 'Aliens'. It was in my youth when I would travel back and forth to Paris three times a year, changing my clothes on the crossing. Going home. In Paris I'd arrive in a sari, in London I'd arrive in trousers.

What was that exactly? Home? Was it a place? Was it a feeling?

My daughter Devi and I arrived in Delhi in early December and were whizzed through a line marked 'Unaccompanied Ladies'. We were booked to leave for Pakistan on the 8th, and after a day to recover from the journey I set out to confirm things. I went to my aunt's house for lunch and to use the phone.

'Well, *Leena Rani*, you can forget about your trip to Pakistan,' said my aunt as I entered. And a momentary flash of satisfaction brushed across her mouth

Did I see that? I thought. 'What do you mean?' I said.

'Haven't you heard?' interjected one of my nieces. 'They've broken the Babri Masjid mosque, Aunty.'

My aunt elaborated. 'What, broken?! They climbed on top of it like a swarm and made the whole thing crumble. There's nothing left. Nothing.'

'I don't understand.'

'It's all this Hindutva business, Aunty,' interjected a guest who was sitting there. 'They've been wanting to destroy the Babri mosque for years and build a Ram temple on it.'

'You can forget about your trip to Pakistan. First, they won't give you a ticket; it's much too dangerous. You can't imagine what Partition was like.'

I wasn't sure I wanted to imagine.

'At Partition, I remember I drove from Amritsar to Lahore. It was very dangerous, because it was the wrong way and Hindus were coming away from Lahore. But I had managed to acquire an army jeep. On each side of the road there were corpses, floating, bloated, stinking, vultures, flies – it was unimaginable. The driver was scared sick. I told him not to look and just drive on.'

'Why were you going there?' asked one of the nieces. 'Wasn't it dangerous?'

'Very dangerous. But I'd left my jewellery in the locker so I had to go to get it.'

Pakistan Airways said that in view of the present situation they might need all available seats to evacuate their diplomatic personnel. It sounded very dramatic.

'You just forget about it,' insisted my aunt. 'It isn't safe. Over there in Pakistan they've gone on a temple-smashing spree. It's all on the BBC.'

I remembered how I'd been told I couldn't go to Punjab some years earlier and decided to telephone Lahore from a public booth.

'Is it safe to come?' I asked.

'Quite safe, just so long as you're not a temple! We'll organise the tickets from here. Just come.'

So on 12 December we flew out, across the invisible border. The plane was only half-full.

'*We didn't just live together with tolerance! We lived together with love.*'

So what happened? How did it happen? Why did it happen? And is it happening again?

We arrived in Faisalabad on the 14th. Jahnara, the Alam's granddaughter, who was Devi's age, was sent to accompany us. Uncle Maqbool met us at the bus station and after a short rest took us to the *mazaar*.

An old woman opened the door to let us in. 'Come in, come in. We have been waiting for you. There might be madness in the city, but here you will find only love,' she said as she stroked our cheeks when we entered. The tabla was being hammered into tune, the Qawali singers were clearing their throats, and the music was just about to start.

'Mummy, this is a good place; I like it,' said Devi with great certainty. 'I'm glad we were able to make it.' My sightless daughter was born with insight.

We were sitting by the inner sanctum of the tomb. It was all marble, and an ornate red-and-gold brocade quilt covered the grave. I spoke to it. Dear Great Uncle Bhajan, Here we are. In spite of, and through, all the noise and fury of riots and curfews, broken mosques and temples, seared hearts, wounded pride and so much pain – into this place of tranquillity and peace – across the border, across many borders. All the way getting here we have felt protected. Even on the bus the driver had the seats in the front next to him vacated for us. All the way he watched over us until now. And now here we are.'

The next morning the girls got a lift back to Lahore and left. I was unable to get out of bed and unable to stop crying. A servant brought me tea and food. After five hours of crying, Uncle Maqbool invited me to have some refreshments with him and suggested I might like to revisit the tomb. Ashraf the driver took me and waited as I went in.

'And, yes, this is a different space.'

I stepped into the *mazaar* complex. It had two tombs and a little mosque. The garlands of light from the festivities of the night before were still around and although the place had been cleared there were still the odd rose petals here and there. The peace was astonishing.

I stepped into the inner sanctum. The quilt covering the grave was strewn with fresh flowers. There was a portrait, but they weren't sure how much it resembled Bhajan Lal because it had been done from memory after his death.

I sat down at the foot of the grave, in front of the portrait of him that perhaps wasn't him.

I spoke again: 'Dear Uncle Bhajan,

'Here I am once more. Yesterday I sang and went to sleep with the *Qawali* ringing in my head. This morning I wept for five hours. Who knows why? I then felt the urge to come here and sit at your tomb.'

I was squatting on the floor, my hands tucked in my lap. Then I opened them, palms upward in the Muslim form of prayer. At first I felt awkward, until the gesture itself spoke to me and I allowed myself to feel its openness, receptivity, surrender.

When I returned home, Uncle Maqbool was waiting for me with Rashid Sahib, the elder disciple who had come to meet me. He got up when I came in, put his hand on his heart, and inclined his head.

'It is a great privilege to meet you, who are a descendant of the Great Man,' began Rashid Sahib, 'but equally it is a great privilege for you. We don't believe that you just come; we believe that you are called. Many are called, but not all who are called come. But you have come. And because you have come, now your life will change. Something in your life, which should have happened and didn't happen, will now happen. It will happen soon. Very soon. It will be a surprise. And you will know then that you were called. There is not much time today, but one more thing I need to tell you.' He looked at me earnestly. 'Remember this: God dwells in the heart. Whatever you believe, the place where God dwells is the same. And that is why in your heart you must not entertain *ghum or parishani* ("grief" or "worry").'

'Oh dear,' I laughed, 'I'm afraid I entertain those two quite a lot.'

'From now on, entertain them less. Acknowledge them when they come, but don't entertain them.'

The next morning, Uncle Maqbool drove us to the bus station.

'I have become fond of you,' he said, 'and this morning you both came to me in my prayers. Every morning, at the end of my prayers, I think of my daughters. From now on, when I think of my daughters I will think of you and Devi, too.'

'Thank you, uncle. Thank you very much.'

Back in Lahore I tried to get in touch with Mr Batalvi. When I'd left Delhi, my mother had asked me to. 'He promised he'd give me something of mine from my house and I've got nothing now since I lost the painting. So ask him for me.' I'd written a letter and tried to call, but there was no reply. Secretly I was relieved; it was a distressing errand.

Then a friend of my parents appeared. 'Call me Azgari Appa,' she said, 'I knew you when you were a baby.' I knew her, too, from my mother's stories – and also because her brother Azim Husain, at Partition, had opted for India and left his ancestral home in the Punjab to do so; he was in the diplomatic service and when we had first come to London he was the Deputy High Commissioner for India and had invited us to tea at his residence in Hampstead. It was on our way that my mother had told me his story, which to my fifteen-year-old self had sounded dramatic and romantic and strange, and my 'Thank you' card posted on my return, was almost effusive.

She was sorry she had missed seeing my mother the previous year and on hearing of my 'errand' decided she would like to help.

There was joyful triumph in her voice when she told me that she had managed to secure the keys to the house. Mr Batalvi agreed we could go and see if we could 'find anything'.

I was deeply dismayed. What my mother was hoping for was not there. The idea of revisiting that house full of debris of a lost world and a life I hadn't known but inherited as a lacuna of pain gave me a shiver. But Azgari Appa was so pleased, and I didn't want to appear ungrateful.

Azgari Appa took me in her car, but did not alight herself. Her driver opened the door and I went in. It was much the same, even the pamphlet, 'The Case for Pakistan' was still on the ledge.

The library was shuttered, thin glints of light created patterns on the floor revealing books scattered around.

'*Your father had a library of a thousand books, only Niaz Mohommed was allowed to touch them.*'

As I stood there, rooted, a wave came through me ... a huge wave of human experience: I felt – like a Palestinian, a German Jew, a Tibetan refugee, a bombed-out Iraqi, I felt heavy, I felt hot, bewildered and lost.

'Gham *and* parishani – *grief and worry, acknowledge them, but don't entertain them.*'

I picked up a couple of books at random and then, as I was leaving, stopped, and returned for one on the floor, by the door.

'Are you okay?' asked Azgari Appa as I placed the books on the ledge of the rear window and got into the car.

'There was nothing of my mother's there, just a few old books of my father's.'

We drove off. Some friends of Azgari Appa's had invited us for tea. After a long silence she said, 'I'm so sorry. After Partition I came to this house and met Mr Batalvi and told him, "This house was built and belonged to very dear friends of mine; I'd like to have their things for safekeeping." He replied he'd been a student of your father's and everything was in safekeeping with him and would be returned. I believed him. So, I'm shocked to hear that he returned nothing and just kept everything. That he didn't even give back your personal things.' She looked out of her window and I looked out of mine. After a while she added: 'But your father was a noble soul. Think what he might say to you.'

'Can I stay in the car and not come in for tea, please?'

'Of course, darling. Of course.'

Sitting in the car, waiting for Azgari Appa, I picked up the books. The first was by Rabindranath Tagore, called *Broken Ties and Other Stories*, and the place that would have held my father's name had been cut out with scissors and Batalvi had been scrawled large below the wound; in the second, entitled *The Martyrdom of Man* by Winwood Reade, Batalvi's name was scrawled over my father's; the third book, which I'd picked up by the door, was a small embossed volume entitled *Keats' Poems* – here the front page had been ripped out, but on the exposed frontispiece, below a quote by Leigh Hunt, in my father's inimitable small italic hand, was pencilled:

Oh folly! For to bear all naked truths,
And to envisage circumstances, all calm,
That is the top of Sovereignty.

I stroked the writing with my fingers and kissed it with my lips and whispered 'Thank you.'

Before I left for Delhi, Azgari Appa came to see me once more. As she was leaving she said: 'Will you do something for me when you go to Delhi?'

'What would you like me to do?'

'Go and see Sanyal, the artist, and tell him, tell him ... we miss him.'

'I'll do that. He features in my mother's stories of the parties ...'

'Playing the flute?'

I nodded.

'They were wonderful parties. Your parents were stars.'

I went to see Sanyal the day before I left for London and delivered the message.

He, too, reminisced about my parents, the gatherings, the people, the parties: remembering among others Amrita Sher-Gil, Mulk Raj Anand, Roerich ...

'Roerich made a painting of your mother, didn't he?'

'Yes,' I replied, 'And I'm told you made a bust of my father.'

Less than ten days after my return to London, I got a call from Kate Rowland at BBC Radio saying that Rukhsana Ahmed, a Pakistani writer friend, had given my number and suggested me for a part for a radio play and would I come and read for them?

'Really? I don't know why she said that.'

'She said you'd been trained?'

'Yes, but that was donkeys years ago. I've never done anything since, and I really don't think I could.'

'Why don't you come and let us be the judge of that?' said Kate in such a way that it would have been rude to refuse.

I was offered the part and recorded the play. In the play with me was Julie Christie. Although in a different drama school, she had been my contemporary. We had a mutual friend who often told me about her and I knew we'd both played Anne Frank at the same time, in different theatres. I'd been put out that he'd gone to see hers but not mine.

A couple of weeks later came another call, to read for a theatre play! So, some thirty years after drama school, I had my debut, playing a lead at the wonderful Bush Theatre, a wonderful company and a resurrected career.

'Imagine, darling, nobody knew about you. Then Julie told us,' said John Dove, my lovely, life-enhancing director.

Well, I didn't know about me, either, I thought. I remembered Rashid Sahib: '*Something in your life that should have happened, will now happen, and you will know you were called ...*'

'*Daddy, what do you want me to become when I grow up?*'

'*An actress, of course.*'

'*Really Daddy! How can I become what I already am?*'

The rehearsals were in the National Theatre studio, down by the Old Vic in The Cut in Waterloo, where I'd had the fateful failed audition and run away and where I'd walked down to the India Office library. Sitting at the top of the 168 bus, I smiled all the way. I couldn't have imagined this.

47.

16 AUGUST 1909: AMRITSAR

Dr Ditta cherished the hope that there would be a reprieve, that the authorities would understand and that the 'real culprits' would be apprehended. Even though he said: 'God's will be done', he couldn't believe that God's will meant that he should lose his son. But when Behari came with a letter in his hand he knew and started to shake his head.

'It is from Colonel Dunlop Smith, Father.'

He didn't want to read it. He was sure that Dunlop Smith had done his best, that the letter was kindly worded, but what words can you use to tell a man that you are going to hang his son?

Later, they sat up the whole night, the whole family. A long and painful vigil. All night there were prayers; the daughters-in-law would take it in turns to read prayers while others filled the oil lamps so that the flame continued to burn.

Mother and father sat together, wondering if they would 'know'. When it finally registered, Dr Ditta's body became a dead weight. Like lead. He couldn't move or feel any sensation. He would never see his son again and nothing would ever be the same. 'Why?

Why? Why?' he asked. The tears streamed down his face and he couldn't feel them until his wife started to wipe them away with her *duputta*. 'He was lost and searching,' she said. 'He has now found himself.' But Dr Ditta dissolved into a bundle and howled with grief.

16 August: Pentonville Prison, London
'The silence that descends on a prison after a hanging is the most fearful thing ...'

Throughout the night, there was someone with me. At first I was annoyed, but then gradually there grew a kind of bond, an intimate and silent sharing, and by the morning I was even grateful for the company. There was restlessness around. It felt as though no one in the prison was sleeping.

I thought of Ammaji.

I became quiet and the prayer came. Soft, like Ammaji's touch:

> *Om Bur Bhuva swaha,*
> *Tat Savitur Varenium ...*

Then, one by one, they appeared before my mind's eye, and I said my farewells: Ammaji, Baoji, Bhajan, Behari Bhai, Kundan Bhai, *Tatya* ... one by one they all came, my family, my friends. And Wyllie, to whom I was now bonded. I wondered if we would meet again.

My last wish? they asked. I said: 'A bath and a shave.' I have always liked to look my best, especially before a journey ...

'*I have fed the sweet rice to the fish, you will have a safe journey, my son.*'

48.
1909: THE STATEMENT

Daily News, 18 August 1909
DHINGRA HANGED
Text of His Astounding Statement

'Dhingra, the Hindoo murderer of Sir Curzon Wylie and Dr Lalcaca, was executed yesterday morning at Pentonville.

'A copy has been placed in our hands of the statement, which he drew up before the murder, intending it to be read as if it had been subsequently drawn up. To this document the prisoner referred in the course of the trial, but it was not given to the public. We may add that a copy has been for some time in the possession of certain of Dhingra's compatriots. The statement is as follows:

CHALLENGE

"I admit the other day I attempted to shed English blood as a humble revenge for the inhuman hangings and deportation of patriotic Indian youths. In this I have consulted none but my own conscience, I have conspired with none but my own duty. I believe that a country held down by foreign bayonets is in a perpetual state of war. Since open battle is rendered impossible to an unarmed race, I drew forth my pistol and fired.

"As a Hindu, I feel that wrong done to my country is an insult to God. Her cause is the cause of Shri Ram. Her service is the service of Shri Krishna. Poor in wealth and in intellect, a son like myself has nothing else to offer to the mother but his own blood and so I have sacrificed the same on her altar. The only lesson required in India today is to learn how to die and the only way to teach it is by dying ourselves; therefore I die and glory in my martyrdom.

"My only prayer is that I may be reborn of the same mother and I may re-die in the same cause till the cause is successful, and she stands free for the good of humanity and the glory of God. *Bande Mataram*."

'At the police court, it will be remembered, Dhingra claimed his right to commit the deed as a patriot, and at the Old Bailey he denied the Lord Chief Justice's power to pass sentence upon him. After one of the shortest trials of a capital charge on record, lasting hardly an hour, he was found guilty by the jury, and listened to the passing of the dread sentence without a tremor of his features.

'Some little time before the execution took place, a large crowd gathered outside the approach to the prison, but it was noticeable that there were very few Indian students among those present. Shortly after nine o'clock, the Under Sheriff left the prison, and in reply to a question as to how the execution passed off, said that everything had been in order, and that death had been instantaneous. Pierrepoint was the executioner. An application for leave to have the body cremated was refused, and it will be buried, in accordance with the usual custom, within the walls of the prison.'

W. S. Blunt: *My Diaries*

'19 August – Lyne Stivens was here ... He talked about the Dhingra assassination, which seems to have at last convinced his royal friends that there is something wrong about the state of India. People talk about political assassination as defeating its own end, but that is nonsense; it is just the shock needed to convince selfish rulers that selfishness has its limits of imprudence. It is like the other fiction that England never yields to threats. My experience is that when England has her face well slapped she apologises, not before.

'22 August – Among the many memorable things that Churchill said was this: talking of Dhingra he said that there had been much discussion in the Cabinet about him. Lloyd George had expressed to him his highest admiration on Dhingra's attitude as a patriot, in which he (Churchill) shared. He (Dhingra) will be remembered 2,000 years hence as we remember Regulus and Caractacus and Plutarch's heroes, and Churchill quoted with admiration Dhingra's last words as the finest ever made in the name of patriotism.'

49.

1909: FAMILY PAPERS

'It is said that after the execution Madan's father lost the will to live and eventually died of grief. Most of the sons dropped the Dhingra from their names, but not your grandfather.'

For Dr Ditta, the mourning never ceased, neither did a single day go by when he didn't think of his son, hanged, in a prison, in a distant place, a place he couldn't visualise beyond the cold, flat, black-and-white photographs. It was an alien world that had now taken away his son. There had been no body to grieve over, no cremation to heal, no ceremony to transform, just a deafening silence, an emptiness. It was as though a stitch had fallen in the closely-knit family; everything was unravelling.

He felt as though he had lost a limb and thereby his balance. To walk properly he now used a walking stick that he had purchased some years earlier when he'd gone to see Madan in Simla when he was working for the Kalka to Simla *tonga* service. It was a finely crafted stick that gradually started to assume the presence of Madan. Sometimes he would even talk to it and imagine he was telling his son things he had forgotten to say. Sometimes he could even sense a reply, and in those moments the sorrow that clung to him like a dark shadow would lighten for a while.

'You know I never wanted to send him,' he kept repeating to his wife. 'It was all of you who said I should let him go.'

'He was your son,' she reminded him. 'Could anyone stop you, once you had made up your mind? In any case,' she consoled him, 'we only go when it is our time. We all have to go.' Her conviction of this gave her strength, and while her husband grieved she quietly took charge of the whole household – even the English drawing room where the *diva*, now regularly replenished with oil, was kept alight. Fresh flowers were placed beside it every morning in front of an ornate box that contained little mementoes: a catapult, some polished stones, a pocket knife, cufflinks. There was no picture, but in a way that made the presence stronger.

'One day his body will be returned. India will be free. And his bones will be immersed in *Gangaji*.' She said this with the same conviction.

The business had left Dr Ditta feeling very exposed. He had stopped riding in the mornings and the city had noticed. He wound up his private practice, and only at the insistence of his wife, after his sons had tried and failed, did he agree to keep up the free clinic he ran in the city. There, although nothing was ever discussed, he started to realise that these simple people quietly cherished the memory of his son with admiration and awe. As he observed he started to question everything.

Dr Ditta looked at the framed certificate of which he had been so proud.

LAHORE MEDICAL SCHOOL
instituted

in the
YEAR OF THE CHRISTIAN ERA 1860
We the undersigned, having carefully examined
Sahib Ditta of *Sahiwall, Zilla Shahpore*
IN MEDICINE, SURGERY, MIDWIFERY, & FORENSIC
MEDICINE,
do hereby certify that he is qualified to practice as a Sub-
Assistant surgeon.
Lahore 31 July 1867

For forty-two years, the certificate had adorned his walls, occupying pride of place. Now, looking at it, he decided to remove it. He propped up his walking stick, stretched up and lifted it down. 'The ten great blessings of British rule.' He looked at the mark on the wall, the outline of dust where the frame had previously hung, and called a servant to clean it away.

He sent for his lawyer and told him that he wanted to add a clause to his will, to specify that no money from his trust fund was ever be used to send any member of the Dhingra family overseas. At his desk he pulled out a sheet of paper, dipped his pen into the inkwell and wrote:

'*Madan Lal Dhingra*
A brief account of his early life
Murder by him of Dr Lalcaca and Sir Curzon Wyllie
His trial and execution in London
by
Bereaved and unfortunate father'

He stopped and looked at what he had written, scratched out the last line, and rewrote:

'*by bereaved father as a last duty to his ill-fated, ill-guided, yet firm and determined son. Sahib Ditta Mal Dhingra.*'

He looked again at what he had written and started to weep, and then sobbed uncontrollably until he could be heard in the inner courtyard below.

Gradually he took to wearing only Indian clothes, then he started to accompany his wife on visits to holy men and shrines in search of some solace.

'*They will meet again in the house of God. Your son and your friend Wyllie Sahib. There they will understand each other and become friends. Both loved India.*'

50.

1909: BHAJAN LAL

It was very strange. Very strange and the strangeness grew. In one fell swoop I no longer had a brother or a name. And it seemed to me that I no longer had a past, as that past had happened to another name. Why it should have made a difference I don't know. But it did.

I was summoned to the solicitor's office, Mr Tindal Atkinson KC. I had met him before, and I knew he had attended the trial. Indians were not allowed to. I was anxious, but he put me at ease. I was 'advised' that the sensible thing to do in the 'interests of family and in my own best interests' was not to use the name 'Dhingra' any more. As there was a surname spelt Lall, it was suggested I adopt it. It would simply mean adding an 'L' to my middle name. A letter would be despatched to Gray's Inn informing them, and I would be called to the bar as Bhajan Lall.

The solicitor was very sympathetic and kind. Curzon Wyllie also had a kindly face. I sent flowers to Lady Wyllie anonymously. I felt for her, for Madan and when I thought of the family at home the pain felt unbearable.

I left the solicitor's office as Bhajan Lall. I felt bereft and completely alone.

I asked myself, 'Who am I?'

I walked down to the river almost instinctively. It was a relief to watch something flow. I looked at the river and became aware that there was a 'me', or something inside 'me', or a 'not me', something quite untouched by the story I'd been in. It was an energy that flowed through me, the river, the people around, the light, everything. I was alone. But by adding another 'L' and a hyphen, I was all-one.

Who am I? The question grew in me. It was really the only question.

51.

1997: FIFTIETH ANNIVERSARY OF INDIAN INDEPENDENCE

'Well,' Diane lifted her wine glass, 'here's to new beginnings: our writing, your theatre tour, 1997 and the fiftieth anniversary of Indian Independence.'

'Bless'em all,' we clinked.

'I must say it does seem a bit unimaginative to be doing a play about the Raj yet again. I thought we'd done with that in the 1980s. And for the fiftieth anniversary of Indian Independence, too!'

'Well, it's for the audience here. It wasn't their Independence.'

'*Staying On* is the one about the two Raj relics, living out their time in some Indian hill station, isn't it?'

'That's the one.'

'And it might come to the West End, you say?'

'Well, that's the plan. Good if it does as I'll have security and salary for a few months.'

We ate our food silently for a while.

'You know I had this fantasy, wish or aspiration, that I could revive my film career and it could somehow be a vehicle for my homecoming.' I put my hand on my heart in declamation mode: 'the return from Exile.'

Diane laughed. 'Yes, I seem to remember you telling me that some years ago.'

'Well, that was a time of innocence or deep delusion fed by my insecurity. I learned that India was not going to happen, there was no welcoming bosom of the family to return to. I was just a foreign visitor. They were my mother's family.'

'You should be nicer to your mother,' said Diane.

'I know. It maddens me that she allows that level of abuse.'

'Well, she did go on hunger strike outside her sisters' house. I think that was pretty plucky thing to do. She's a feisty lady is your mum.'

'There's a mean bully gene in her family that some people have.'

'And against which she puts up a great nonviolent resistance. You should be proud of her.'

The following week, I prepared my bag to take to rehearsals and checked that I had all I needed: wallet, script, keys, highlighters, pens. I opened the envelope to check the time and venue and work out the best way to get there. Inside there was a map. I looked at it and double-checked: the rehearsal rooms were just off The Cut in Waterloo, near the India Office Library. Was there some meaning in this? How was it that I kept going back to that same area?

On the bus I thought about it all and once I got to the theatre, the old haunting returned alongside the excitement of meeting the new company for our shared venture. As the play was set in Independent India, all the characters in it were 'brown', apart from the elderly English couple who had stayed on and were played by Prunella Scales and Richard Johnson. Looking around the company, I wondered what they considered themselves to be: Indians, Pakistanis, Asians, British? I reflected on all the various identity labels that had been placed on me: a girl from India, an Indian, a coloured, a Paki, a wog, a black, an Asian, an ethnic minority – 'visitor from foreign'.

'It's not beautee-ful its byoot-ful.'

Now I was well past the age of Cordelia and Miranda, and once again had to learn to say beautee-ful for my part as Suzy Williams, the Anglo-Indian Hairdresser. Or Mrs Patel in the corner shop, the other roles I was offered.

During the lunch break, I wandered off on my own to the India Office Library. It had changed and had been refurbished. I stood on the pavement briefly and looked at it. I knew that it was in the process of being relocated to the upcoming British Library in King's Cross.

At the weekend I brought out the case in which I had stored all the documents of my research. I had meant to classify them before putting them away, and although they were in files they were all mixed up. Maybe I could put them in order as a way of marking the fiftieth anniversary. I pulled out one of the files and opened it.

Telegram: 14 Aug. 1909
From His Majesty's Secretary of State for India.
To His Excellency, the Viceroy

'Please inform relations of Dhingra that after considering all circumstances including evidence of father and brothers, Home Secretary regrets that he cannot advise His Majesty to interfere with the due course of the law.'

I put it back and shut the box. I couldn't go there now. I needed to keep my head space for rehearsals. But I didn't put the box away. I found a place for it on my desk. It would be there when I was ready. The tour would finish with a week in Richmond. I would look at it then.

Staying On opened at Guilford, and every evening the foyer was filled with 'India Hands', the old colonels of the Raj – who had never died but had only faded away. They all remembered India with nostalgia; for some it was the magical land where they had been born and they cherished its warmth in their bones. For me these people were a familiar lot who reminded me of my childhood and also of my Anglicised Indian family. For the younger 'Asian' actors, they were a strange anachronism; they were the people you read about in plays and they found them patronising. Ironically, I found myself cast in the role of explaining and even defending them.

'But the English *are* patronising,' insisted Kate, a fellow actor and Prunella's understudy, during our long chats in the dressing room we shared. 'I'm Scots, I should know. We've had them around for much longer than you.'

'Well,' I replied, 'not all. Not in my Quaker school, for instance.'

'Oh aye! I think you're very forgiving.'

'I don't know. I spent years and years barricading myself against Englishness, trying to escape, to run away.'

'I don't blame you.'

52.

1997: FAMILY PAPERS

The file was marked 'Family Papers'. Into it I folded away my great-grandfather's medical certificate on its strong parchment paper, the will, with its little holes where the insects had feasted, and the photocopy of the A5 page that I had found in a book written in Punjabi, as a plate in the frontispiece. It was in Sahib Ditta's handwriting. '*Ill-fated, ill-guided, yet firm and determined...*' and he'd crossed out 'unfortunate'. I wished he had made his peace.

There wasn't much else in the file – plans of Sahib Ditta's enormous mansion, a chart of symptoms and remedies for various poisons, my grandfather's death certificate and his obituary:

The Times

London, 4 July 1936

SIR BEHARI LAL DHINGRA

DEWAN OF JIND

'Sir Behari Lal Dhingra, who died at Hampstead yesterday after a serious illness, was a notable figure in Indian States politics and administration.

M.R.C.S., L.R.C.P., M.D., Kaiser-i-Hind Gold medal (First Class), Chief Minister of Jind, C.I.E. and Knighthood.

An ardent loyalist he had many English friends and was deeply opposed to terrorism, which he believed could only postpone the political advancement of his country ... he will be long remembered and mourned by a great circle – English and Indian – to whom he had endeared himself by his charming manners, loyal friendship, and sincere devotion to India, whose fulfilment he regarded as wrapped up in the British connection.'

I decided to go for a stroll and have a look at the house in Fitzjohn's Avenue where my grandfather had lived and died: 'fulfilment ... wrapped up in the British connection'. Indeed, I thought, as I walked up Hampstead High Street, what about fulfilment thwarted by the British connection? It was too unequal a connection.

My grandfather, like so many others, had bought into the colonial theory of progress – modernising and opening up frontiers of new knowledge. But even though he could send his daughter to Oxford in the 1920s, when it came to the crunch she had to be pulled out and abandon her studies. As an undergraduate my aunt had been shadowed everywhere and once attended a meeting about Indian freedom, whereupon her father was 'advised' that she be withdrawn lest she follow in the steps of her uncle. So in the end, in spite of Oxford, she was married off and silenced.

The house, number 108, was near the village, not far from the shops. I looked at it. So this was where my grandfather had lived and died! The road my father avoided walking down. The 'ardent loyalist'. As I looked at the house I thought that my grandfather had had to pay a high price for his 'loyalty', just as Madan had had to pay a high price for his 'rebellion'. For my grandfather had died at the early age of sixty-three. The complicated name for his medical condition was basically cancer of the throat. The throat – the chakra of self-expression. The price of silence.

'*Your grandfather was not a toady. He genuinely admired the British.*'

Surely that was also possible, I conceded, as I came into the High Street and stopped to look at it. I could almost imagine it with horses and carriages in Madan's day, with the opening of the Underground, the deepest in London. Or during my grandfather's time, with honking cars and useful shops. I crossed the road into Well Walk, past Hyndman's house and into the tree-lined avenue on Hampstead Heath. I was sure that all of the Dhingras had at one point taken that route. As I walked I felt I was dispelling shadows, shadows of sadness, of grief, of anger, of history, of years of silencing. I tried to imagine them dissolving away as I walked home. Could I really dispel shadows retrospectively? For my forebears? Could I set them all free?

The Heath opened out and I stopped to take it in, the rolling green, the wise and ancient trees, the careful, lovingly created landscape. Just looking at it, my spirits lifted. Well, I said to one of the Highgate spires, if one is to live in exile, this really isn't a bad place to be an exile in. '*Not a bad place*'! I shook my head. God, how English I'd become! Not a bad place indeed! It was a beautiful place – quite magical. And it was also because of its Englishness. 'Not such a bad place.' I smiled.

Back in my room I looked at the piles of papers on my desk. The acting tour had ended and for the previous two months I'd been trying to work on my book about Madan Lal. It was proving to be very difficult. Something was blocked. I could feel it. But what was it?

'*17 August 1909. Name: Madan Lal Dhingra. Male. 25 years old. Cause of death: Fracture of the cervical vertebrae. Executed by Law.*'

I had pinned the death certificate next to the photograph and was looking at it. Then, I looked out over the London sky and thought of Paris.

Paris! Of course! I had to go to Paris. That's where it happened, our dislocation and exile was enacted against the backdrop of that beautiful city.

'*We met this man in Paris. He'd been there in the room with Uncle Madan. "Only he who could hold his hand on the candle for the longest would do it."*'

I tried to locate my envelope on Madhava Rao as I thought of my father meeting him. On 19 August 1947, Free India was only four days old. My parents probably didn't know about Partition then. I wondered where they were when they first learned of the massacres and mass migrations, and realised they were refugees. August in Paris in 1947. India was free, and they were refugees in Paris, their children in a school in India, waiting for their return. They left their home with just a suitcase each. My father's sabbatical, a short stay abroad. Now Partition. A story that couldn't be told.

And that's the way we stayed: as refugees. In Paris. Paris, the city I grew up in. The city that had taken my father from me and to which I had vowed never to return. Why did I do that? What did I cut it out? Paris, Partition, *Pitaji*, Papa! A large tear fell on my papers and then another and another ...

I had recreated Partition for myself. It had taken me all this time to realise it.

Department of Criminal Intelligence

'Information regarding the activity of the Revolutionary Party in London and Paris since the middle of the year 1910.

'After the arrest of V. D. Savarkar on 13-3-10 and his removal to Bombay on 1 July 1910, the Revolutionary Party in London seem to have, for the time being, been completely demoralised. The usual Sunday meetings of the "Free India" society ceased. Two of the principal revolutionaries, viz Chattopadhya and Madhava Rao fled in hot haste to Paris on 9 June 1910, leaving their luggage behind them, in order to escape arrest as they heard from N. Pal (son of B. C. Pal) that warrants were out against them ...

'The latest information of the party of Paris was that there was considerable dissension amongst them, each accusing the other of selfishness and treachery and squabbling over their methods of work and disposal of funds.'

53.
1997: August – Paris, Partition, Papa

I was sitting with my sister in the back of Polly's Tea Rooms, where there was no view except the one in our minds.

She looked at me with that kind of ever-knowing elder sister sideways glance.

'So you're going to Paris?'

'Yes. The play's not going to the West End so I thought I'd go to Paris.'

'When was the last time you were there?'

'1979.'

'You mean you haven't been since Daddy died?'

I shook my head. 'Well, I lost touch with Alix and there was nowhere to go.'

'So where are you staying?'

'I met this man in Lahore, Etienne, and he invited me.'

'*Où est ce qu'il habite?*' My sister suddenly reverted to French.

'*Dans la banlieue quelquepart*' I replied, shrugging my shoulders, French-style.

'*Il viens me chercher à la gare.*'

'*C'est bien, ça.*'

'What made you decide?'

'It sort of bubbled up, really. Then I thought about how in homeopathy, in the cure you recapitulate the history of the condition. And I thought – it all goes back to Partition – and for me – that's Paris.'

My sister nodded.

'Do you remember the house in Lahore?'

I shook my head.

'I suppose you were too small.'

I shrugged my shoulders, French-style. 'Even when I went there, I didn't recognise the place. Except maybe the front steps where I played with the dog and my little red shoe.'

'And you had to have those rabies injections.'

'I don't remember the dog hurting me at all. But I remember the doctor who lied.'

My sister gave me another sideways glance and said, 'Have you ever thought what life might been like if the Partition hadn't happened?'

'No. Never. Have you?'

'Yes. Many times.'

'Tell me.'

'Well, Daddy would've had his work at the College, his students, his writer and artist friends. They would have had their parties and gatherings. Mummy would have gone off on her jaunts and journeys. When she was away, Niaz Mohommed would have run the house and if it was for a long spell, Aunty Danti would have come and overseen things. But for us, well, we would have had a home, stability, a place to be and belong to.'

'Gosh. I can't imagine that,' I said. And Mummy wouldn't have lost her stuff, I thought. And then I remembered something.

'You know, years ago I did a workshop called "Healing as Self-healing".'

'Yes. It was very significant for you, wasn't it?'

I nodded. 'Well, we had a guided meditation in which we had to imagine a house and the image that came into my head was Val D'or, that house in St Cloud. Strange as I must have been seven or so and had never thought of it since.'

'Not strange at all,' said my sister. 'It was our last family home. After that it was that small flat where we could never fit together and we were all over the place.'

'I know. When I came to London it was my tenth educational establishment in ten years.'

'Honestly! I don't know what Mummy and Daddy were thinking!' my sister frowned, then softened: 'I suppose they were just improvising as they went along.'

'Yes. I don't suppose it was easy for them,' I said.

'And what about me, running around and trying to support you all?' she snapped.

I looked at my sister and felt a pang and remembered, another time, in the same café and her telling me: '…when you have an unsettled life … you lose touch with your instincts.' She had said it as though about me, but now, as I looked at her … suddenly she caught my eye and said in French, 'This interest you have in Madan Lal – are you deflecting from finding out about your father?

'*Je ne sais pas*,' I replied, shrugging my shoulders, French-style.

Sometime later I was on the Eurostar to Paris. My first visit since my father had died eighteen years earlier. For me, the fiftieth anniversary of Indian Independence had to be spent in Paris, to commemorate the Partition of India and the Partition of our family. Paris was where it had all happened for us and where I needed to be. It was the city of my childhood.

Etienne met me at the Gard du Nord. 'So you're here at last. That's good,' he said. 'I've got you a map and a mobile phone, and when we get home I'll show you how to find your friends on the *minitel*. You type in the name and address and it will give you the phone number.'

I located Alix, who was delighted to hear from me and invited me to stay! Two days later as I walked down the rue Broca I remembered my father coming to visit me there, the year before he died. That was the last time I saw him. The memory stabbed my heart, a sharp pain and tears.

Dearest Papa, maybe in the end this is really all about you. My loss, my search, my partition from you, my dearest Papa, so that when you died I was left with an aching emptiness. What happened? How did you so disappear from my life? Why did I allow it?

So many partitions.

Alix opened the door. '*Ah ma vieille! Te voilà vachement sympathique!*'

'Paris isn't only your father. It's the city of your childhood,' said Raza, an artist friend of my father's whose phone number I found on the *minitel*. 'I can still remember you, aged ten, dancing around at my first exhibition singing: "Padamsee, Raza, Souza!"'

I saw myself, five years old, blowing soap bubbles at the *Trocadero*.

I went to sleep singing: '*Maman les petits bateaux qui vont sur l'eau ont ils des jambes ...*'

The next day I went to Montmartre, to the Marché St Pierre, to pick up some cloth ... and I loved it, that after all these years I knew where to go and that the bargains were still there. My mother would buy French chiffon in sari lengths to take to India. She would never wear it. She wore only Indian silks; the French chiffon was too westernised. But it sold for a profit in India and the extra money was needed to replace the lost home.

'*It's not "vee vee", Mummy, it's "ooee ooee". Your parents didn't teach you anything, did they? They didn't teach you to speak French properly.*'

Around the Sacré Coeur I remembered the holy pictures – which I longed to be able to collect like my street playmates. Mary and Jesus, beautiful in pastels, silver and gold.

'*You must find and follow your swadharma, the path of your true nature. It must be your way, not anyone else's way, but your own way.*'

Maybe I had lost myself for a long time. Maybe that's why I couldn't see my father. History and mystery. I passed the Galeries Lafayette and remembered Marie-Thérèse, my first perfume, Houbigant's *Quelques Fleurs* and my 'special going-away dress'. Going home to India ...

The bus advanced along the Seine and I remembered the time when there were no cars along its banks.

Paris, The city of my childhood. The city of happy times. Of snatches of family life.

'*Just observe, darling, then sit down and write.*'

Dearest *Pitaji*, Papa, Daddy. I have called you all these names at different stages of my various identities: part Indian, part French, part English. Mama didn't like me calling you Daddy. It was too colonial, so I censored it. I censored a lot of things. But Daddy was what I first called you. The letters I wrote to you and which you so carefully preserved, from all my many schools in so many countries, I always addressed you as 'Darling Daddy'.

Partition didn't only dismember India; it dismembered us: from India, as a family, from each other, from ourselves. It was the beginning of strings of partings, of partitions ...

The night before my departure we were sitting in the restaurant.

'I love to see you in a sari,' exclaimed Alix as she leant over to touch it, 'and this fuchsia pink with the orange, so vibrant, *c'est merveilleux.*'

'You know, Alix, when I used to come "home to Paris", three times a year, six journeys. I always arrived in a sari. And when I returned to London, I was always in trousers. I changed my clothes on the boat.'

'Ahh. Why?'

'Growing up as an ex-colonial subject in England was a very ... how can I put it? You needed to shrink. To fit in you had to cut out bits of yourself, and then, I suppose, they got lost.'

'Ahh oui, but you don't have to do it now,' replied Alix, ordering the wine at the same time. 'I tell you what, this time wear a sari when you arrive in London.'

'No. It wouldn't be convenient, wheeling my baggage wearing a sari.'

'You can do it ... The world has changed since we were young. We don't have to stay the same. Try the wine, it's really good.'

The wine was good.

'It's true. Things have changed. When I was younger, India didn't really exist except as a place where there were beggars and tigers, which the English had tried to "civilise". Now, for the fiftieth anniversary of Independence, they've all gone there: the Queen and the entire establishment. They've even visited Jallianwala Bagh, where a massacre had taken place. It's as though they're beginning to admit to their invisible history, the one that happened on distant shores that they weren't taught about.'

'I definitely think you should return to London in a sari. It will help you to look at all those issues. Have some more wine.'

I wore the same fuchsia-pink printed crepe silk sari for my return journey. At the Gare du Nord I noticed a man with a shaven head clocking me and felt myself getting tense. Of all days to collide with a skinhead, I thought. I hastened my pace towards the train. My wheely toppled.

'Let me help you,' came a voice. The skinhead was smiling, folding his hands together. 'Namaste,' he said, 'let me take your bag. I've hardly any luggage of my own.'

'Oh. Thank you. Namaste,' I replied.

'*When you say Namaste ... remember the meaning: I bow to the divine in you ... Yes, Daddy.*'

'Where did you learn Namaste?' I asked. 'Have you lived in India?'

'No,' he replied, 'but I lived some years in East Ham. I suppose it's the nearest I'll ever get to India. But I loved it there. I picked up a few words.'

'Really?'

'I can say Namaste, Sat Sri Akal, Salaam Aleikum and of course Accha, with the head shake, too. My name is Alasdair, by the way.'

Having discovered our seats were in the same compartment, we chatted as we walked down the platform. He told me he had come to deliver a very large suitcase and got a paid holiday. And I told him of my writer's block, which I hoped a visit to Paris would dislodge.

'I'll fix the wheel on your case before we get to London ...'

'I think we live in the most amazing time, in cities where all the cultures of the world exist side by side. One can learn so much. I come from Aberdeen. I only knew about my own culture and that was all. Now, all around us, we can experience other ways of being, of thinking, of eating. I can't to go to the West Indies, but I can go to Brixton and it's all there. For a person like me, who can't really afford to travel, it's wonderful. It's such a privilege.'

'Well, I must say that it's refreshing to hear you talk like that. I've always been trying to disappear and not to be found out.'

'Yes, I know about that, too.'

'Do you? But how can you?'

'You can be settled in one place where you don't fit and so feel unsettled in yourself. I've never understood bigotry or people who want to close the world. Even as a boy I was into "Rock against Racism". Gradually people will come to realise. Did you hear about Robin Cook offering to help sort out the messy imperial legacy of India and Pakistan? I think he might have put his foot in it rather. His heart was in the right place though.' Alasdair laughed. 'Scots also feel that they were colonised, you know. They don't like the English.'

'Yes, I do know. I shared a dressing room and digs with a Scottish actress friend Kate and she never tired of telling me. But in India, all the British were English. It's all rather funny, really. India is coming out of invisibility. Maybe so can I.'

'That's good. It's when we can admit our own stuff that we can heal, because you can never heal others if you're wrong.'

'That sounds a bit of a conundrum. Who are we to judge anyway?'

'Exactly. And why should we accept anyone else's judgements? I'm sure you'll get on with writing your book now. Good Luck. I'll look out for it.'

Back home, I opened my case, pulled out the photograph. I looked at it for a long time before pinning it once again on the board above my desk. And started to write.

THE PHOTOGRAPH

On the board above my desk I have pinned up a photograph of you. You are wearing a striped lounge suit with a contrasting waistcoat in lighter material. You are sitting in a chair, in a garden ...

VISITATION

I feel as though until now
I have been a character in the story of another.
A family? A country? A history? Who knows?
I've spent my life in a book I didn't fit into
Not knowing my part or what I was supposed to do
Losing my way and missing all the cues.

So now I'm walking out of that book and that story
Which I didn't create, and which wasn't my own.
For I have touched my own mystery
And will now allow that mystery to unfold.
History: his story. Mystery: my story.

(Maybe I'll write a book of the story I'm leaving
And in doing so discover my own?)

EPILOGUE

August 2020

Dear Uncle Madan,

In Amritsar today, not far from where you were born, there stands a tall statue of you: 9 foot 5 inches of bronze standing on an equally tall white plinth, set in the centre of a raised two-tier circular platform with floodlights and further encircled by bronze posts linked with a loosely looped chain, creating the effect of a garland. You are dressed in a suit, hand in your pocket, just like the descriptions of you at time: looking relaxed, defiant and focused. And the whole effigy/structure is prominently placed by the Town Hall, a short pedestrianised walk from the Golden Temple and Jallianwala Bagh, where ten years after your death in 1919, the Amritsar Massacre took place and where there is statue of Uddam Singh, who would later travel to London to avenge it and also be executed at Pentonville. Only two freedom fighters were executed in London, both Punjabis, both from Amritsar. Both finally exhumed in the 1970s and returned to India.

We are presently living at a time when statues are being toppled, their presence and purpose interrogated: Who placed them there? To what end? What narrative do they serve?

Very recently, in Bristol, a demonstration supporting 'Black Lives Matter' pulled down a contentious statue of Edward Colson whose plinth said: *'Erected by citizens of Bristol as a memorial of one of the most virtuous and wise sons of their city AD 1895.'*

But the rage that drove those who pulled it down derived from what was not said: *Colston's wealth came from slave trading … the transportation of approximately 84,000 African men, women and young children (of whom 19,000 died on voyages) from West Africa to the Caribbean and the Americas.*

Your plinth says: *Shahid Madan Lal Dhingra. Indomitable Hindustani challenged the mighty British Empire with his courage and valour. The brave disciple of Veer Savarkar …*

In your story the young Savarkar, who was your friend, was just a few months older than you. You met when you were both twenty-three. You both respected, admired and had a deep affection for each other. Of that I have no doubt.

You were comrades, fellow revolutionaries and both dreamed of an India that was free and for the benefit for all its inhabitants. And Savarkar himself put it rather well. Speaking in 1907, he said: *'Hindus are at the heart of Hindustan. Nevertheless just as the beauty of the rainbow is not impaired but enhanced by its varied hues, so also Hindustan will appear the more beautiful across the sky of the future by assimilating the best in the Muslim, Parsi, Jewish and other civilisations.'*

And that was the vision of India you both shared, struggled to realise and for which you gave your life.

But the Savarkar to whom you are linked on the plinth, whose disciple you are purported to be, changed his views and wrote

Hindutva, which stigmatised Muslims and advocated unequal citizenship.

Would you have given your life for that? I think not, if I extrapolate.

You are from the Punjab. The land of the five rivers, which has also been watered and nourished by the rivers of Hinduism, Sikhism and Islam.

You come from Amritsar, home of the Great Golden Temple whose foundation stone was laid by a Muslim saint.

I would recall that the Guru Nanak, the founder of Sikhism, was revered not only by Sikhs, but by Hindus and Muslims, too.

I might also tell you this about your fellow patriot from the Punjab and Pentonville, Uddam Singh: *'While in custody, he called himself "Ram Mohammad Singh Azad": the first three words of the name reflect the three major religious communities of Punjab (Hindu, Muslim and Sikh); the last word "Azad" (literally "free") reflects his anti-colonial sentiment.'*

In the Punjab today, I am told, Muslims are not stigmatised. When the attacks – on Muslims – took place in Delhi a few months ago the Sikhs rescued them. The Akal Takhat, the highest temporal seat of the Sikh faith, issued a *hukamnama* – an order – to save and protect fellow citizens. That food, shelter, support be made available.

Your plinth also declares: 'I am a Hindu.' I imagine today there must be many people grappling with that question. Years ago, I asked my father, 'What does it mean for me to be a Hindu?'

'It means that you must find and follow your *swadharma*, the path of your true nature. But it must be *your way*. Not Mummy's way, or my way, or anybody else's way, but your own way.'

The country, too, will have to find its *swadharma*.

BIBLIOGRAPHY

Books

Blunt, W. S., *My Diaries: Part, Two* Alfred A. Knopf, 1921

Brown, Emily C., *Har Dayal, Hindu Revolutionary and Rationalist*, University of Arizona Press, 1975

Brown, Judith M., *Modern India: The Origins of an Asian Democracy*, Oxford University Press, 1985

Datta, V. N., *Madan Lal Dhingra and the Revolutionary Movement*, Vikas, 1978

Garnett, David, *The Golden Echo*, Chatto and Windus, 1953

Maighovalia, B. S., *First Indian Martyr to be Executed at Pentonville*, Hoshiarpur, 1975

Raghavan, G.N.S., *M. Asaf Ali's Memoirs: The Emergence of Modern India*, Ajanta, 1994

Sethna, Khoshed Ali, *Madame Bhikaji Rustom Cama*, Government of India Publications Division, 1987

Tolstoy, Leo, *A Letter to a Hindu*: https://www.gutenberg.org/files/7176/7176-h/7176-h.htm.